The British and the Sikhs

Discovery, Warfare and Friendship (c.1700–1900)

Gurinder Singh Mann

Helion & Company

Helion & Company Limited
Unit 8 Amherst Business Centre
Budbrooke Road
Warwick
CV34 5WE
England
Tel. 01926 499 619
Email: info@helion.co.uk
Website: www.helion.co.uk
Twitter: @helionbooks
Visit our blog at blog.helion.co.uk

Published by Helion & Company 2020
Designed and typeset by Mach 3 Solutions Ltd (www.mach3solutions.co.uk)
Cover designed by Paul Hewitt, Battlefield Design (www.battlefield-design.co.uk)

Text © Gurinder Singh Mann 2020
Images and maps © as individually credited

Cover: General Baghel Singh and the Khalsa forces conquest of Delhi in 1783. The smouldering Red Fort, Delhi can be seen in the background with the British looking on. Image created by and © Harjinder Singh Sunner.

ISBN 978-1-911628-24-8

British Library Cataloguing-in-Publication Data.
A catalogue record for this book is available from the British Library.

For details of other military history titles published by Helion & Company Limited contact the above address or visit our website: http://www.helion.co.uk.

We always welcome receipt of book proposals from prospective authors.

The period 1815-1914 is sometimes called the long century of peace. It was in reality very far from that. It was a century of civil wars, popular uprisings, and struggles for Independence. An era of colonial expansion, wars of Empire, and colonial campaigning, much of which was unconventional in nature. It was also an age of major conventional wars, in Europe that would see the Crimea campaign and the wars of German unification. Such conflicts, along with the American Civil War, foreshadowed the total war of the 20th century.

It was also a period of great technological advancement, which in time impacted the military and warfare in general. Steam power, electricity, the telegraph, the radio, the railway, all became tools of war. The century was one of dramatic change. Tactics altered, sometimes slowly, to meet the challenges of the new technology. The dramatic change in the technology of war in this period is reflected in the new title of this series: From Musket to Maxim.

The new title better reflects the fact that the series covers all nations and all conflict of the period between 1815-1914. Already the series has commissioned books that deal with matters outside the British experience. This is something that the series will endeavour to do more of in the future. At the same time there still remains an important place for the study of the British military during this period. It is one of fascination, with campaigns that capture the imagination, in which Britain although the world's predominant power, continues to field a relatively small army.

The aim of the series is to throw the spotlight on the conflicts of that century, which can often get overlooked, sandwiched as they are between two major conflicts, the French/Revolutionary/Napoleonic Wars and the First World War. The series will produced a variety of books and styles. Some will look simply at campaigns or battles. Others will concentrate on particular aspects of a war or campaign. There will also be books that look at wider concepts of warfare during this era. It is the intention that this series will present a platform for historians to present their work on an important but often overlooked century of warfare.

Submissions

The publishers would be pleased to receive submissions for this series. Please contact series editor Dr Christopher Brice via email (chrismbrice@yahoo.com), or in writing to Helion & Company Limited, Unit 8, Amherst Business Centre, Budbrooke Road, Warwick, Warwickshire, CV34 5WE.

Books in this series:

1. *The Battle of Majuba Hill: The Transvaal Campaign 1880-1881* John Laband (ISBN 978-1-911512-38-7)*

2. *For Queen and Company: Vignettes of the Irish Soldier in the Indian Mutiny* David Truesdale (ISBN 978-1-911512-79-0)*

3. *The Furthest Garrison: Imperial Regiments in New Zealand 1840-1870* Adam Davis (ISBN 978-1-911628-29-3)*

4. *Victory over Disease: Resolving The Medical Crisis In The Crimean War, 1854-1856* Michael Hinton (ISBN 978-1-911628 31-6)*

5. *Journey Through the Wilderness: Garnet Wolseley's Canadian Red River Expedition of 1870* Paul McNicholls (ISBN 978-1-911628-30-9)*

6. *Kitchener: The Man Not the Myth* Anne Samson (ISBN 978-1-912866-45-8)

7. *The British and the Sikhs: Discovery, Warfare and Friendship (c.1700–1900)* Gurinder Singh Mann (ISBN 978-1-911628-24-8) *

* Denotes books are paperback 246mm × 189mm, other books are hardback.

Contents

List of Illustrations

In text

In colour plate section

Acknowledgements

There have been many individuals and groups who have supported me in completing this project. I would like to thank Dr Paramvir Singh and the Department of Encyclopaedia, Punjabi University, Patiala. The Panjab Cultural Association, UK, deserves credit for the foresight to undertake the Anglo–Panjabi initiative and bringing out the translations of Dr John Leyden. I would like to thank Anurag Singh and use of the Dr Trilochan Library, Ludhiana, and access to his manuscripts and rare books. I would like to thank the staff at the British Library, Victoria and Albert Museum, the Royal Collection Trust, Ancient House Museum, Thetford, and other UK institutions that have been most helpful in my quest. Thanks to Christine Bernath (Gurkha Regimental Museum), Captain Mick Holtby (Royal Lancers & Nottinghamshire Yeomanry Museum) and Simon Dixon (University of Leicester) for the exchange of ideas related to Anglo–Sikh history and the discussion around artefacts in their respective institutions.

Thanks to all the staff at Helion & Co Ltd, especially Dr Christopher Brice, for the great support they have provided me throughout the process of publishing this book. Thanks to Harjinder Singh Sunner for a well-crafted portrait for the cover incorporating General Baghel Singh's conquest of Delhi. Other mentions include: Peter Bance, Bobby Bansal, Sukhbinder Singh Paul, Neil Carleton and Susan Stronge (Victoria and Albert Museum), Attul Jetha, Rajinder Singh, Gurnam Singh (University of Coventry), Dr Opinderjit Takhar (University of Wolverhampton), Raj Mann, Kartar Singh, Taranjit Singh, Dr Kamalroop Singh, John Coster, Avtar Singh Bahra, Jeevandeep Singh (Ludhiana), Rav Singh ('A Little History of the Sikhs'), Steven Purewal (Indus Media Foundation), Dr Kashmir Singh (Punjabi University, Patiala), George Anderson, Harjinder Singh Lallie (University of Warwick), Jasmohan Singh Obhi, Matthew Mee, Iain Smith and to the Mann family who have supported me throughout my career as a historian.

I would also lastly like to thank visitors to my website: www.sikhscholar.co.uk. Their comments and questions provide me with the daily motivation to write and ensure that projects like this have value. This project has also been endorsed by the Sikh Museum Initiative (SMI), www.sikhmuseum.org.uk, which is bringing out new research on Sikh artefacts and relics in the UK.

The Accounts

It was in 1997 as part of my MA in South Asian Religions at De Montfort University, Leicester, that I started looking closely at many descriptions of the Sikhs from British and other Western sources. Some of these I used for my dissertation, 'The Role of the Dasam Granth in Khalsa', namely the work of Lieutenant Colonel John Malcolm, *The Sketch of the Sikhs*, published in 1812. I also became familiar with British accounts of the Sikhs after reading the work of J.D Cunningham (1812–51), *A History of the Sikhs* (1849). I also considered British sources for several of my essays published in the Sikh Journal, *Sant Sipahi*, between 2000 and 2010. This included the 'Descriptions of the Dasam Granth from the "Sketch of the Sikhs" in view of Sikh History' and 'Sri Takhat Harimandir Sahib Patna Sahib: A Perspective of its History and Maryada', both published in 2008. Information from these essays is included in the accounts within this book.

It was in 2001 that I became familiar with the accounts suggesting that a British surgeon tended to the Tenth Guru, Gobind Singh (1666–1707), in his last days at Hazur Sahib, Nanded, in the state of Maharashtra. Many sources have been silent on any British surgeon at Nanded, and the first account in this volume considers this prospect. In 2011, as part of a project initiated by the Panjab Cultural Association, I delivered a lecture on rare translations of Sikh texts, 'The Lost British Accounts of Sikh Texts.' The project considered the works of Dr John Leyden (1775–1811), who translated Sikh texts predating the translations of the German philologist Ernest Trumpp (1828–85) of the *Adi Granth* and the works of Max Arthur Macauliffe (1841–1913), who wrote his magnum opus *The Sikh Religion* in six volumes. Dr Leyden translated Sikh texts as early as *c.*1808. Some of these translations are considered within the book, as well as the Sikh translation project set up by the British, undertaken by Ernest Trumpp.

During 2011, I started researching the various laws which were enacted by the British in India, including the Charter Act (1813), their impact, as well as considering the role played by the missionary movement in the Panjab. I presented some of this information on my website www.sikhscholar.co.uk, as well as delivering the paper 'British and the Sikhs: The Impact and Legacy of Colonial Dominance in the Panjab' at the Punjab Research Group, University of Wolverhampton, in 2012.

The Anglo–Sikh Wars (1845–46 and 1848–49) were the defining moment where several pitched battles solidified the position of the British within the Panjab. The

wars culminated in the British armies annexing the Panjab. The Sikhs have always felt aggrieved that their leaders let them down once the first Anglo–Sikh War had commenced, together with whether their crossing of the Sutlej actually was an invasion of British territories. After the various treaties were initiated by the British, they also took over the Lahore treasury, or *Toshkhana*, which housed the wealth of the Sikh government. As a result, many Sikh relics and artefacts were taken as spoils of war. This included Sikh manuscripts, weapons and other important artefacts of the Sikhs. Many relics were found on the battlefields of the Anglo–Sikh Wars and some of these are now spread across the UK in private collections, regimental museums and other larger museums. Some relics from these battles were displayed in the exhibition which I curated entitled 'Anglo–Sikh Wars: Battles, Treaties and Relics' in 2017. This narrative is also developed within the book to consider how many Sikh artefacts were gifted to the British during British Indian rule by the Maharajahs of the Panjab. Lavish examples of arms and armour and other expensive items were given to the various members of the Royal Family during the 19th century.

One institution which had its origins before the ascension of the Tenth Guru was the Buddha Dal (older guard), a vanguard army, credited to the veteran and pious Sikh, Baba Buddha (1506–1631). These 'knights errant' would be known as the Akali Nihangs, whose influence would be instrumental throughout Sikh history. We consider the account of General Baghel Singh, who, part of the Buddha Dal forces, conquered Delhi and became a *defacto* ruler. Rather than extending his territories, he levied taxes from the Mughal rulers. His conquests have remained relatively neglected, and as a result, it was this area which I felt required further discussion. These references will make this historic event more known in the mainstream as it defined the rise of the East India Company, together with the rise of the Khalsa. The Akali Nihangs were defiant against British rule during the 19th century. An analysis of their role is considered throughout the book; however, one incident is deliberated on and relates to several Akalis who were under siege by the British: threats to blow up a Sikh institution led to their arrest.

After the annexation of the Panjab, many Sikhs were left without employment and as a result, many former soldiers enlisted into the British Indian Army. Whilst there was an initial reluctance by the British, the Sikhs demonstrated their loyalty to the British through various campaigns, especially during the so-called Indian Mutiny of 1857. This resulted in many Sikh and Panjab units forming within the army. The Battle of Saragarhi (1897) was also a seminal moment for the Sikhs, who maintained their positions against tribesman on the North-west Frontier and became martyrs in the process. The gradual development of army enlistments led to Sikhs fighting in both the First and Second World Wars, providing a valuable resource for the global effort to defeat the forces of tyranny.

This book is not intended to be a complete reference guide highlighting the relationship between the British and the Sikhs, but more of a sample of anecdotes and history which shows how their histories have been intertwined between 1700 and 1900. The book is also supplemented with rare documents which include letters of

friendship between Jassa Singh Ahluwalia – leader of the Buddha Dal – and the British envoy James Browne, Anglo–Sikh treaties and proceedings from a Christian missionary conference. Honorific terms have been omitted and various spellings of common words have been used by commentators, as would be expected through a time spanning 200 years.

Gurinder Singh Mann
Leicester, UK
October 2019

Introduction

The word Panjab refers to the 'land of the five rivers' and falls in the regions now in India and Pakistan. These five rivers are the Beas, Ravi, Sutlej, Chenab and Jhelum, which are all tributaries of the Indus River. Panjab has a long history and rich cultural heritage. Some of the most important events related to India and Pakistan have taken place in Panjab. The famous Harappan civilization (*c.*3000 BC) was founded within this area and was a cradle of culture. The battles witnessed in the *Mahabharata* were again a Panjab-based epic. The Greek leader Alexander the Great (356–323 BC), invaded and conquered the Panjab in 326 BC, leaving behind a legacy. There were other dynasties, including the infamous one led by the Buddhist king, Ashoka (d. 232 BC), of the Maurya dynasty.

The people of the Panjab are called Panjabis and the language they speak is labelled the same. The fertile territory has a rich history dating back thousands of years and is the homeland to the world's fifth-largest religion, Sikhism. The Panjab has witnessed many invasions and the frontier has had to defend and repel various incursions, including the Mughals and Afghans, who set up their dynasties in India, firstly under Emperor Babur (1483–1530). During the same period, the Sikh religion was formed under Guru Nanak (1469–1539), who was opposed to the religious hypocrisy within the Hindu and Muslim religion at the time. The Sikh religion was a monotheistic faith which was opposed to ritualism and blind faith. The development of the religion was continued by a further nine preceptors, culminating with Guru Gobind Singh (1666–1708).[1] There was also a transformation in the faith, incorporating a military strain formalising the Sikhs into the Khalsa or 'fraternity of the pure' through the *Khande ki Pahul*, or initiation of the double-edged sword. Spiritual guidance and teachings were consecrated within the scripture, named Guru Granth Sahib. As a result, the Sikhs follow the Guru Granth as a 'living Guru'. The Sikh faith has sometimes been described as syncretic, i.e. absorbing ideas from the Hindu and Islamic faiths, but this loose description fails to consider the faith as revealed and as a result,

---

1   The 10 Gurus are Guru Nanak (1469–1539), Guru Angad (1539–52), Guru Amar Das (1552–74), Guru Ram Das (1574–81), Guru Arjan (1581–1606), Guru Hargobind (1606–44), Guru Har Rai (1630–61), Guru Harkrishan (1656–64), Guru Tegh Bahadur (1621–75) and Guru Gobind Singh (1666–1708). Guru Granth Sahib is sometimes known as the 11th Guru.

Sikhism is referred to as *tisra panth*, or the third way.[2] The Tenth Guru left writings of his own termed Dasam Granth, or 'scripture of the Tenth King', the compositions of which bear martial undertones.

The British entered the territories of India as far back as 1600 through a trading company. The royal charter was given by Queen Elizabeth I (1533–1603) in the same year. It was initially called The Company of Merchants of London Trading into the East Indies,[3] which traded in commodities including cotton, silk, saltpetre (used to produce gunpowder) as well as opium. It was later named the Honourable East India Company, the name under which it is famously known. So rather than the British government conquering parts of India, a private company expanded its interests through treaties, negotiations and, at times, sheer might. Like the Portuguese and the Dutch who had been trading in India, they recruited native armies which would protect the Company's interests. It was the capture of Arcot (1751) and the Battle of Plassey (1757), where they fought against the Nawab of Bengal and the French, that gave the British a solid foundation in India. These successes came under Major General Robert Clive (1725–74), better known as 'Clive of India.' The Battle of Buxar in 1764 was pivotal to the Company, where they defeated the armies of the Mughals, Oudh and Bengal. The Mughal ruler, Shah Alam II (1728–1806), and in signing the Treaty of Allahabad in 1765 effectively gave away *Diwani* rights, or the right to collect taxes on behalf of the emperor from the eastern provinces of Bengal-Bihar-Orissa. Whilst Clive did not have much direct contact with the Sikhs, he was to say they were only the power to impede the threat of Shah Abdali and was "extremely glad to know that the Shah's progress has been impeded by the Sikhs… As long as he does not defeat the Sikhs or come to terms with them, he cannot penetrate into India. And neither of these events seems probable since the Sikhs have adopted such effective tactics, and since they hate the Shah on account of his destruction of the Chak [Guru Chakk, i.e. Amritsar]."[4] Clive, however, courted controversy for his methods and was subject to a Parliamentary enquiry.[5]

The Company's initial moves did not consider the religions of the East; trade was their only concern. The Sikhs, however, were familiar with the Christian religion,

2   A reference to *tisra panth* can be seen in the apocryphal composition of Guru Gobind Singh entitled the *Uggardanti*. See mine and Kamalroop Singh's *The Granth of Guru Gobind Singh: Essays, Lectures and Translations* (Delhi: OUP, 2015).
3   Other names included John Company.
4   Imperial Record Department, *Calendar of Persian Correspondence: Volume 2 (1767–9)* (Calcutta: Superintendent Government Printing, 1914), letter 52, 2:20. He also commissioned Major Antoine Louis Henri Polier (1741–95) to write a detailed account of the Sikhs.
5   On his return to England he served as an MP for Shrewsbury. However, he was part of the enquiry which looked at the EIC's practices. In 1772, Clive was accused of embezzling Company money and blamed for the famine in Bengal between 1769 and 1772 which greatly reduced the population of the area. He was exonerated of these charges. However, his reputation was tarnished.

as testified within the Sikh scriptures. The accounts of the British from the 17th century are limited. One early Western account is a letter written by the Jesuit priest Jerome Xavier in 1606. The letter narrates the *Shaheedi* (martyrdom) of the fifth guru of the Sikhs, Guru Arjun (1563–1606). The execution of General Banda Singh Bahadur (1670–1716) in Delhi appears to be the first known account of the Sikhs by the British. The Mughal authorities captured the 'rebel Guru' and paraded him in the streets of Delhi, subjecting him to horrific torture before executing him.[6] The account was captured by John Surman *et. al.* in 1716 in the *Madras Diary Consultation Book, 1715–17*. This account is included in this volume. These references shed important light on the lives and manners of the Sikhs, as well as imparting information from a political perspective. The Western perspectives of the Sikhs were described by Christian preachers, travellers and most notably by military officers.

The Sikhs fought against tyranny and protected religious freedoms of all faiths. Banda Bahadur, at the start of the 18th century, was given the leadership to continue the fight in the Panjab, together with other Khalsa generals. The Khalsa army was eventually divided into Sikh Misls, or confederacies, that covered and protected various parts of the Panjab. The 18th century was a period of great upheaval and a battle for survival; persecution of the Sikhs was commonplace, with bounties placed on their heads. Early Sikh leaders like Kapur Singh (1697–1753)[7] formed the Khalsa into battalions, the Buddha Dal (older guard) and Taruna Dal (younger guard). He was succeeded by Jassa Singh Ahluwalia (1718–83), who continued the Sikh struggle against the imperial Mughal forces. His leadership witnessed the holocausts known as the *Choota Ghallughara* (smaller holocaust) and *Vadhha Ghallughara* (bigger holocaust), where thousands of Sikhs were killed.

There are several interesting British accounts from the 18th century, including those of Forster (1783), Brown (1788) and Francklin (1798). This was during the successful leadership of General Baghel Singh of the Karorasinghia Misl, who succeeded in conquering Delhi in 1783 and hoisting the Khalsa battle standard. However, the Sikhs did not subjugate the area and the main Sikh leaders went back to the Panjab and received regular payments or taxes from Shah Alam II, the deposed king. Sikh sovereignty also extended to having permanent reminders of their struggle in Delhi, and as a result, Baghel Singh's terms included the building of several Sikh temples, or Gurdwaras, related mainly to the Gurus. The British, also present in Delhi, were alarmed by the Sikh incursions. Numerous letters were exchanged by the administrators of the first Governor-General of the Presidency of Fort William (Bengal), Warren Hastings (1732–1818). They sought to loosen the grip of the Sikhs around

---

6   Many early Mughal and British sources refer to Banda Bahadur as a Guru. Even frescoes within the Gurudwara of Banda state that he was a Guru. This is incorrect, as the last living Guru of the Sikhs was Guru Gobind Singh. Whilst military authority was given to Banda, he appears to have resembled the Tenth Guru. These factors may have contributed to the erroneous view.

7   The title of Nawab was given to him by the Mughals to confer rights and sovereignty.

Delhi and other territories to the east. Hastings understood the Sikhs were a buffer between the Afghan incursions and British territories. He had continued from where Clive of India had left off, and on his return to Britain was impeached by Parliament but later acquitted.

However, it was deemed that no direct confrontation should take place and terms of friendship should perhaps be sought. The British sent correspondence to the Sikh chiefs with the aim of securing friendship, as the Sikhs were bordering on British interests at Awadh (Oude) near the River Ganges. This was probably one of the most important junctures of Anglo–Sikh relations, yet these interactions have gone unnoticed in both modern Sikh and British history. As a result, prominence is given to General Baghel Singh, who was in contact with the British envoy James Browne. The cover of this book depicts Baghel Singh and the Khalsa forces amongst the burning Red Fort, the seat of the Mughal king of Delhi, with the British looking on.

However, it was the British who took Delhi in 1803 as part of the Second Anglo Maratha War. During this time, Ranjit Singh (1780–1839), head of the Sukerchakia Misl, absorbed many of the existing confederacies and declared himself Maharajah of the Panjab. This ushered in a glorious period for the Sikhs and led to much-needed stability in the Panjab. The Sikh Empire lasted from 1799–1849. It was during this period that the British met the 'Lion of Panjab', and many interactions took place. These included the historic meeting with Charles T. Metcalfe (1785–1846), Governor-General of the East India Company, leading to the Treaty of Amritsar in 1809, as well as the Anglo–Sikh Treaty of 1831, signed by William Bentinck (1774–1839).[8] The treaty of 1809 essentially created a split in the Panjab, with several Sikh states (known as the Cis-Sutlej States) such as Patiala, Jind and Kalsia opting to be part of the British protectorate.

British perspectives form the bulk of references in this book; however, we do consider a plethora of Panjabi and European sources, together with Persian ones. Persian was the state and courtly language for many hundreds of years, and there are many descriptions by Muslim writers as would be expected. Yet some of these accounts may have been biased due to the hostilities between the ruling establishment and the Sikhs. However, the British interaction with the Sikhs is our focus, and this sheds light on the incursions made by the British in India, notably the Panjab. The interactions between them led to an increase in Sikh descriptions in English tracts and papers. The EIC also took many writers to the East, and consequently it became an active policy by the British to collect information on India, its religions and – most notably – any weaknesses they may have had. Many intelligence reports were produced which aided British designs in the sub-continent. Also instrumental in the expansionist plans was the role of cartographers, who mapped out the terrain and territories of India. James Rendell's maps from the 1780s were highly accurate, and his

---

8   See appendices for this treaty.

depiction of the Sikh territories also highlights how many territorial gains had been made by this small community.[9]

A few writers described the situation in the Panjab, and these contributions ended up in well-known newspapers of the period. One of the most popular British newspapers in the 19th century was *The Illustrated London News* (ILN), established and first printed in 1842. It covered many major world events, from the Victorian period all the way through to the last edition in 2003. It was one of the first fully illustrated weekly newspapers which gave coverage of the British across the world. With the presence of the British in the Indian sub-continent, the paper gave an interesting perspective of the East India Company.[10] The Panjab and the Sikhs were given ample coverage, with numerous illustrations. It appears, based on the reporting of the Sikhs in the 19th century, that the British public was more aware of this hardy race than at present. Notable events covered included the earliest 19th-century accounts of the Sikhs during the Anglo–Sikh Wars (1845–46 and 1848–49), the annexation of the Panjab and the Indian Mutiny (1857), as well as the numerous campaigns involving Sikhs as part of the British Indian Army. There were also some wonderful illustrations in the newspaper of the Akali Nihangs, the warriors who were to face the wrath of the British in numerous encounters.

There were many travellers, adventurers and poets who passed through the Panjab and recorded and even illustrated what they saw. Emily Eden (1797–1869) sketched many portraits of rulers and princes in her *Portraits of the Princes and People of India* (1843).[11] Due to her access to the Sikh Court, she was able to undertake sketches of Maharajah Ranjit Singh, his son Maharajah Sher Singh (1807–43) and the Akali Nihangs, all drawn with excellent accuracy, for which she received much acclaim. Eden wrote of the Akalis:

> Akalees or Immortals, Sikh religious devotees, being very wild in appearance and turbulent characters. They formerly were largely employed in the Sikh armies and were often remarkable for acts of desperate courage, but their licence renders them formidable to any regular Government and Ranjeet Singh gradually reduced their numbers, and broke their power by distributing them in small companies among his disciplined battalion; their blue dresses, their high-peaked turbans, the rings of steel, which they wear as the peculiar emblems of their devotion to the first great military leader of the Sikhs Guru Gobind Singh, and the profusion and variety of their arms make them very picturesque objects.[12]

---

9   What is not recorded on the map is the tributaries of the Sikhs. This however has been created in the map which follows the Introduction.

10   From here on refered to as the EIC.

11   Emily Eden was a poet and novelist. She accompanied her brother George Eden, 1st Earl of Auckland, who served as Governor-General in India from 1835–1842.

12   Emily Eden, *Portraits of the Princes & Peoples of India by the Honorable Miss Eden Drawn on the Stone by L. Dickinson* (London: J. Dickinson & Son, 1844), Plate 5. Other descriptions

Artists captured the glory period of the Sikh Empire through their paintings of Maharajah Ranjit Singh and the Lahore Court in all its majestic glory. Artists like William Carpenter (1818–99) became synonymous with depicting the Panjab religious institutions and rulers. His many drawings include depictions of the Harimandir Sahib, popularly known as the Golden Temple, titled 'Tank & Marble Causeway the Sikh Temple Amritsar and The Golden Temple at Amritsar', and of the Akal Takht, titled 'The Akalis Tower at Amritsar'.[13] His illustrations were used in the ILN and were later acquired by the Victoria and Albert Museum.[14] Another painter, described as a 'war artist', was William Simpson (1823–99), who was famed for his reporting of the Crimean War. He dedicated his sketches from India to Queen Victoria, published in the book *India, Ancient and Modern*.[15] His works related to the Sikhs were similar to those of Carpenter focusing on Amritsar, and included 'Sikh priest reading the Grunth, Umritsur', a depiction of a priest reading from the scripture Guru Granth Sahib, and 'Akalis at the Holy Tank, Umritsar', showing an Akali Nihang wearing the *Dastar Boonga* (crowned towers), the signature Turban of the Sikh warriors.

Felice Beato (1832–1909), the Italian–British photographer, is credited as the first to capture through lense the different cultures in East Asia. He was present at the Crimean War (1853–56) as well as the Opium Wars of 1839–42 and 1856–60. His works of the Sikhs include the Golden Temple, the Akali Nihangs as well as the Sikhs in the British India Army. However, he is widely known for the photography of skulls and corpses during the Indian Mutiny, particularly one labelled as the 'Interior of Secundrabagh after the slaughter of 2,000 rebels' (1858). The title of the first war photographer is sometimes given to John McCosh (1805–1885), who used a groundbreaking calotype process for his works. He took part in the second Anglo–Sikh War, where he was able to photograph the key players of the time such as Diwan Mulraj, Hugh Gough as well as the soldier Patrick Vans Agnew.[16]

With the advent of the Anglo–Sikh Wars, coverage was given to the battles of Mudki, Ferozeshah Chillianwallah and Gujarat, amongst others. The annexation of the Panjab was covered in detail, and war booty and prizes were seen in many editions. These included Sikh cannons, as well as captured battle standards, together with the *Koh-i-Noor*, or mountain of light, diamond. Many Sikh relics and artefacts made their way to the UK, including Sikh scriptures and Gurumukhi works which

of Sikhs by Emily Eden appear in her *Up the Country: Letters Written to Her Sister from the Upper Provinces of India* (London: Richard Bentley, 1867).

13   V & A Museum numbers IS.54-1882, IS.50-1882 and IS.40-1882.

14   In 1881, he showcased 275 of his paintings in the South Kensington Museum, London.

15   William Simpson, *India ancient and modern: a series of illustrations of the country and the people of India and adjacent territories; executed in chromo-lithography from drawings by William Simpson; with descriptive literature by John William Kaye* (London: Day and Son, 1867).

16   His other Sikh representations include areas of Lahore, including the tomb or *Samadhi* of Ranjit Singh. Much of his work can be found at the National Army Museum, London.

were deposited in the India Office Library (the British Library) in London. Other manuscripts and relics went to the Victoria and Albert Museum, Royal Armouries, the British Museum, the Wellcome Trust and regimental museums, as well as many private collections in the UK. The Royal Collection Trust also holds many Sikh items (these are discussed within the book). The plethora of Sikh items which have appeared in British auction houses shows the many different types of Sikh relics which have found their way to the UK held within personal collections.

After the Anglo–Sikh Wars, the Sikhs were still in need of jobs and the militant strand breathed into them by Guru Gobind Singh was still a passion which needed stirring. Sikhs were employed as part of the British Indian Army and contributed to conquests in faraway places such as Sudan and Abyssinia (Ethiopia). One of the pivotal moments was the Sikhs loyalty to the British in the Indian Mutiny or rebellion of 1857, when the Maharajahs of Panjab sent their troops to quell the disturbances. Whilst some parts of the subcontinent were besieged by pockets of resistance against the British, the Sikhs in the Panjab provided much-needed support in the campaign.

This book concerns itself with relations between the British and Sikhs until 1900, but it is still useful to understand the effect of the Sikhs within the British Indian Army. The culmination of the Sikhs being part of the Allied forces would be seen with their recruitment and participation in the First and Second World Wars. The Sikhs at this time were part of the military units set up in the Panjab. When Sikh soldiers returned to the Panjab, they saw their brethren being treated as second-class citizens and witnessed indiscriminate killings by the British in incidents such as the Jallianwala Bagh massacre in 1919.[17] A reform movement also started taking shape, known as the Singh Sabhas, which culminated in the formation of a religious orthodoxy known as the SGPC (Sikh Gurdwara Prabandhak Committee) in 1920. Their role was to look after Gurdwaras and ensure their sanctity was preserved. It was also at this time that the political party known as the Akali Dal came into being, working to ensure that the Panjab was free from British control.

Prior to 1947 and the partition of India, Panjab covered a major area. A significant part of Panjab was then given to the newly formed Pakistan, including many shrines related to the Sikh Gurus, Sikh Empire and a good number of Sikh personalities and martyrs. The British separated the Panjab into two based on boundary demarcation, as created by Cyril Radcliffe (1899–1977). The Indian Independence Act of 1947 stipulated that British rule in India would come to an end on 15 August that year. This had a devasting effect on the people of India, with sectarian violence taking place between Muslims, Sikhs and Hindus.

Whereas the script of Panjabi in India is Gurmukhi and is related to the Sikh scripture, the Guru Granth Sahib – the script of Panjabi in Pakistan – is Shahmukhi. The British held a presence in the Panjab for many years, but they formally ruled between 1849 and 1947. The Cis-Sutlej states were under a British protectorate since 1809. As

---

17   There are regular calls for the British Government to apologise for this incident.

a result, much of the Panjab and British history is intertwined. However, this relation-ship would not end there, and with the advent of the movement of labour, many Sikhs came to the shores of the UK in the 1960s to make their homes. So the story has come full circle, with Sikhs today playing a prominent part within British society, including the armed forces.

Map depicting Sikh Misl territories and conquests around Delhi, and the British protectorate areas after 1765. (Map drawn by George Anderson © Helion & Company 2020).

1

'Dr Cole' and Guru Gobind Singh

We start our narrative by considering the relationship of a British surgeon and the Sikhs. Guru Gobind Singh, the Tenth Guru of the Sikhs, had solidified the Sikhs into a vanguard army known as the Khalsa, or fraternity of the pure. The Sikhs had been transformed into sainted soldiers in 1699 by a ceremony known as *Khande Ki Pahul*, or initiation with a double-edge sword. Tradition asserts the religious symbols of the '5Ks' were worn by the Khalsa to distinguish them from any other religious group.[1] The Sikhs under the Guru became formidable around the Panjab but faced opposition from the Mughal Empire and the so-called hill Rajahs/Hindu kings who wanted to protect their hegemony in the region.

The Guru witnessed his sons being martyred by the Mughals, but his faith in God was unflinching and he set a moral code amongst the Sikhs. He taught the Sikhs the art of war known as *Shastarvidia*. Each initiated Khalsa would be known as *Sawa Lakh*, equal to 125,000 on the battlefield, and he led his Khalsa forces in numerous battles. He also created a literary court the like of which had not been seen before, encouraging Hindus and Muslims to translate world literature into the common language. Themes including philosophy, medicine and warfare were discussed, and many Indic texts, such as the *Bhagavad Gita* and *Puranas*, were presented to the Guru. The scholars in his Durbar were the best-paid and most highly regarded amongst his Khalsa.

The Guru gave the Sikhs the final instruction that there would be no more physical living Gurus after him, and the Sikhs should place faith in the Sikh scripture – Guru Granth Sahib – as the living Guru. The Guru commanded Banda Singh Bahadur, together with five prominent Sikhs, to start taking back territories in the Panjab and to avenge the injustices taking place there. The battle standard was given to the Khalsa, together with a sword, one gold coin and five arrows, signifying the temporal authority vested in these Khalsa to continue the mission of the Guru.

---

1   The keeping of the *Kesh* (uncut hair), *Kara* (a steel bracelet), *Kanga* (a wooden comb), *Kaccha* (underwear) and *Kirpan* (steel sword).

Within the final days of the Guru, whilst he was encamped at Nanded, Maharashtra, in 1708, he began undertaking his courtly activities and the congregation came from far and wide to catch a glimpse of him. After the Khalsa warriors were sent to the Panjab we hear of an interesting description of a doctor who is said to have attended to Guru Gobind Singh in 1708. On the fateful night when the Guru was about to sleep, a Pathan entered the tent and reverently bowed before the Guru, behaving in a most courteous manner. As the Guru raised his head to bless him, the Pathan took out his dagger and stabbed the Guru, who managed to deflect the attack with his shield or *Dhal*. Some accounts state that the Guru killed the Pathan, whilst others say Sikhs within the camp executed him. However, the Guru had been seriously injured and bled profusely.

The news reached the camp of the Mughal Emperor, Bahadur Shah (1643–1712), also known as Shah Alam I, who despatched one of his medics. The wounds were stitched up by the medic with great skill, thanks to which the Guru appeared to have recovered. He was later sent several arrows to test, and it was said that using his bow and arrows split open his wound, from which he did not recover. The Guru breathed his last at Nanded sometime in 1708. Thus ended the human form of the Gurus which began with Guru Nanak in 1469. However, the spiritual heir would be consecrated in the scripture, Guru Granth Sahib, and regarded as a 'living Guru'.

Who was the doctor that attended to the Tenth Guru? Several sources mention that a doctor did attend to the Guru, and that he was in the service of Emperor Bahadur Shah. It was assumed that the doctor would most likely have been a Muslim. However, a ruler would employ the best people from their court, so that need not necessarily be so. There are several Sikh and British sources which describe these events and differ in their assessment regarding who this medic might have been. It is in the late account by Dhian Singh in the relatively small work *Daswan Patshah Ka Antam Kautak*[2] that we first hear of a British doctor. There had already been British surgeons working in India, and one who became famous in the court of Mughal Emperor Farrukhsiyar (1685–1719) was William Hamilton (d. 1717), who had accompanied the mission of John Surman from Patna to Bengal. However, the services of a British doctor in the aftermath of Guru Gobind Singh's wounds have captured the thoughts of many writers.

Dhian Singh writes within his text the following: "*Das Mohran Roz Sahib Dewain Jarahdar Kau, Kal Usih Da nam, Angrez si*" ("he was an Englishman, Cole by name, and the Guru paid him 10 Mohurs a day".[3] He tells us that the doctor was British and that he was paid handsomely for his services in tending to the Guru. We thus need to consider some early sources on Sikh history and determine if a British doctor named Cole did indeed attend to Guru Gobind Singh. One early account of these events

---

2   Dhian Singh, *Daswen Patshah ka Antam Kautak*, quoted in Dr Gurbachan Singh Nayer, *The Panjab-Past And Present*, Vol. XXV-I, April 1991, No. 49 (Patiala: Punjabi University, 1991).

3   Mohur was a gold coin, hence a reference to the currency used. Dhian Singh, *Daswen Patshah ka Antam Kautak* (publication details not known).

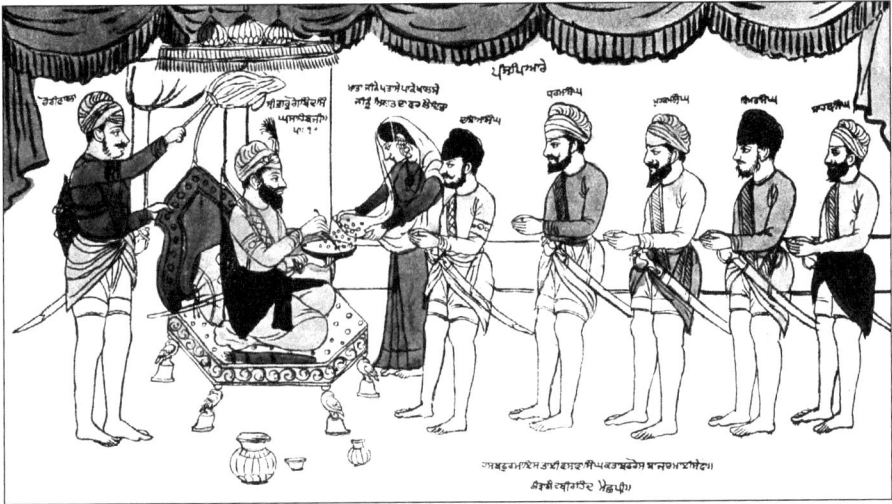

Guru Gobind Singh mixing nectar for his disciples at the birth of Khalsa.
(Wellcome Collection. CC-BY)

was by the court poet of Guru Gobind Singh, Sainapat, who wrote his *Gursobha*, or *Splendour of the Guru* (1711), considered to be completed at Nanded. Sainapat is silent on any British doctor in his work.[4] The document referred to as *Amarnama*, said to be written by the bard 'Dhadi' Nathmal, also refers to the final days of the Tenth Guru at Nanded. This was reputed to have been completed at the time of the Guru's ascension, but again does not mention a British doctor.[5] A rare document which was found by Dr Trilochan Singh also refers to the ascension of the Tenth Guru, yet again there is no mention of a Dr Cole.[6] Turning to British accounts, George Forster of the EIC referred to the Guru's last days in his Letter No. XI of 1783. He states in his *A Journey from Bengal to England* that: "Gobind Singh was assassinated during this expedition of Emperor Bahadur Shah to the Deccan by a Pathan soldier and he died of his wounds in 1708 at the town of Nanded without leaving any male issue; and a tradition delivered to the Sicques, limiting their priests to the number of ten, induced them to appoint no successors to Govind Singh."[7] Lieutenant Colonel John Malcolm,

---

4   Kulwant Singh (trans.), *Sri Gur Sobha Sainapati* (Chandigarh: Institute of Sikh Studies, 2014).
5   It is stated that the account was completed on 31 October 1708.
6   Dr Trilochan Singh, 'Guru Gobind Singh's Ascension', *Sikh Review*, October 1963, pp.13–38. It was an important intervention by Trilochan Singh, who prevented the manuscript from being destroyed.
7   George Forster, *A Journey from Bengal to England: Through the Northern Part of India, Kashmire, Afghanistan, and Persia, and into Russia by the Caspian Sea* (London: Printed for R. Faulder, 1798), Vol. I, p.263.

who is credited with the start of Sikh histography from a British perspective, states that the Guru's last days were at Nanded, and he again is silent on a British doctor treating the Guru.[8]

Dr Ganda Singh (1972) gives many accounts of the last days of the Tenth Guru, but none of these mentions a British man named Cole.[9] However, there is one account which stands out from the others: this is by Sukha Singh, who wrote his *Gurbilas Patshahi 10*, or *Splendour of the Tenth Guru*, in 1797. In his account of the final days of the Guru, he states that: "The Emperor was still at Nanded when he sent his own surgeon, a *Ferengi*, Call or Cole by name when the Guru was stabbed."[10] This is interesting, as the word '*Ferrengi*' appears in various accounts in the 18th and 19th centuries. The term, however, does not necessarily mean British, but is more likely to mean European. The word even appears in Guru Gobind Singh's scripture, the Dasam Granth. It appears that this may be the closet source suggesting a European doctor attending to the Tenth Guru. However, this does not specify that it was a British doctor. So, if he was not British could the account by Sukha Singh be pointing to a European medic? This is certainly the assertion made by some writers,[11] who claim the doctor in question was not British, but a medic named Nicolas Manucci (1638–1717), this assertion being based on the text *Storia Do Mogor* (*The Story of Mogul India*).[12]

According to this view, Nicolas Manucci was with the Emperor at the time of the Tenth Guru, and thus must be the so-called 'Dr Cole' who attended to Guru Gobind Singh. Let us consider this idea in more detail. Dr Nicholas Manucci was born in Venice and hence was a Venetian medic, not British. He left home at the age of 14 and was employed by Viscount Bellomont (1616–56),[13] who took him to Surat, India, in 1656. After his master passed away he became an artilleryman in the employ of Dara Shukoh (1615–59.[14] Later he moved to to work for Emperor Bahadur Shah.

8   Interestingly, John Malcolm verifies the place of death based on the internal evidence of a manuscript of Guru Granth Sahib which he had in his possession. It is not clear whether this manuscript is extant. See Lt Col John Malcolm, *The Sketch of the Sikhs: A Singular Nation Who Inhabit the Provinces of the Punjab Situated Between the Rivers Jamnu and Indus* (London: John Murray, 1812), p.70.
9   Dr Ganda Singh, *Guru Gobind Singh's Death At Nanded: An Examination of Succession Theories* (Faridkot: Guru Nanak Foundation, 1972).
10 Dr Ganda Singh, *Guru Gobind Singh's Death*, p.30.
11 Harpal Singh, 'An European Surgeon Who Attended Satguru Gobind Singh in 1708', https://satguru.weebly.com/european-surgeon-who-attended-satguru-gobind-singh-in-1708.html (accessed 10 June 2018).
12 Niccolao Manucci, *Storia Do Mogor or Mogul India 1653–1708 By Niccolao Manucci, Venetian*, Translated with Introduction and Notes by William Irvine, 4 Volumes (London: John Murray, 1907).
13 Henry Bard, 1st Viscount Bellomont.
14 Edward Farley Owen, *European Travellers in India: During the Fifteenth, Sixteenth and Seventeenth Centuries, the Evidence Afforded by Them with Respect to Indian Social Institutions, & the Nature & Influence of Indian Government* (Delhi: Asian Educational Services, 1991), pp.214–26. Originally published in 1909.

The text *Storia Do Mogor* covers his work as a surgeon during this period, as well as commenting on the life of Mughal Emperor Aurangzeb (1618–1707).

We learn that Dr Manucci started writing/dictating the fourth volume of his text between 1706 and 1709 whilst he was at Madras. We should note that the Guru passed away in 1708, when most of the book had been written. He had already started sending manuscripts of his work to France, and one early addition appeared in 1705, compiled by the French historian and Jesuit Priest Francois Catrou (1659–1737).[15] There were further variants of the work published in 1708 and 1715, and it was later translated into Italian, Portuguese and English.

Manucci, whilst originally based at Lahore, also passed through Patna, stayed at the Deccan and was present at Aurangabad. These locations were all related to the Sikhs in some form or other. Whilst it is probable that he may have encountered the Sikhs, there is no mention of Dr Manucci meeting any Sikh in his work. Prince Dara Shukoh (1615–59) of the Mughal Empire, whom Manucci was working for, had been in contact with Guru Har Rai (1630–11), the seventh Guru. Sikh tradition narrates that the Guru had sent herbs to Dara when his son fell ill. The story goes that he was cured due to this act. Manucci does not, however, mention this incident; more importantly, if Manucci was held in high regard, why was he not consulted on the health of the Emperor's son? However, our concern is with Bahadur Shah, and whether under any conditions he was to meet Guru Gobind Singh.

Manucci had deserted the camp of Bahadur Shah and ended up at the court of King Abul Hassan Shah in Golconda. When Bahadur Shah heard of this, he arranged for Manucci to be brought to him. Manucci left the court and eventually ended up in Fort St George, Madras, in 1702, moving later to Pondicherry. It was only in 1712 that he looked to resolve his differences with Bahadur Shah, but this was not to be as the Emperor died in 1712.[16] Whilst the history and accounts of Dr Manucci are interesting, there is no evidence to support the idea that he was in the employ of Emperor Bahadur Shah in 1708, working on his behalf or sent by him to tend to Guru Gobind Singh.

This then begs the question who the doctor was, and if indeed he was European at all. The case remains open, but at least some of the theories that have been circulated can be dismissed. The tradition at Hazur Sahib also suggests that there was a European doctor who tended to Guru Gobind Singh, and a modern painting depicts this event.[17] However, the enigma of the British doctor tending to Guru Gobind Singh remains unresolved.

15   For complexities of the text and possible tampering, see Niccolao Manucci, *Storia Do Mogor*.
16   See Rao Bahadur Iyangar, 'Manucci in Madras', in *The Madras Tercentenary Commemoration Volume* (Chennai: Asian Educational Services, 1994; first published in 1934).
17   This painting is kept at the museum at Gurdwara Banda Ghat at Hazur Sahib.

2

The Execution of Banda Singh Bahadur in Delhi

The line of the Sikh Gurus that had begun with Guru Nanak (1469–1539), the founder of Sikh religion, came to an end with the 10th and last Guru, Gobind Singh, who bequeathed spiritual heritage of Sikhism to the scripture, Guru Granth Sahib, and the temporal leadership of the Sikhs to the general body of the Khalsa.

The military leadership would be passed to a relatively unknown within the Sikh faith: Banda Singh Bahadur (1670–1716), a sadhu (ascetic) of the *bairagi* order. Armed initially with just five followers, a battle standard, war drum and some weapons, his mission as the commander of the Khalsa forces was to take revenge on the enemies of the Guru and makes some advances in the Sikh cause.[1] Banda made major inroads in fighting against Mughal tyranny and persecution towards the Sikhs. The initial incursion at Khanda in the Sonipat district (1709) sent a strong message to the Mughal authorities and was followed by the sacking of Samana in the same year. Banda had his base at Lohgarh (the Fortress of Steel) and started issuing coins with the symbol of Sikh sovereignty, *Deg-Tegh-Fateh.*[2] The town of Rahon was captured in 1710, together with Jalalabad being attacked.

The Battle of Chaapar Chiri (12 May 1710) was an important milestone where the Sikhs killed Wazir Khan (governor of Sirhind) and Dewan Suchanand, the individuals who were responsible for the martyrdom of the two infant sons of Guru Gobind Singh.[3] Two days later, Sirhind was also sacked by the Khalsa but was later recaptured by the Mughals. Banda made Lohgarh his capital between 1710 and 1713, and as a

---

1   *Bariragi*: a believer in the Hindu deity Vishnu and a member of the caste of Hindu Brahmins. The five Sikhs were Baj Singh, Binod Singh, Ram Singh, Daya Singh and Kahan Singh. They would later be the foundations of the Buddha Dal, with Binod Singh being chosen as the leader.

2   The concept was devised by Guru Gobind Singh. It denotes three processes: that of *degh* (nourishment), *tegh* (sword) and *fateh* (victory). So, the nourishment (of the poor) and the use of the sword leads to victory. See mine and Kamalroop Singh's *The Granth of Guru Gobind Singh: Essays, Lectures and Translations* (Delhi: OUP), pp.210–17.

3   The *Fateh Burj*, or Victory Tower, commemorates Banda's victory.

Coin minted by
Banda Singh Bahadur,
Lohgarh, 1711–1712.
(American Numismatic
Society)

result the fort there was attacked several times. The fight was then taken to Jamnu, with a great battle taking place in 1712.

Bahadur Shah, the Mughal emperor, died in 1713. Farrukhsiyar then took to the throne, and appointed Abdus Samad Khan (d. 1737) as the governor of Lahore, who together with his son Zakariya Khan was sent to fight Banda in Jammu. The siege of Gurdas Nangal (1715) was the final battle for Banda. The fort was besieged for eight months, during which many Sikhs broke away from Banda and deserted the defences. The imperial forces of the Mughals under Abdus Samad Khan assembled Pathans, Bundela Rajputs and the Rajputs of Katoch and Jasrot. The combined forces were able to penetrate the defences of the fort, leading to the capture of Banda.

This happened in December 1715, when Banda was carried to Delhi as a prisoner along with 694 other Sikhs, shackled in chains and in cages. They were all, with the exception of Banda and a few chosen leaders, executed in the maidan opposite the Chandni Chowk Kotwali at the rate of 100 a day, beginning on 5 March 1716.[4] The turn of Banda Singh Bahadur himself and his associates came three months later on 9 June, when he was taken out to the Qutb Minar and torn to pieces near the tomb of Emperor Bahadur Shah.[5]

Writing from Delhi in 1716, John Surman and Edward Stephenson informed Robert Hedges, the British governor of Fort William in Calcutta, about what was happening to Banda Singh Bahadur and his fellow prisoners.[6] The embassy of the

---

4   This is also the location where Guru Tegh Bahadur (162175), the ninth Guru, was executed by the Mughals. Gurdwara Sis Ganj Sahib was built by General Baghel Singh (whom we discuss later) to symbolise the Guru's martyrdom.

5   Also spelt Qutab Minar, this is the tallest minaret in the world made up of bricks, forming part of the Qutb complex, a UNESCO World Heritage Site. It was constructed by Qutab-Ud-Din-Aibak (1150–1210), founder of the Delhi Sultanate which ruled the India subcontinent from 1206–1526.

6   The account appears in the Madras Diary and Consultation Book for 1715–19, No. 87, Range 237. It later appeared in various sources, with commentary, including C.R. Wilson's *The Early Annals of the English in Bengal*, Volume II Part II (Calcutta: The Asiatic Society,

governor of Fort William was present at the court of Mughal Emperor Farrukhsiyar and witnessed these executions, leaving an important and eye-watering account of Banda's death. They wrote of the remarkable calm with which the Sikhs accepted their fate:

Letter XII

The Honourable Robert Hedges Esq.,
President & Governor of Fort William & Council in Bengal.
Honourable Sirs. etc.

We wrote your Honour on the 7th ultimo since which we have received no letters.

The great Rebel Gooroo [Banda Singh] who has been for these 20 years so troublesome in the Subaship [suba] of Lahore is at length taken with all his family and attendance by Abd-us-Samad Cawn the Suba [subedar, i.e., governor] of that province. Some days ago they entered the city laden with fetters, his whole attendants which were left alive being about seven hundred and eighty all severally mounted on camels which were sent out of the City for that purpose, besides about two thousand heads stuck upon poles, being those who died by the sword in battle. He was carried into the presence of the King, and from thence to a close prison. He at present has his life prolonged with most of his *mutsuddys* [officers] in the hope to get an Account of his treasure in the several parts of his Kingdom, and of those that assisted him, when afterwards he will be executed, for the rest there are 100 each day beheaded. It is not a little remarkable with what patience they undergo their fate, and to the last it has not been found that one apostatised from his new formed Religion.

Dilly, March the 10th, 1716
We are,
Honourable Sir & Sirs,
Your most obedient humble servants,
John Surman,
Edward Stephenson.
Cojee Seerhaud assenting.
Hugh Barker. Secretary

It must also be qualified why Banda might be called 'Gooroo' in some quarters after the death of Guru Gobind Singh, the Mughals and Sikhs alike mistakenly seeing Banda as a Guru. There are some suggestions by his opponents that it was Banda who called himself a Guru, leading to divisions within the Sikh forces. Something

---

1911), pp.120–21, and J. Talboys Wheeler's *Early Records of British India* (London: Trubner and Company, 1878), p.180.

significant which is missing from this account is the gruesome detail where the son of Banda (Ajai Singh) was killed in front of him and his body parts fed to Banda, an extreme act of barbarity which most people cannot fathom to this day. Banda had his eyes gouged out and was hacked to pieces in front of the onlooking crowds. However, Banda and his followers did not flinch when the met their executioner. There now stands at Mehrauli in Delhi a brick wall and a Gurdwara commemorating the spot where he was killed.[7]

This British account is one of the first giving details of the Sikhs, as well as confirming the ascendancy of the EIC in the Mughal Empire. In 1717, Emperor Farrukhsiyar issued a *farman* (grant) giving the EIC the right to reside and trade in the Mughal kingdom; essentially it was the 'Magna Carta' of English trade in India. They could trade freely, except for a yearly payment of 3,000 rupees. This was said to be because William Hamilton (d. 1717), a surgeon associated with the company that witnessed Banda's execution, cured Farrukhsiyar of a disease.[8]

Mehrauli, Delhi. Location commemorating the martyrdom of Banda Singh Bahadur. (Photograph by Gurinder Singh Mann)

7   Gurdwara Shahidi Asthaan Baba Banda Singh Bahadur is situated at Mehrauli near the historic Qutab Minar in memory of his martyrdom.
8   Philip J. Stern, *The Company-State: Corporate Sovereignty and the Early Modern Foundations of the British Empire in India* (USA: Oxford University Press, 2011).

3

Charles Wilkins and the Throne at Patna

An early description of the Sikhs comes from a British writer from 1781. It was made by Sir Charles Wilkins (1749–1836), who came to India in 1770 and began his career in the EIC's service. He undertook the translation of various Hindu religious scriptures, namely the *Bhagavad-Gita*,[1] the *Hitopadesha* Sanskrit fables[2] and the *Shakuntala*. He wrote *A Grammar of Sanskrit* as early as 1779,[3] and also started the research papers known as the *Asiatick Researchers* in Calcutta. It was here that he was informed by a Sikh gentleman that he should visit the birthplace of Guru Gobind Singh. On his way to Benares, he did exactly that, which led to him writing an interesting description of the Sikhs at Patna in Bihar.

The population of the Sikhs was mainly based in Panjab, but the mission of the Gurus was to spread knowledge of the Sikh religion beyond this area. This was initiated by the first Guru of the Sikhs, Guru Nanak, who undertook numerous missionary visits throughout India and beyond, including Sri Lanka, Afghanistan and even as far as Iraq. Guru Nanak visited Patna on his *Udasis*, or journeys, and his stay at Bihar is venerated by a Gurdwara commemorating his visit.[4] The establishment of *Manjis* (diocese) throughout India ensured the Sikh religion was being disseminated. The ninth Guru, Tegh Bahadur, also visited the congregation at Patna and during his tenure established the religion in the area. His family set up home there during his visit to the eastern parts of India. It was in Patna that Guru Gobind Singh was born in 1666, the Gurdwara which commemorates his birth known as Takht Harimandir Sahib.[5]

---

1   The British Library has reprints of these translations. All references are See: 14060.a.12. and W.P.9530/76.
2   See: W.P.9530/137.
3   See: T 45289
4   Gurdwara Gai Ghat, Patna, Bihar.
5   A very informative account on the history of the Sikhs at Patna has been undertaken by Dr Ved Prakash with his *The Sikhs In Bihar* (New Delhi: Janaki Prakashan, 1981).

When Charles Wilkins visited Patna, he was to see one of the most important locations in Sikh history. Wilkins wrote his account of the Sikhs for the Asiatick Society on 1 March 1781. Entitled 'The Seeks and their college at Patna', it is one of the first Western accounts explaining the rights and rituals of the Sikhs. It was published some years later in the *Transactions of Asiatick Society* in 1788. His observations were quoted throughout the 19th century but remained confined to British tracts and books. It was not until Dr Ganda Singh, the eminent Sikh historian, rediscovered it in the late 1930s that Wilkins' account saw the light of day for the Sikhs.[6] Wilkins begins his account by describing how he located the temple, which he refers to as a 'college'. He states:

> They said it was a place of worship open to me and to all men; but, at the same time, intimated that I must take off my shoes. As I consider this ceremony in the same light as uncovering my head upon entering any of our temples dedicated to the Deity, I did not hesitate to comply, and I was then politely conducted into the hall, and seated upon a carpet, in the midst of the assembly, which was so numerous as almost to fill the room.[7]

A Western definition of what a college represents compared with that of an Indian description would likely have differed. I am inclined to say that the actual 'college' may have been some form of *Taksal* (educational learning centre) set up by Guru Gobind Singh. The 10th Guru was a formidable poet and retained a large contingent of the poets within his own *Durbar*, or court, highlighting the importance of education to locations related Guru Gobind Singh. The practice of entering a Gurdwara without shoes and covering one's head continues to this day, as does the main philosophical notion of the Gurdwara being open to all people of all faiths and creeds. Wilkins describes other facets of the temple, which would again seem consistent with modern Sikh practices:

> The congregation arranged themselves upon the carpet, on each side of the hall, so as to leave a space before the altar from end to end. The great book [Guru Granth Sahib], desk, and all, was brought, with some little ceremony from the altar, and placed at the opposite extremity of the hall. An old man, with a revered silver beard, kneeled down before the desk with his face towards the altar; and on one side of him sat a man with a small drum, and two or three with cymbals. The book was now opened, and the old man began to chant to the time of the drum and the cymbals; and, at the conclusion of every verse, most

6   The importance of his visit was analysed in my paper 'Sri Takhat Harimandir Sahib Patna Sahib: A Perspective of its History and Maryada', *Sant Sipahi*, Jullunder, September 2008.

7   Charles Wilkins, 'The Seeks and their college At Patna', 1 March 1781, *Transactions of the Asiatick Society* Vol. 1 (Calcutta: 1788), pp.288–94. All further quotes from this text.

of the congregation joined chorus in a response, with countenances exhibiting great marks of joy. Their tones were by no means harsh; the time was quick; and I learnt that the subject was a Hymn in praise of the unity, the omnipresence, and the omnipotence, of the Deity. I was singularly delighted with the gestures of the old man: I never saw a countenance so expressive of infelt joy, whilst he turned about from one to another, as it were, bespeaking their assents to those truths which his very soul seemed to be engaged in chanting forth. The Hymn being concluded, which consisted of about twenty verses, the whole congregation got up and presented their faces with joined hands towards the altar, in the attitude of prayer. A young man now stood forth; and, with a loud voice and distinct accent, solemnly pronounced a long prayer or kind of liturgy, at certain periods of which all the people joined in a general response, saying Wa Gooroo! They prayed against temptation; for grace to do good; for the general good of mankind; and a particular blessing to the Seeks: and for the safety of those who at that time were on their travels. This prayer was followed by a short blessing from the old man, and an invitation to the assembly to partake of a friendly feast. The book [Guru Granth Sahib] was then closed and restored to its place at the altar.

This description tells us most importantly that the Sikh scripture, Guru Granth Sahib, was brought to the front of the Gurdwara and certain passages were read, after which the ceremony was concluded with the *Ardas*, or petition.[8] The whole congregation got up with joined hands and sought blessings. The ceremony ended with a "friendly feast", which Wilkins describes as follows:

[T]wo men entered bearing a large caldron, called a Curray,[9] just taken from the fire, and placed it in the center of the hall upon a low stool. These were followed by others with five of six dishes, some of which were of silver, and a large pile of leaves sewed together with fibres in the form of plates … It was a kind of sweetmeat, of the consistence of soft brown sugar, composed of flour and sugar mixed up with clarified butter, which is called Ghee. Had not the Ghee been rancid I should have relished it better.

The description now moves to the offering of the *Prashad*, or 'sacrament', to the congregation. The use of flour, sugar and butter pertains to the way *Prashad* is still distributed in modern times. These remarkable descriptions, made in 1781, inform us that many of the principles are remarkably similar to what we see in the Gurdwara setting in the present day. Whilst there have been reformations in the Sikh religion with the advent

8   The *Ardas* is the most important prayer of the Sikhs and is recited daily during and after many rituals and ceremonies.
9   Literally *Karahi*, or a large cauldron.

of the Singh Sabha Movement and the coming of the SGPC (Sikh Gurdwara Prabandhak Committee), much of the religious tradition has remained relatively unchanged.

The description continues and sheds light on the reverence and recital of the secondary scripture of the Sikhs, Dasam Granth, authored by Guru Gobind Singh. Whilst in most Gurdwaras the Guru Granth Sahib is given absolute authority in terms of veneration, there was a praxis started in the 18th century also giving authority to the writings of Guru Gobind Singh.[10] Wilkins writes:

> THEY told me further, that some years after this book of Naneek Sah had been promulgated, another made its appearance [Dasam Granth], now held in almost as much esteem as the former. The name of the author has escaped my memory; but they favoured me with an extract from the book itself in praise of the Deity. The passage had struck my ear on my first entering the hall, when the students were all engaged in reading. From the familiarity of the language to the Hindoovee, and many Shanscrit words, I was able to understand a good deal of it, and I hope, at some future period, to have the honour of laying a translation of it before the Society. They told me I might have copies of both their books, if I would be at the expense of transcribing them.

Portrait of Charles Wilkins. '1788 Painted by J.G. Middleton, engraved by J Sartain. Charles Wilkins Esq. L.L.D. F.R.S & c. London Published Jan 1st 1830 by Moon, Boys & Graves, Pall Mall & J Sartain, 6 Howland Street, Fitzroy Square'. (RS.11374. © The Royal Society)

The secondary Granth, according to Wilkins, was given similar reverence to the Guru Granth Sahib. The scripture, the Dasam Granth, has been subject to much debate of late, especially in relation to authenticity. However, all early sources from the 18th century, including manuscript and historical evidence, confirms that Guru

---

10   See Gurinder Singh Mann and Kamalroop Singh, *Sri Dasam Granth Sahib: Questions and Answers* (London: Archimedes Press, 2011).

Gobind Singh authored the scripture.[11] Wilkins' eyewitness account is an early source confirming the importance of the second scripture. Wilkins comments that he would translate the scriptures in the future, something he was unable to accomplish. It would remain a task for the orientalist Dr John Leyden to translate one composition of the Dasam Granth, as well as other Sikh works (which we discuss later). In a catalogue of Sanskrit manuscripts from 1869, the author, whilst noting a manuscript of Guru Granth Sahib, also describes that recitations of both scriptures take place at Patna, which he witnessed.[12] Interestingly, nearly 100 years after Wilkins' description, Monier Williams described a similar picture in his *Religious thought and Life In India* (1883), in which he also refers to a visit to the Takht at Patna:

> The temple dedicated to the tenth Guru Govind, at Patna, was rebuilt by Ranjit Singh about forty years ago. I found it, after some trouble in a side street, hidden from view and approached by a gateway, over which were the images of the first nine Gurus, with Nanak in the centre. The shrine is open on one side. Its guardian had a high-peaked turban encircled by steel rings (cakra), used as weapons. He was evidently an Akali – or 'worshipper of the timeless god' – a term applied to a particular class of Sikh zealots who believe themselves justified in putting every opponent of their religion to the sword … on one side of the recess – supposed to be the actual room in which Govind was born more than two centuries before – were some of his garments and weapons, and what was once his bed, with other relics, all in a state of decay. On the other side was a kind of low altar, on which were lying under a canopy a beautifully embroidered copy of the Adi-Granth and the Granth of Govind [Sri Dasam Granth]. In the centre, on a raised platform were a number of sacred swords, which appeared to be as much objects of worship as the sacred books.[13]

---

11   Several early recensions of the Sikh scriptures are kept at Patna Sahib. This includes an early Guru Granth Sahib revision with the signature of Guru Gobind Singh together with a Dasam Granth manuscript dated 1698. For more information on this manuscript, see Singh and Mann, *The Granth of Guru Gobind Singh.*

12   T.H. Aufrecht, *A Catalogue of Sanskrit Manuscripts in the Library of Trinity College* (Cambridge: Deighton, Bell, & Co., etc, 1869), p.91.

13   Monier Williams, *Religious thought and life in India. An account of the Religions of the Indian peoples, based on a life's study of their literature and on personal investigations in their own Country* (London: J. Murray, 1885), pp.174–75. See also another early description of Patna and Sikh Takht, but rather a confusing one, Robert Montgomery Martin's *The History, Antiquities, Topography, and Statistics of Eastern India : comprising the districts of Behar, Shahabad, Bhagulpoor, Goruckpoor, Dinajepoor, Puraniya, Rungpoor, & Assam, in relation to their geology, mineralogy, botany, agriculture, commerce, manufactures, fine arts, population, religion, education, statistics, etc* (London: W.H. Allen and Co., 1838), pp.211–14.

The guarding of the Takht by the Akali Nihang order was something which differed from Wilkins' account, but other similarities can be seen.[14] Wilkins also notes that there was a presence of weapons at the Takht, similarly to Williams: "A little room, which, as you enter, is situated at the left hand end of the hall, is the chancel, and is furnished with an altar covered with a cloth of gold, upon which was laid a round black shield over a long broad sword." Essentially, the account by Charles Wilkins is one of the earliest British writings which explains and chronicles the religious activity at a Gurdwara and acknowledges the importance of the Sikh scriptures.

---

14   The Akalis are seen as the original order of the Khalsa, so called as they believe in Akal, 'the Timeless', a reference to God. They are armed to the teeth, wearing conical Turbans, or *Dastar Bungas*, and always dressed in blue attire. The term 'Nihang' also refers to them as being fearless and without care. They saw the British as an imperial power, and as a result, many skirmishes took place throughout the 19th century. Even after the annexation of the Panjab, the Akalis never wavered from their duty as guardians of the Sikh faith; see the chapter 'The British attack the Akal Takht and Capture the Nihangs.'

4

General Baghel Singh, the Conqueror of Delhi

During the 18th century, the Sikhs were constantly fighting for survival after the demise of Guru Gobind Singh. The Sikhs were persecuted, and their first military leader, General Banda Singh Bahadur, was executed in Delhi after being captured by the Mughals. As we have seen, he was put in a cage and paraded together with his followers. As the seat of power, Delhi was the place where all administration, justice and sentencing took place. After Banda's death, the Sikhs rallied around several Khalsa leaders. Akali Darbara Singh (1644–1734) was one of the earliest, having been brought up by Guru Gobind Singh, and became a martyr in 1734. There was then a major progression of the Sikhs under 'Nawab' Kapur Singh (1697–1753) and his Singhpuria Misl.[1] He earned the title 'Nawab' in 1733, the honour being given to him by the Muslims. It was Kapur Singh who reconstructed the army of the Akalis, previously named Buddha Dal (army of veterans) and Taruna Dal (younger Sikhs), into the Dal Khalsa, or 'army of god'. He would also initiate Sikhs into the Khalsa order and was deemed a person of great merit.

During the lifetime of Kapur Singh, the leadership of the Buddha Dal was passed to Jassa Singh Ahluwalia (1718–83). Kapur Singh remarked that, "The Panth [congregation] made me only a Nawab, they will entitle you to be a Sovereign." Jassa Singh *Kalal* came to be known as *Shah* (king).[2] He was brought up in Delhi under the tutelage of Mata Sundari (1666–1708), the consort of Guru Gobind Singh. He fought many battles and Kapurthala became his capital in 1745. He also fought against the Afghans led by Ahmed Shah Abdali (*c.*1722–72), who made many incursions into the Indian subcontinent.[3] It was Jassa Singh who had led a rescue of over 2,000 women

---

1   The town of Kapurgarh in Nabha and the Bharatpur Fort in Ropar are all related to Singhpuria Misl. I have seen various Sikh relics at these locations.

2   Kulwant Singh (trans.), *Sri Gur Panth Prakash* (Rattan Singh Bhangoo) Volume II, (Episodes 82–169) (Chandigarh: Institute of Sikh Studies, 2008), p.97. Jassa Singh's surname was 'Kalal', after the caste name denoting the distiller profession. Hereafter, Bhangu.

3   Also known as Ahmad Shah Durrani, founder of the Durrani Empire.

kept captive by Abdali's forces, and in 1761 he captured Lahore. Jassa Singh led the Khalsa during the testing times of the two holocausts known as *Vadhha/Choota Ghallugharas*, or big/smaller holocausts.

A *Sarbat Khalsa*[4] (conclave) took place at Amritsar on Baisakhi, 29 March 1748; the entire force of the Khalsa was divided into 11 Misls or divisions, each under its own chief or (Sardar). These confederacies and their leaders were as follows, with the estimated number of horsemen they could muster:

1   Ahluwalia Misl under Jassa Singh Ahluwalia (3,000 horse).
2   Singhpuria (Faizullapuria) Misl under Nawab Kapur Singh (8,000 horse).
3   Karorasinghia Misl under Karora Singh (12,000 horse).
4   Nishanvalia Misl under Dasaundha Singh (12,000 horse).
5   Shahidi Misl under Baba Deep Singh (2,000 horse).
6   Dalewalia Misl under Gulab Singh (7,500 horse).
7   Sukerchakia Misl under Charhat Singh (2,500 horse).
8   Bhangi Misl under Hari Singh Dhillon, 10,000 horse.
9   Kanhaiya Misl under Jai Singh (3,000 horse).
10   Nakai Misl under Hira Singh (2,000 horse).
11   Ramgharia Misl under Jassa Singh Ramgharia (3,000 horse).

(There was also the Phulkian Misl under Baba Ala Singh (5,000 horse).[5]

The Dal Khalsa, with its total estimated strength of over 70,000, consisted of primarily cavalry, with very little artillery or infantry. There have been widely varying estimates of the strength of Sikh forces. Forster claimed that the Sikh military strength was a highly exaggerated 200,000,[6] while James Browne, in 1785, estimated it at 98,200.[7] Each Misl was given a drum and a battle standard to mark their designation. Whilst there were smaller bands of Sikh military forces, the Buddha Dal were the only Sikhs who could undertake the investiture of new battalions. It was during the rise of the Sikh Misls that the great holocaust took place in February 1762. George Forster

4   This is a reference to the congregation of the Sikhs coming together to resolve any
     differences and agreeing to collective action.
5   Henry Prinsep, *Origin of the Sikh Power and Political life of Ranjit Singh with an account
     of the Religion, Laws, and Customs of Sikhs* (Calcutta: G.H. Huttman, 1834), pp.29–32.
     Harbans Singh, *The Encyclopedia Of Sikhism – Volume III M–R* (Patiala: Punjabi University,
     2001), p.98. Sometimes Patiala is not counted within the main list of Misls, as they
     operated independently and sometimes against the interest of the Khalsa.
6   George Forster, *A Journey from Bengal to England: Through the Northern part of India,
     Kashmire, Afghanistan, and Persia, and into Russia by the Caspian Sea* (London: Printed
     for R. Faulder, 1798), Vol. 1, Letter XI, p.289. Forster's travels give some important
     observations of the Panjab and the Sikhs. His works were published posthumously after
     his death in 1792.
7   Bhagat Singh, *A History of the Sikh Misals* (Patiala: Punjabi University, 1993).

(1752–91) was a traveller who went through Panjab as part of the EIC and served as a diplomat, and his observations give us important descriptions on the character and military strength of the Sikhs. He writes:

> Amrut Sir was razed to the ground, and the sacred waters choked up with its ruins. Pyramids were erected, and covered with the heads of slaughtered Sicques; and it is mentioned, that Ahmed Shah caused the walls of the principal mosques which had been polluted by the Sicques, to be washed with their blood, that the contamination might be removed, and the ignominy offered to the religion of Mahomet, expiated. Yet these examples of ferocious rigour did not quell the native courage of the Sicques, who still continued to issue from their fastnesses, to hover on the rear of the Afghan armies, and to cut off their scattered parties.[8]

After the forces of Shah Abdali retreated to their own borders around 1767, the Sikhs started capturing territories and returning some normality to the provinces. This was a major period for the development towards Sikh supremacy. The main cause of their success lay in their superior cavalry, the rapidity with which they marched and the guerrilla tactics they employed. The hit-and-run tactics that Forster refers to were known as *Dhai Phat*, or two-and-a-half strikes. William Francklin states, "The men are accustomed to charge on full gallop, on a sudden they stop, discharge their pieces with a deliberate aim, when suddenly wheeling about, after performing three of four turns, they renew their attack."[9] According to Rattan Singh Bhangu (d.1846), who was asked by the British to write a history of the Sikhs, comments, "The wise and the experienced were of the opinion that in battle there are two and a half movements. Rushing on the enemy and retreating make two and to strike is the half. The Guru [Gobind Singh] has taught us to run away and to come back again to fight. This is a great tactic. The Guru himself adopted these and in it there is no dishonour."[10]

Baghel Singh was born in 1730 in the village of Jhabal Kalan, in the district of Tarn Taran, Amritsar. The Karorasinghia Misl had its origins under Sham Singh and Karam Singh (d.1748), its foundations being built by one Karora Singh (d.1761), from whom the Misl name is taken. Baghel Singh took command of the Misl after Karora Singh's death,[11] increasing his military strength. During his lifetime he fought

---

8   Forster, *A Journey from Bengal*, Vol. 1, Letter IX, p.278.
9   William Francklin, *The History of the Reign of Shah-aulum, the present emperor of Hindostaun: Containing the transactions of the court of Delhi, and the neighbouring states, during a period of thirty-six years: interspersed with geographical and topographical observations on several of the principal cities of Hindostaun* (London: Cooper and Graham, 1798), pp.86–87.
10 Bhangu, *Sri Gur Panth Prakash*, pp.345–46.
11 The strength of the Misl is defined by Rattan Singh Bhangu: "Kroresinghia Misl was the biggest in the Majha region. It also had territorial rights over one fourth of Doaba. From

Tomb of General Baghel Singh, Hoshiarpur. (Photograph by Gurinder Singh Mann)

against the Mughals, Afghans, the Marathas and – more importantly – his Misl fought against the British. As well as his military skills, his diplomacy in negotiating treaties made him a worthy individual to uphold the Buddha Dal name. Other Misls joined him, notably the Bhangi Misl (Rai Singh Bhangi) and Dalewalia Misl (Tara Singh Ghaiba) in his campaigns in and around Jamnu-Ganga Doab. Several incursions by the Khalsa had taken place around Delhi during the mid-1700s, involving various Misaldars, most notably Jassa Singh of the Ramgharia Misl. In 1781, Baghel Singh continued his raids around Delhi and headed towards the centre of the Mughal capital. He was joined by the Buddha Dal leader, Jassa Singh Ahluwalia, and a force of 40,000 troops,[12] and they started to lay siege to Delhi.

George Forster made the following observations between February and April 1783 in describing Baghel Singh and the Khalsa making an approach towards Rohilkund, an area neighbouring British protectorate territories (see Map 1 in the Introduction):

the foot hills of Doaba region up to the Ganges, this Misl would collect revenues without any hindrance." Kulwant Singh (trans,), *Sri Gur Panth Prakash*, p.691. Karora Singh died fighting in Karnal against the Nawab of Kurjipura.

12   Estimates vary on the exact number.

> In the beginning of the year 1783 a party of Siques traversing the Ghous Ghur districts, approached the Ganges, where it forms the western limit of Rohilcund, with an intention of crossing the river, and invading the country of the Wazir.[13] Being at the time in Rohilcund, I witnessed the terror and general alarm which prevailed amongst the inhabitants, who deserting the open country, had retired into forts and places inaccessible to cavalry.[14]

These descriptions show the Khalsa on the verge of crossing the Ganges, but they encircled and camped at Ghaziabad, moving to Bulandshahr, Khurja and then towards Aligarh and Agra. The Sikhs were sacking areas with impunity and sending a clear message to all the surrounding areas and rulers. The Khalsa,, under Baghel Singh and Jassa Singh Ahluwalia, acquired many spoils and sent one-tenth of their wealth to the Harimandir Sahib in Amritsar, as per the custom at the time.

On 8 March 1783, Baghel Singh and Jassa Singh Ahluwalia encamped at a place later named as *Tis Hazari* (30,000, after the number of troops of the Buddha Dal). This location has become synonymous with the name of Baghel Singh.[15] After some hard-fought battles with the Delhi armies of Emperor Shah Alam, the Muslims were defeated. On 11 March 1783, the Buddha Dal made for the Red Fort, where the royal palace was located, virtually entering without a fight and hoisting the Khalsa battle standards. Jassa Singh Ahluwalia was placed on the throne of Delhi, and hence the name was given to him of *Padshah* (king).[16] It was a triumphant honour for the Khalsa after their persecution under the Mughals and a salute to Guru Gobind Singh, who forged the identity of the Khalsa. Within 20 years of nearly being wiped out by the Afghan and Mughal forces, the Sikhs had seriously dented the Mughal Empire with relative ease.[17]

Jassa Singh Ramgharia and his Misl were part of the victorious forces, and he literally ripped the seat of power – a sill or stone slab – from the Red Fort.[18] The sil was wrapped in chains like a prisoner and taken back to the Panjab. This is now located at the Ramgharia Bungas, a fortress-type enclosure within the Golden Temple complex

13   Reference to Nawab Wazir of Oudh, Asaf-ud-Daula (1748–97).
14   Forster, *A Journey from Bengal*, Vol. 1, p.283.
15   This location is now the main courthouse of Delhi. There is no reminder of Baghel Singh's stay here. However, in September 2018, I located a small Gurdwara at the back of the Courts which was set up to remember the sacrifices of the General. Unfortunately, it is in an unknown place and hidden from view. I would like to thank Kashmir Singh (Punjabi University Patiala) for helping me locate this Gurudwara.
16   However, it is also claimed that Jassa Singh Ramgharia objected to Jassa Singh Ahluwalia taking the throne. As a result, he withdrew from the throne, so as not to mar the important victory.
17   It should be noted that the Mughal Empire was in decline, but it still required a large Sikh force and tactical measures on their part to reach the ramparts of the Red Fort.
18   See the colour section for a portrait of Jassa Singh Ramgharia.

at Amritsar.[19] The Sikh chronicler Rattan Singh Bhangu describes the situation at Delhi when it was taken:

> The Khalsa Panth moved to the area surrounding Delhi.
> As a Delhi ruler felt concerned at this development,
> A sense of panic gripped the inhabitants of Delhi.
> As commotion and havoc spread among the Mughals,
> Whosoever heard about the Khalsa felt scared.
> Declaring the Khalsa as the violent 'Kharanjdal' sect,
> The Muslims felt it had all the signs of that sect.
> As the Mughal ruler of Delhi felt highly scared,
> He called an assembly of all the Islamic sects.
> The Khalsa Panth would not spare the Mughals, said he,
> As they had ransacked the entire territory around Delhi.
> It was now the turn of the Mughals to face adversity,
> As they did not have an adequate army to fight the Khalsa.
> Without the army how could they survive and be safe,
> Truly had the Mughals fallen into Khalsa hands.
> As the Mughal ancestors had slaughtered the Guru's sons,
> Their ancestors had been ungrateful to the Sikh Gurus.
> The way the Mughals had been torturing the Khalsa Panth,
> So would the Singhs wish to pay them in the same coin.[20]

Baghel Singh was given the honour to negotiate the settlement with the King of Delhi. Whilst it would have been the convention and possibly the right of the Khalsa to stay in Delhi, the vast resources needed to maintain their sovereignty of these lands would not have been sustainable. There was also the issue of inter-Misl rivalry, but at this juncture, it was still a victory for the Sikhs the like of which had never been seen before.

Jassa Singh Ahluwalia returned to the Panjab, leaving Baghel Singh to start negotiations with the Mughal Court. Begum Samru (1753–1836), a female commander of an army and ruler of Sardhana,[21] was summoned by the Mughal Emperor to negotiate with Baghel Singh, whom she knew. The Begum was considered a daughter to Shah Alam

---

19   Most people would fail to notice this important slab if it was not pointed out to them. For a recent history of the Ramgharia Misl, see Colonel Iqbal Singh, *The Quest for the Past – Retracing the History of the Seventeenth-Century Sikh Warrior* (US: XLIBRIS, 2017).

20   *Sri Gur Panth Prakash*, p.721.

21   Also known as Joanna Nobilis Sombre, but popularly known as Begum Samru, she inherited a European army after the death of her husband Walter Reinhardt Sombre (*c.* 1725–78). She was to become the only Catholic ruler in India, controlling the area of Sardhana, Meerut (the present-day state of Uttar Pradesh). Her story is fascinating, to say the least.

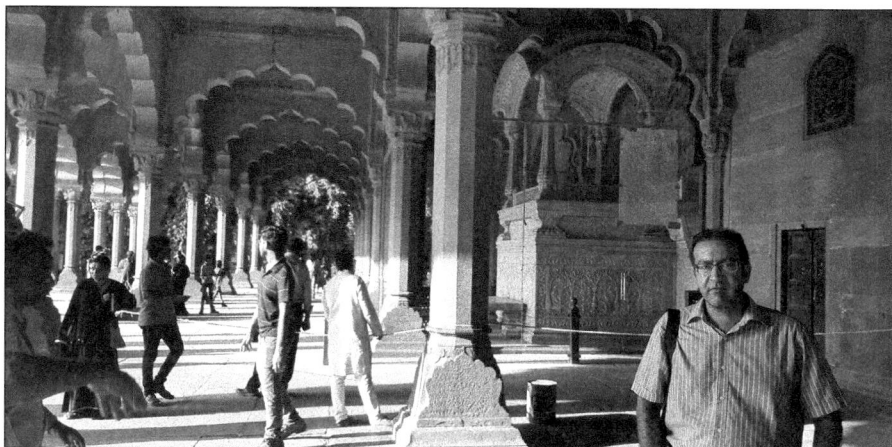

The author inside the Diwan-E-Am, Red Fort, Delhi.
(Photograph by Gurinder Singh Mann)

and was trusted entirely by him to prevent the destruction of Delhi by the Sikhs. Her negotiations resulted in the Sikhs being given permission to build several Gurdwaras in honour of the Sikh Gurus and other important figures. They would also receive income from octroi duties in the capital, and as a result, Baghel Singh would retreat from the fort and base himself at *Sabzi Mandi* (the marketplace) with 4,000 troops.[22]

Rattan Singh Bhangu further describes the negotiations with Begum Samru:

> Thereafter, did Begum Samru send the messengers,
> To Baghel Singh with elephants loaded with palanquins of gold.
> As the Mughal messengers brought Baghel Singh along with them,
> S. Baghel Singh's forces put up their camp near Delhi…
> Thus was Begum Samru instrumental in negotiating a deal,
> Between Baghel Singh and the Delhi ruler with solemn vows.
> Baghel Singh got a written deal signed by the king,
> That he would permit the construction of seven (ancient) Sikh shrines.[23]

At the construction of each of the Gurdwaras, the Khalsa battle standard was hoisted to show Sikh supremacy.[24] After eight months, the job was completed and Bhangu remarks,

22   Jaspreet Kaur Sandhu, *Sikh Ethos: Eighteenth Century Perspective* (Delhi: Vision & Venture, 2000).
23   *Sri Gur Panth Prakash*, p.723.
24   These Gurdwaras were as follows and have historical associations with the Sikhs: Gurdwara Mata Sundri, Gurdwara Bangla Sahib, Gurdwara Rakab Ganj, Gurdwara Sis Ganj, Gurdwara Majnu Ka Tilla, Gurdwara Bala Sahib and Gurdwara Moti Bagh. See M.K. Pal, *Historical Gurdwaras of Delhi* (Delhi: Niyogi Books, 2013).

"After planting the seventh Khalsa flag at this site, the sacred Sikh shrines were constructed by S. Baghel Singh. As *Karah Parshad* [holy sacrament] was distributed with the beat of war drums, the Sikhs converged happily at this place from all sides."[25] He also showed his statesmanlike influence, obtaining signatures from opposing Muslim chiefs and presenting these to the Delhi king to show that there was no threat to security by having the shrines built. In a final act, Shah Alam met Baghel Singh and the Khalsa were presented with gifts and money, "The highest title that belonged to the Muslim royal court, Did the Mughal emperor confer on S. Baghel Singh. An elephant fitted with a big palanquin did the king offer. War drums loaded on camels were beaten in Singh's honour."[26]

Portrait of Warren Hastings, 1783–1784, by Johan Joseph Zoffany. (Yale Center for British Art, Paul Mellon Fund)

This resulted in the main army of the Khalsa leaving Delhi, but some of the men of Baghel Singh's Karorasinghia Misl would remain, "Did S. Baghel Singh's contingent stay at Delhi for many years. Receiving ransom from the surrounding provinces, did he make the Marhattas his allies as well. Bringing Delhi under his own command and control, did he collect revenues at six annas out of every rupee."[27] The Mughal Emperor thereby thought that the Sikhs would stop their incursions, but this was not to be and the following two decades witnessed a number of raids in the vicinity.

The Governor-General of Bengal, Warren Hastings (1732–1818), was receiving reports on the rise and military threat of the Sikhs.[28] He remarked that, "They carried their depredations to the very suburbs of Delhi, where Two of their officers actually reside in a quarter called Subzee Mundee, which is chiefly occupied by shroffs and shopkeepers, for the double purpose of levying their *rauky* (which is the name given to that species of contribution) and protecting the inhabitants from the marauders of their own nation."[29]

---

25   *Sri Gur Panth Prakash*, p.732.
26   *Sri Gur Panth Prakash*, p.740.
27   *Sri Gur Panth Prakash*, p.744.
28   The English statesman was the first Governor of the Presidency of Fort William (Bengal), before the title of Governor-General of India was invoked in 1828.
29   Forrest, *Selections*, III 1123-5, National Archives of India, New Delhi, Secret Proceedings, 14 December 1784, pp.537–44.

I recently came across a series of letters which shows the concerns outlined by the British at the incursions by the Sikhs in the Delhi area. They make it clear that the Sikh threat had to be assessed and ask whether some of the regional Muslim rulers had adequate defences to repel any Sikh attacks. As there were many skirmishes with the imperial forces of Delhi, the raids of the Sikhs had come to the notice of the British. In January 1783, John Bristow, at the Vizier's court, started communications with Warren Hastings at Calcutta. The Sikh incursions alarmed the British, and after March 1783 their presence within Delhi would affect their interests. The British had created outposts near Oude, and incursions by the Sikhs might have led to them either receiving tributes from British-aligned rulers or encroaching on their territories. At this stage the British viewed Sikh dominance as territorial at best. The lack of influence of the EIC at Delhi would play into the hands of the various players like the Marathas and Rohillas, who would have had an upper hand in negotiations in trade and commerce. This led to the EIC being lower down the pecking order of their interests. It thus appeared that the Sikhs would be a threat.[30] The *Vakils* (emissaries) of the Khalsa now had access to the emperor and tributes were being sent to Baghel Singh's Misl after Begum Samru's negotiations. A few weeks before the Khalsa took over Delhi, John Bristow, in a letter dated 28 February 1783, attached testimony from other Mughal chiefs regarding the Sikhs to make his case:

> Under date the 27th January, I had the honour to transmit you information relative to the Seiks, who have since that period committed depredations on the neighbouring Countries, and made several attempts against the Vizier's dominions. The small force with which their attacks have been repulsed, flatter me with hopes that little is to be apprehended, if timely precautions be taken.[31]

William Francklin (1763–1839) was another EIC officer who wrote on the Sikhs, and we can ascertain some descriptions of events at the court of Shah Alam in relation to the Sikhs.[32] Francklin describes the rise of the Sikhs as follows:

> In the reign of Ahumud Shah [Abdali] the tribe became very formidable. Profiting by the disturbances which then prevailed in every part of the empire,

---

30   John Bristow also looked to George Forster's observations to understand the threat of the Sikhs.
31   East India Company, *An Authentic Copy of the Correspondence in India: Between the Country Powers and the Honourable the East India Company's Servants: Containing Amongst Many Others the Letters of Governor Hastings, J. Macpherson, Esq., J. Stables, Esq. … &c., Together with the Minutes of the Supreme Council at Calcutta: the Whole Forming a Collection of the Most Interesting India-papers, which Were Laid Before Parliament in the Session of 1786*, Volume 4 (London: J. Debrett, 1787), pp.19–20.
32   In 1782, Francklin was appointed as an ensign of the 19th Regiment of Bengal Native Infantry. He was later made lieutenant colonel. His works include that of his travels in Persia, as well as numerous other tracts. He was a member of the Royal Asiatic Society as well as the Asiatic Society of Calcutta.

the Seiks again made head against the government, and with far better success. They conquered the whole of the Panjab, (or country included within the five rivers which fall into the Indus) and even pushed their arms beyond it.

In the last reign (Aulum Geer the Second) their dominions were bounded on the west by the country of Cabul, and extended east-ward to the vicinity of Delhi, north by a range of high mountains, and to the southwest they embraced the province of Moultan and the city of Tatta, situated on the banks of the Indus. Lahoor,[33] the capital of Punjab, was selected as their chief city of residence, and as such has since continued.[34]

He further states that Warren Hastings had sent an envoy in the form of Major James Browne to aid Shah Alam, and he was greeted with anticipation:

In the beginning of 1784, Major Brown, who had been commissioned on a deputation to the king by the supreme council of Calcutta, arrived at the capital. The Major was received with high respect; and in behalf of the British government, presented Shah-Aulum a handsome paishcush [tribute].

The arrival of this deputation excited various emotions in the minds of the Delhians; some were of opinion that the period was at hand when Shah-Aulum would return to the protection of his oldest and, in truth, his best friends, the English: others again conjectured that the intent of the embassy was, to arrange with the minister the concerns of the royal family. These, during the late commotions, had arisen to a height which was truly distressful.

But the real cause of Major Brown's arrival was in consequence of orders he had received from his government, not to decline any overture that might be made for affording a military aid to the royal cause. The Seiks had for several years back, by their predatory incursions into Doo Ab and Rohilcund, excited alarm in the government of Majud Al Dowla: and Mr. Hastings, the British governor, with his usual discernment, deemed the exertions of the court of Delhi might, at the present juncture of affairs, prove a beneficial counterpoise to the rising power of the Seiks.[35]

Major Browne contacted various Sikh chiefs, including Jassa Singh Ahluwalia, Lahina Singh, Sahib Singh, Karam Singh Shaheed and Baghel Singh. He had taken a line contrary to Warren Hastings' orders and now started to embroil himself directly in political and military affairs. The *Vakil* of Baghel Singh, Lakhpat Rai, was based at the court and corresponded with Browne, and it appeared that the "Sikh chiefs were willing to establish friendly relations" with the British. Baghel Singh, however, was

---

33   Lahore.
34   Francklin, *The History of the Reign of Shah-Aulum*, p.74.
35   Francklin, *The History of the Reign of Shah-Aulum*, pp.115–16.

concerned with the building of the Gurdwaras during 1783 and deferred communications to the head of the Buddha Dal, Jassa Singh Ahluwalia, referenced as the
"highest and greatest and in that country called Badshah Singh".[36] There were also
hints of a possible treaty that would keep the Sikhs from gaining more territories and
threatening British interests. (See appendices for the letter of friendship between Jassa
Singh Ahluwalia and James Browne.)

Over the next few years, the incursions by the Sikhs would continue and Browne's
correspondence led to nothing. Jassa Singh Ahluwalia passed away in 1783, so there
was no de facto leader of the Khalsa. The Sikhs may have missed their chance to have
a power base in Delhi, but they would form a treaty with the Marathas instead, who
had now taken a major footing at Delhi and were a formidable power in India. They
signed a short-lived treaty with the Mahratta leader, Mahadji Scindia (1730–94),
in 1785, which worried the British. Browne stated, "[S]urely a confederacy of two
such formidable powers as the Sicks and the Mahrattas, close to the Vizier's frontier, must afford matter for very serious apprehension, to every person who is anxious
for the safety of the Company's possessions in India."[37] However, the power base
of the British was increasing and Baghel Singh would come into contact with the
British army officials, including the Irish mercenary George Thomas (1756–1802).[38]
The fact that Baghel Singh and the Khalsa forces had reached the territories to the
east controlled by the Nawab of Oudh – a British protectorate state – shows the vision
of Baghel Singh in conquering lands and obtaining tributaries.[39] From 1765–1803,
the Khalsa continued to raise tributaries from locations and neighbourhoods around
Delhi. Major James Rennell (1742–1830), a cartographer for the EIC, wrote in 1788,
"It is fortunate that the Oude dominions have the Ganges for a barrier between them

36   Krishna Dyal Bhargava (ed.), *Browne Correspondence* (Delhi: Pub. for the National
     Archives of India by the Manager of Publications, Government of India, 1960), pp.74–82.
     Browne states: "From all these letters the Readiness of these Sirdars to enter into a
     friendly communication with the English Nation, is sufficiently evident, at the Same
     Time they are in some Degree alarmed at the apparent Union between Us and the Shah's
     Servants, which they are apprehensive may lead to some attempts on their Possessions."
37   Major J. Browne, *India Tracts: Containing a Description of the Jungle Terry Districts, Their
     Revenues, Trade, and Government: with a Plan for the Improvement of Them. Also an History
     of the Origin and Progress of the Sicks* (Black-Friars: Logographic Press, Printing House
     Square, 1788), p.30.
38   Thomas was unsuccessful in creating any lasting power base of his own, and whilst carving
     out a short-lived territory of Hisar in Haryana between 1798 and 1801, was defeated by
     the combined forces of the Marathas and the Sikhs. The forces of Mahratta leader Daulat
     Rao Sindhia (1779–1827) were led by French adventurer General Pierre Perron (d.1834).
     Baghel Singh also fought in this battle, together with the Karorasinghia Misl chiefs
     Bhanga Singh and Gurdit Singh.
39   My lecture 'General Baghel Singh: the "Conqueror of Delhi" – An assessment of his
     achievements through statehood and heritage' at the Fifth International Sikh Research
     Conference, University of Warwick, July 2018.

Janesier May 8th

My dear Madam

I had the honour to address you yesterday evening immediately on receipt of yours most kind favour of the 5th instant I am just now told that Bunga Sing will arrive here in the course of this day and as I know not after that whether I may be allowed the use of pen ink and paper or not I seize the opportunity whilst in my power to request that whatever you intend in my favour may be conducted with the utmost secrecy for I have reason to believe they have the earliest and best intelligence of every thing done at Jerdennels and Gungepoora indeed they are so perfectly on their guard that I am of opinion no plan or stratagem can succeed from their caution and apprehensions those last three nights I conceive they have received information of some new plan for my service perhaps from that scoundrel alyeh Shawn or from my equally unworthy domestick monsavam but come through whatever channel it may intelligence of something that is meditated against this place they have had how my heart would beat with joy to see it surrounded by a powerfull body of cavalry Bunga Sing himself within its walls and a party of your troops and a couple of guns advancing towards it by such a spirited measure the nabob quiet here I have Shawn and goodwit Sing would possess themselves of the whole here of their enemy and the expence necessary for the executing the plan I am willing to defray should I have at last found his way to serve me be cautious how you repose any confidence in him

Adieu may god for ever shelter you with the wings of his mercy is the sincere prayer of my dear Madam

your faithfully devoted and very

Hble Sert   R Stuart

Letter from Colonel Robert Stuart to the Begum Sombre of Oudh, 8 May 1791.
(Perth & Kinross Archive, MS115/papers/266/17)

and this army of plunderers."[40] However, in 1791 the Karorasinghia Misls of Bhanga Singh (d.1815) attacked the Wazir's territories and abducted Colonel Robert Stuart (1744–1820) from Anupshahr and kept him a prisoner at Thanesar, in the district of Kurukshetra.[41] This was a highly unusual act at the time. Rai Singh Bhangi and Gurdit Singh made enquiries to have Colonel Stuart released, but Bhanga Singh was not interested. Even at this juncture, the British did not try to send a force to have the colonel released. It was considered a risky prospect, as they would have to cross Maratha territories and they were also aware that the Sikhs had never led any large military incursion against them. As a result, this was a seen as an isolated incident. Eventually a counter-move was undertaken where the ransom was paid by Begum Samaru, who in turn received payment from the British.[42] After many months in captivity, Colonel Stuart was finally released.

The legacy left by Baghel Singh and his Misl is still a work in progress: his accomplishments are still to be fully understood. It was only in 2014 that the Sikhs of Delhi started commemorating the victory of Baghel Singh on a major scale, and this at the Red Fort itself, and the day is referred to as 'Fateh Diwas'(victory day).[43] For all the major players vying for power in Delhi, the Sikhs of the 18th century had accomplished their victory over the Mughal Empire. Bhangu states:

Such a great historical landmark did S. Baghel Singh establish,
That his name would shine in history till eternity.
Such a great service did he render unto the Guru,
That surely would he stand honoured in the Divine Court.[44]

40   James Rennell, *Memoir of a map of Hindoostan; or The Mogul Empire: with an introduction, illustrative of the geography and present division of that country: and a map of the countries situated between the head of the Indus, and the Caspian Sea* (London: Printed by M. Brown, for the author, 1788), p.cxxli. Rennell also based his descriptions on the works of George Forster.
41   Referred to as Robert Stuart of Annat and Rait, who rose to become a lieutenant general in the EIC. His tomb at Kilspindie Churchyard, Perth and Kinross, bears an inscription of the title given to him by Shah Alam II.
42   Julia Keay, *Farzana: The Woman Who Saved an Empire* (London: I.B. Tauris, 2013), p.208. The letters from Colonel Stuart to Begum Samru are kept at Kincross and Penrith Archives, Scotland, with whom I am working to make these known to the mainstream public.
43   In March 2019, statues of Jassa Singh Ahlulwalia, Baghel Singh and Jassa Singh Ramgharia were unveiled at Delhi Fateh Memorial Park commemorating this important event.
44   *Sri Gur Panth Prakash*, p.731

5

Dr Leyden, the 'polymath' First Translator of the Sikhs

John Casper Leyden (1775–1811) was born in Denholm, near Hawick, in Scotland. His parents were John Leyden, a shepherd, and his wife Isabella Scott. He was the first born of six – four sons and two daughters. His family moved to a small cottage in the remote area of Helawshiels. Leyden's appetite for learning was encouraged by his grandmother, who read the *Bible* to the young boy; he learnt to commit whole passages to memory.

At the age of 9, at Kirktown Parish School, he began his foundation in languages, beginning with Latin. It was here where his drive and passion for learning gathered pace. His parents encouraged him to train for the ministry, and he preached at the Presbytery of St Andrews. He was placed under the tutorage of Rev. James Duncan. Leyden came across the classical Greek works of Homer, which opened his mind to ancient literature. His thirst for reading continued. One anecdote tells of how his father wanted to buy a donkey to transport the young Leyden to school. This idea did not appeal to him, as he felt his school counterparts would ridicule him. However, once he learnt the deal involved a book written in 'strange languages', he soon changed his mind. This turned out to be a Latin dictionary written in different languages, including Latin, Hebrew, Italian, Spanish and German.

In November 1790, Leyden qualified to attend the University of Edinburgh, where he studied mathematics and logic, whilst also building on his Greek and Latin knowledge. In the following years, he attended lectures on divinity and church history, which was required if he was to take Ministerial office in Scotland. In 1795, his family relocated to Cavers in the Scottish Borders. The small gloomy church there provided him with the ideal location to carry out his studies. However, while there he gained a reputation as being a reader in the occult, as he was reading books with 'strange characters'. At the library at Cavers House, he found many valuable English works and foreign literature to read. He had progressed in Hebrew and Arabic, and was now moving his interest towards Eastern learning. In 1798, Leyden received his licence to preach. He set his sights on collecting and publishing information which was not known to Europeans. As a result, he published his *A Historical and Philosophical Sketch*

of the Discoveries and Settlements of the Europeans in Northern and Western Africa, at the Close of the Eighteenth Century in 1799.

It was this idea of understanding other cultures and their writings that eventually made him consider going to India, where he could study more languages. However, he could only do this if he was appointed as a surgeon. To facilitate his goal, he trained as a surgeon in an incredibly short period.[1] He managed to secure an appointment in Madras through the EIC in 1802, and sailed for India the following year.

Arriving in India, Leyden oversaw the Madras General Hospital. In 1804 he was appointed to survey the provinces of Mysore which were taken from Tipu Sultan.[2] It was here that he met Lieutenant Colonel John Malcolm, another Scottish adventurer, a future

Sketch of Dr John Leyden by George Elliot (1811). Adapted from John Reith, *Life of Dr John Leyden Poet and Linguist* (Galashiels: A. Walker & Son, 1908).

Governor of Bombay. A year later, in 1805, Malcolm visited the Panjab and developed his interest in Panjabi and the Sikhs. In October 1805, Leyden arrived at the EIC base in Penang to study the Malay language, but while there he became increasingly ill, being cared for by the statesman Thomas Stamford Raffles (1781–1826), who founded Singapore and British Malaya. However, he continued to study night and day from his sickbed. In February 1806, he travelled to Calcutta, where many Orientalists had gathered a large number of manuscripts. He buried himself in the grammar and dictionaries of many of the Indian languages, and it is most likely that Leyden learnt Panjabi here. In 1807, at Fort William College, Calcutta, he became Professor of the Chair of Hindustani, after which he became Commissioner of the Courts at Calcutta and, two years later, the Superintendent of the Calcutta Mint.

Dr Leyden sent much of his income to his parents, with the rest being spent on his pursuit of acquiring Indian manuscripts. Leyden then accompanied Lord Minto (1751–1814), the Governor-General of British India, to the Malayan Islands as an

1   Leyden had earlier in his career studied medicine, and received a diploma in Surgery within the record time of just six months.
2   James Morton, *The Poetical Remains of the late Dr. John Leyden, with Memoirs of his life by the Rev. James Morton* (London: Longman, Hurst, Rees, Orme and Brown, 1819), p.xxxv.

interpreter,[3] after which he went with British troops to Java. His only motive was to find any manuscripts and further his learning. He learned of a library which contained Oriental manuscripts, and rushed to discover what was there. However, it was an unventilated room, and he succumbed to sickness there, which was attributed to the 'pestilential air' in the room. Two days later, on 28 August 1811, Leyden died in the hands of Thomas Stamford Raffles. Dr John Leyden was buried at the cemetery at Tanabang in Java. After his death, the name and importance of Leyden grew and many of his works were published posthumously. A few years later, John Malcolm met Leyden's father and advised him that Leyden's instructions were that the proceeds of his works were to be given to him. His father replied, "I pray therefore that you publish nothing that is not for my son's good name."[4]

Malcolm would use some of Leyden's Panjabi translations in his famous, *Sketch of the Sikhs*, published in 1811. Dr Leyden was a genius, who in his short life of 36 years had mastered more than 30 languages; he was a preacher, surgeon, traveller, author, linguist and orientalist.[5] Before his death, Leyden had completed translations from the Persian, Arabic, and Sanskrit languages. Henry Thomas Colebrooke (1765–1837), who founded the Royal Asiatic Society, commenting on Leyden's translations in Malay and Pracrit languages, "expressed his satisfaction with Leyden's execution of this arduous and useful labour".[6]

The translations of Dr Leyden's manuscripts

There are two manuscripts in relation to Leyden within the British Library which focus on Sikh history: 1) Euro MSS Mack General 40; and 2) Add. 26558.

These manuscripts contain the translations of various Panjabi works into English. The original works were written at the end of the 17th century and the early 18th century. The translations of these works were undertaken by Dr Leyden between 1805 and 1809. These translations have remained neglected at the British Library, and the

---

3   Known as Sir Gilbert Elliott between 1777 and 1797 and The Lord Minto between 1797 and 1813. A Scottish diplomat and politician, he sat in the House of Commons between 1776 and 1795 and then become Governor-General of India.

4   Morton, *The Poetical Remains*, p.lxxxiii.

5   He contributed several small pieces to a collection of poems, called the 'Minstrelsy' of the Scottish Border, which he published with his celebrated friend, Walter Scott. Another important poem was the 'Ode on the Death of Nelson'. Morton, *The Poetical Remains*, p.lxxvi.

6   Morton, *The Poetical Remains*, p.lxii. Colebrooke was no stranger to Sikh texts, having donated a manuscript of the Janamsakhis to the India Office Library. This version of the MS has been referred to as the *Vilayat Wali Janamsakhi* (manuscript from Britain) but is popularly known as the Colebrooke Janamsakhi. MSS Panj. B6 is kept at the British Library. See Harbans Singh, *Guru Nanak And The Origins Of The Sikh Faith* (Bombay: Asia Publishing House, 1969), p.26.

only person who commented on the work of Leyden was Lieutenant Colonel John Malcolm in his famous *Sketch of the Sikhs*. It was in 2004 that I discovered the existence of these writings. I was excited and intrigued to know more about them. They were grouped under the Mackenzie Collection (Euro MSS Mack General 40), the original manuscript of which was kept at the British Library. This made me wonder if there were any other works that may have been translated by Dr Leyden. I began my search in 2006 and eventually discovered a set of writings in a different collection, Add. 26558. These were brought into the limelight in 2011. The Panjab Cultural Association created a project to present the works online and for a small booklet to be produced.[7] I undertook lectures at various locations related to the project, highlighting the importance of his writings.[8]

Translations of the first manuscript, Euro MSS Mack General 40, appear in the collection of Colonel Colin Mackenzie (1754–1821), the first Surveyor General of India, employed by the EIC to undertake historical and cultural research.[9] It is this part of the collection which contains Leyden's work. There are several compositions within this MS, some written by Dr Leyden and others which are letters. The Panjabi translations are as follows, numbered according to the entry in the manuscript:

No.6: *Sri Bachitra Natak* by Guru Gobind Singh. A composition from the Sikh religious Scripture, Dasam Granth. An autobiographical account of the 10th Guru of the Sikhs that narrates his battles and the balance of power in the Panjab in the 17th century.

No 7: *Kuraka* on Guru Gobind Singh from the Panjabi of Nund. An unknown text highlighting the death of Guru Gobind Singh's son, Ajit Singh, and the Battle of Chamkaur.[10]

7   *Dr Leyden's Panjabi Translations* (London: Archimedes Press, 2011). This project was undertaken with Dr Kamalroop Singh. The information was on www.drleyden.co.uk (this website is no longer available).
8   I undertook lectures at Oxford and Leicester to show the importance of his translations, and a small booklet was also released. This took place in 2011, a fitting tribute to the orientalist on the 200th anniversary of Leyden's death. *The Lost British Accounts of the Sikhs: Lecture report*, 3/12/2011, http://www.sikhscholar.co.uk/2011/12/lost-british-accounts-of-sikhs-lecture.html (accessed 24 November 2018).
9   An officer of the Madras Engineers, he came to India in 1783, where he collated thousands of paper manuscripts, at least 1,700 drawings and 521 palm leaf manuscripts which now form the British Library's Mackenzie Collection. See 'Bringing Colin Mackenzie Home' at https://blogs.bl.uk/untoldlives/2016/05/bringing-colin-mackenzie-home.html (accessed 24 November 2018).
10 After some analysis, I can firmly place the writer of the text as Nand Ram, a poet in the literary court of Guru Gobind Singh. The Battle of Chamkaur (1704) took place between the Khalsa and Mughal forces of Wazir Khan.

No 8: The chapter of Guru Gobind Singh from the 'Doogur Dialect of the Panjabi'. Another unknown text, recounting the Battle of Chamkaur and the martyrdom of the Guru's sons.

No 9: On the Tenth Padshah. In the *Ram Kulli* verse from the Panjabi. Portions of this text conform to the 18th-century text *Var Sri Bhaugati Ji* by the court poet Bhai Gurdas II.[11]

No 10: *Bhagat Ratnavali* or *Sikhian di Bhagatmala* (Garland of Sikh saints), attributed to Bhai Mani Singh (1670–1737), Head Custodian of the Harimandir Sahib. An account of the pious Sikh Gurus and saints – from the reign of Guru Nanak to Guru Gobind Singh.

No 11: *Gyan Ratanvali*, attributed to Bhai Mani Singh. A *Janamsakhi* of Guru Nanak's life.

The choice of texts is interesting as they are a miscellaneous set of texts and appear to be from one single manuscript, as opposed to select translations. The source of these translations is not known.

The second translations are from manuscript Add 24450. It was after coming across the first set of translations that I discovered the second set in 2006. In this manuscript there are only two Panjabi texts:

Prem Sumarag Granth (the true way to love). The original manuscripts of this text cite and attribute it to Guru Gobind Singh, while Dr Leyden has ascribed it to Bhai Gurdas, neither of which seem correct, as there is no historical evidence to confirm either. It seems more likely that the instructions were written sometime after Guru Gobind Singh's passing, which is favoured by historians. The text is a set of prescriptions and rules for a Sikh state. It is sometimes referred to as a *Rahitnama*, or 'code of conduct'. The Leyden manuscript contains two versions of the *Prem Sumarag Granth*, one of which is a complete version and the other a rough draft. The text bears the date of the work as 1808 on one of its folios. The second brief text is commentary on the *Japji Sahib* of Guru Nanak.

This find led to historians redating the original text. Dr W.H. McLeod, a leading scholar in the field of Sikh studies, had in 2006 completed a translation of the text. He wrote to me regarding the text:

11   This is essentially a ballad recounting the exploits of the Khalsa and Guru Gobind Singh. It is said to be dated to from the time of Guru Gobind Singh. Not much is known about Bhai Gurdas II. However, the verses of this text are used within the recital of *Kirtan* and *Katha*.

The Prem Shumar Grunth
by Bhai Guidas.

Ek ony har Satt Guru Prasauk. Sri Guruje ki Tateh.

The present Prem Shumar Grunth is composed according
to the Doctrines of the Ten padshas by thy favour.
By the order of akal puruk the Guru the first chapter
is set forth for instruction & remembrance of the proper
mode of worship. —
The first Adyay. —

I

The immortal being (akal Purukh)
said to this insect I bear the form of a sword; from
this my own form creation with its carcous forms &nodes
has received exastance for the purpose of manifesting
a bul for the Universal world, a seet which may be
the residence of Dharm (Iustice) which my destroy
error (Kubudh) and illustrate subrudh.) I am the
Supreme being (Param Purkh) excepting the
Knowledge of me there is no other Knowledge, therefore
have I manifested this bul. & placed ten incarnations
in the world for the preservation of the werd among
living men. Untill though the world is put to Shame
by them, error is not extirpated, and if any know

(acts

English translation of the *Prem Sumarag Granth* by Dr John Leyden.
(© The British Library Board; Add_26588-030)

How did you find out about Leyden and his activity as a translator? I have always assumed that he was merely the collector of manuscripts which he subsequently gave to the British Museum. Clearly, I was wrong.[12]

He eventually changed his view on the date of the text:

In the *Sikhs of the Khalsa* I expressed the view that the dating of the work [Prem Sumarag] was located in the first half of the nineteenth century, the middle or the later years of Ranjit Singh's reign. This has proved to be incorrect … I was informed of its existence by Gurinder Singh Mann of Leicester in the United Kingdom.[13]

It is truly remarkable that Dr Leyden worked on this 18th-century text, which in turn has provided evidence of dating in the modern day. The significance of the texts is that they are the first known translations of Sikh works, predating those of Ernest Trumpp (1828–85) and Max Arthur Macauliffe (1841–1913). These works were also recognised by Lieutenant Colonel John Malcolm, and his *Sketch of the Sikhs* became the blueprint of Sikh historiography in the 19th and 20th centuries. According to Malcolm, he used Leyden's translations throughout his book:

This slender stock of materials was subsequently much enriched by my friend Dr. Leyden who has favoured me with a translation of several tracts written by Sikh authors in the Penjabi and Duggar dialects, treating of their history and religion; which … contain the most valuable verifications of the different religious institutions of the Sikh nation.[14]

Leyden was guided by a thirst for knowledge; as a result, his translation work can be considered highly accurate. He never visited the Panjab, but his linguistic abilities guided his work, as opposed to any political pressure from British authorities to assess the works. What made Leyden translate the *Bachitra Natak* and the *Prem Sumarag* in their entirety? It could be argued that the two works discuss the worldview of the Sikhs, the lineage and purpose of the 10th Guru and political ideas including the formation of a Sikh state. These works were precolonial in the sense that the Panjab was not part of the Sikh territories at the time of writing. It seems his motivations can be appraised as follows: "Perhaps the first British traveller that ever sought India, moved neither by the love of wealth or of power. … [He] was guided solely by wish of

12   Dr W.H. McLeod had regular communications with me regarding this important text. This was a personal email sent to me, dated February 2006.
13   Dr W.H McLeod, 'Reflections on Prem Sumarag', *Journal of Punjab Studies*, Volume 14, No. 1 (Spring 2007).
14   Malcolm, *Sketch of the Sikhs*, p.3.

extending our knowledge of oriental literature, and distinguishing himself as its most successful cultivator."[15]

So whilst the work of Lieutenant Colonel Malcolm is widely seen as the start of Sikh historiography from a European viewpoint, we now need to revise this idea based on these translations. The works of Leyden remained forgotten by translators who followed him, including J.D. Cunningham, Ernest Trumpp and even Max Arthur Macauliffe. His treatment has not fared any better with modern Sikh historians and scholars. Yet in a series of essays and lectures, I have contended that the works of Leyden are of immense importance and now require greater recognition.

15 'Biographical Memoir of Dr Leyden, M.D.', The Edinburgh Annual Register For 811, Vol. Fourth: Part Second (Edinburgh: Longman, Hurst, Rees, Orme and Brown, 1813). pp. xii–lxviii.

6

Maharajah Ranjit Singh and the Sikh Empire

The five most powerful Sikh Misls around the Panjab were the Sukerchakia, Kanhaiya, Nakai, Ahluwalia and Bhangi. They had held sway at the end of the 18th century, but one was to become supreme over them: the Sukerchakia Misl. It was led by Ranjit Singh (1780–1839), who attained its leadership at the age of 12. Through conquests and strategic marriage alliances, he managed to absorb many of the other powerful Misls. He consolidated his strength and control over the Panjab, leading to the rise of the Sikh Empire. General Baghel Singh, whose Misl was dominant around the River Jamnu, passed away around 1802, and Jassa Singh Ramgharia in 1803. This led to the younger Khalsa taking centre stage.[1]

Ranjit Singh's reign introduced reforms, modernisation, investment in infrastructure, a decline in crime, increase in education and a rise in general prosperity. The Khalsa army and government included Sikhs, Hindus, Muslims and Europeans. Ranjit Singh's legacy featured a period of Sikh cultural and artistic renaissance, including the rebuilding of the Sikh Gurdwaras and the thrones of polity, or Takhts. The building of forts, havelis (mansions) and lavish gardens were an important part of the infrastructure projects. Many artisans flocked into the Darbar to provide their expertise and resources, as well as the development of arms manufacture, in places like Gujarat and Sialkot.

Ranjit Singh had over 20 wives, including Mehtab Kaur (c.1782–1813) of the Kanhaiya Misl, Raj Kaur or Mai Nakain (d.1838) of the Nakai Misl,[2] Ratan Kaur (1819–48) and Daya Kaur (d.1843) of the Bhangi Misl, Chand Kaur (1802–42) of the Kanhaiya Misl and his youngest wife, Maharani Jindan Kaur (d.1863). These marriages ensured dynastic links and territorial gains, the latter being the most instrumental following the death of the Maharajah.

---

1   The Karorasinghia Misl of Baghel Singh held many towns, such as Kalsia and Ladwa, and other areas which were remote from the inner workings of the Lahore Durbar.
2   Also known as Datar Kaur.

In 1799, Ranjit Singh's 25,000-strong army, supported by another 25,000 led by his mother-in-law, Rani Sada Kaur (*c.*1762–1832) of the Kanhaiya Misl, took part in a joint operation and attacked the region controlled by the Bhangi Sikhs centred around Lahore. The rulers escaped, marking Lahore as the first major conquest of Ranjit Singh, whose rule was welcomed by the Sufi Muslim and Hindu population of Lahore.[3] This success started his period of dominance and unification of the Panjab; in 1800, the ruler of Jammu ceded control of this region to Ranjit Singh.

In 1801, Ranjit Singh was proclaimed the 'Maharajah of Panjab', and a formal investiture ceremony was carried out by Sahib Singh Bedi – a descendant of Guru Nanak. On the day of his coronation, prayers for his wellbeing were performed across mosques, temples and gurdwaras in his territories. Ranjit Singh called his government the *Sarkar Khalsa*, or rule of the Khalsa. He ordered new coins to be issued in the name of Guru Nanak named the *NanakShahi*, as opposed to coins being minted in his own name like many Indian rulers before him.[4] (See the image of Ranjit Singh coin in the colour section).

In 1802, Ranjit Singh also took Amritsar from the Bhangi Misl. Sukhan Kaur, widow of Gulab Singh, was governing the place after the death of her husband. It was at this juncture that Jodh Singh Ramgharia (1758–1815) and Akali Phula Singh (1761–1823) imposed themselves between the two forces to ensure the sanctity of Amritsar was preserved and avoid major bloodshed. A pension was negotiated for Sukhan Kaur, under which the Maharajah took possession of the infamous Zamzama (Lion's Roar) Gun. This cannon was intrinsically linked with the Bhangi Misl, and was hence referred to as *Bhangian-di-Topp*, the 'Gun of the Bhangis'.[5] The writer Rudyard Kipling (1865–1936), in his novel *Kim* – set amidst the backdrop of the 'Great Game', the political conflict between Britain and Russia in Central Asia – opens with the lines "Who hold Zam-Zam meh, that 'fire-breathing dragon', hold the Punjab; for the great green-bronze piece is always first of the conqueror's loot."[6]

3   The rule of the triumvirate of chiefs of the Bhangi Misl – Sahib Singh, Chait Singh and Mohar Singh – was not liked by the inhabitants. "The three Sikh chiefs in possession were shameless in conduct, profligate and debauched, and neglectful of the means of securing themselves. They had few troops or retainers, and their administration was most unpopular." Henry Thoby Prinsep, *Origin of the Sikh Power in the Punjab and political life of Maharaja Ranjit Singh; with an account of the Religion, Laws, and Customs of Sikhs* (Calcutta: G.H. Huttmann, Military Orphan Press, 1834), p.52.
4   The British Museum has many Sikh coins in their collection, including those from the Misl and Ranjit Singh period. See Museum No 1912,0709.234 (minted in Lahore), and No. 1920,0722.75 and 1850,1121.4 (minted in Amritsar) during 1801. Also see Paramdip Kaur Khera, *Catalogue of Sikh Coins in the British Museum* (London: The British Musem, 2011).
5   The gun was commissioned by Ahmad Shah Abdali and constructed by Nazar Shah Khan. It was used by Abdali in the Battle of Panipat in 1761. See Mesrovb Jacob Seth, *Armenians in India, from the Earliest Times to the Present Day* (New Delhi: Asian Educational Services, 2005), p.118. After the Anglo–Sikh Wars, it came into the hands of the British. However, it can now be seen in Lahore.
6   Rudyard Kipling, *Kim* (New York: Doubleday Page and Company, 1912), p.3. First published in 1901. The passage referred to depicts the character Kim sitting on the Zamzama Gun.

Maharaja Ranjit Singh having the sacred *Granth* read to him. Recreated illustration from the painting by Joseph August Schoefft (1809–1888). (Illustration, *Journal Universel*, No. 126, Volume V, 26 July 1845)[7]

The British were incrementally moving to the north and solidifying their position around Delhi. During the Second Anglo–Maratha War in 1803, General Lake (1744–1808) defeated the Marathas and as a result the British became masters of Delhi.[8] Ranjit Singh had tried his best to negotiate terms with the so-called Cis-Sutlej territories,[9] composed of Patiala, Nabha, Jind, Kaithal, Thanesar, Malerkotla and Faridkot, as well as the state of Kalsia.[10] The rulers who were closer to Delhi than Lahore were not given the assurances needed by Ranjit Singh for protection, and if anything, their territories were more likely to be seized by him. Colonel Major General Ochterlony issued an *Ittalahnama* or proclamation dated 9 February 1809, confirming that the Cis-Sutlej states would be siding with the British and the territories seized by

7   For more information on this painting, see my 'Descriptions of the Dasam Granth from the Sketch of the Sikhs in view of Sikh History', *Sant Sipahi* (April 2008).
8   Gerard Lake, 1st Viscount Lake.
9   A Latin reference to 'On this side [of]' Sutlej by the British because they were on the British, or southern, side of the Sutlej River.
10   Kalsia State was a dominion of the Karorasinghia Misl. The Shaheedi Misl also had a small domain in the Cis-Sutlej State in Jharauli.

the Maharajah would be restored to them.[11] As a result, these domains became part of a British protectorate.[12]

On 25 April 1809, Ranjit Singh signed the Treaty of Amritsar with Governor-General Charles T. Metcalfe of the EIC, whereby the Sikh Empire agreed not to expand south of the Sutlej River and the Company promised it would not attempt to militarily cross the Sutlej into Sikh territories. Article 2 of the treaty states:

> The Raja will not maintain in the territory which he occupies on the left bank of the river Sutlej more troops than are necessary for the internal duties of that territory nor commit or suffer any encroachments on the possessions or rights of the chiefs in its vicinity.[13]

The treaty, however, does not mention tributaries south of the river which the Maharajah had rights and access to. Henry Prinsep (1793–1878) states:

> The British Government has since 1808 been the protector of the Sikh territory lying between the Sutlej and the Jumna: Its officers have been appealed to for the adjustment of all disputes between the chiefs and their neighbours or dependants, and the references to the Supreme Council of Government at the Presidency are frequent, and involve questions of great intricacy, making the management of our relations in that quarter by no means the least troublesome part of the business submitted to its decision.[14]

This was confirmed by Major General David Ochterlony (1758–1825)[15] in July 1809 and a review of Ranjit Singh's territories across the river in 1828 by Captain William Murray[16] stating that that the Lahore Durbar owned 45 *talukas* (territories), including areas such as Anandpur, Ropar, Chamkaur, Machiwara, Himmatpur-Wadni

---

11   See Appendix A in Main Bashir Ahmed Faroodi, *British Relations With The Cis-Sutlej States(1809–1823)* (Delhi, Punjab National Press, 1942).
12   A further edict or Proclamation of Protection dated 3 May 1809 was issued to the Cis-Sutlej states confirming British protection from Ranjit Singh. See Appendix C in Faroodi, *British Relations With The Cis-Sutlej States*.
13   See Appendices.
14   Prinsep, *Origin of the Sikh Power*, pp.v–vi. It is clear that the headache that the Sikh chiefs were creating for the British was overwhelming, and as a result another proclamation was issued asking them to ensure that law and order prevailed amongst the states. See second 'Proclamation of Protection' dated 22 August 1811, Appendix C, Faroodi, *British Relations With The Cis-Sutlej States*.
15   Sir David Ochterlony, 1st Baronet of Pitforthy, 1st Baronet of Ochterlony GCB, was born in the USA and was a general of the EIC. He held the powerful post of British Resident to the Mughal court at Delhi. In a note dated 29 July he refers to 14 different regions under the control of Ranjit Singh. See Gupta, *History of the Sikhs*, Vol. V, pp.86–87.
16   Assistant Political Agent at Ludhiana, Deputy Superintendent of Sikh and Hill Affairs and later Political Agent at Ambala from 1815–31.

(territories of Sada Kaur) and Harikepatan, as well as Ferozepore (until 1835).[17] The truth is that the tributes continued to be paid to Ranjit Singh by domains across the Sutlej. This all feeds into the contested question of whether the Sikhs crossing the Sutlej in 1845 constituted a violation of the Treaty of Amritsar, which led to the First Sikh War (an idea we discuss in the next chapter). Two commanders of the *Fauj-i-Khas*, named as Colonel Chet Singh and Jamadar Hafiz Ibrahim, patrolled around the Sutlej River to ensure law and order, and kept a watchful eye over the Akali Nihangs who regularly crossed the Sutlej.[18] This was common knowledge to the British, and Captain Wade regularly raised complaints; however, Captain Murray understood the sensitivities involved and was at odds with him.[19] However this border patrol was keeping the peace not creating friction.[20] See Map of the Sikh Territory: and of the protected Sikh States, in the neighbourhood of the Sutluj River in the colour plate section.

The treaty was a major mistake on the part of Maharajah Ranjit Singh, who ceded hard-fought territories of the Khalsa which had taken decades to conquer. He was unable to convince the Cis-Sutlej states to create a united Panjab. His hand was also forced by the firm negotiations by the EIC's Metcalfe, as well as the Cis-Sutlej states giving free passage to the British, which allowed Major General Ochterlony to bring a British force through Patiala and other areas to ensure their protection.[21] This effectively led to Ranjit Singh signing the treaty. However, it was also an opportunity for making conquests of Afghanistan, as the border in the south was now secured. The treaty started an uneasy friendship with the British, but nevertheless, it remained intact until the First Anglo–Sikh War in 1845.

17   List drawn up by Captain Murray for Captain Claude Martine Wade (1794 – 1861), Agent to the Governor-General for the Affairs of the Punjab and North-West Frontier between 1823–1840. "Ranjit Singh has 45 Talooks entire, or in share with others, on the British side of the Sutlej." Prinsep, *Origin of the Sikh Power*, pp.184–85. Gupta, *History of the Sikhs*, Vol. 4, pp.87–88. Bikrama Jit Hasrat, *Anglo Sikh Relations 1799–1849. A Reappraisal of the Rise and Fall of the Sikhs* (Hoshiarpur: V.V. Research Institute Book Agency, 1968), pp.112–17. Ferozepore gave a military advantage to the British when war broke out. Anandpur, whilst not paying any tributes to Ranjit Singh, was deemed a religious place of sanctity which should be governed by the Lahore Durbar.

18   For the areas patrolled below the Sutlej, see the statement by Captain Wade 'of the Disposition of the French Sowars employed on the Banks of the Sutlej' in Jean-Marie Lafont, *Fauj-i-Khas – Maharajah Ranjit Singh and his French officers* (Amritsar: Guru Nanak Dev University, 2002), p.199.

19   Tensions broke out between Captain Murray and Wade, with Wade stating that the Sikhs were breaking the treaty of 1809 and Murray proving the Sikh forces had been sanctioned and were effective in ensuring that law and order prevailed.

20   Lafont, *Fauj-i-Khas*, pp.38–42. The Akalis regularly crossed the river to visit sacred places related to Guru Gobind Singh, namely Anandpur, Chamkaur and Machiwara.

21   Major General Ochterlony crossed the River Jamuna in January 1809 with 30,000 troops and restored areas of the Cis-Sutlej states taken by Ranjit Singh. See Gupta, *History of the Sikhs*, Vol. 5, pp.238–39.

During this time the Sikh conquests continued. Hari Singh Nalwa (1791–1837), one of the ablest Sikh commanders, took part in his first victorious incursion into Afghan territories, known as the Battle of Kasur (1807). This was followed by the Battle of Sialkot (1808),[22] whilst in 1813, Ranjit Singh wrestled the *Koh-i-Noor* Diamond from Shah Shuja. This was coupled with a striking victory over the Durrani Empire at the Battle of Attock.[23] The fort at Attock was a strategic replenishment point for all armies crossing the Indus. The stranglehold over Kashmir was contested in 1814, but it was something of an abortive affair, and the Sikhs had to wait until 1819 to wrestle control of the region from the Afghans. In 1818, due to non-payment of taxes, Ranjit Singh sent his son, Prince Kharak Singh (1801–1840), and a strong Khalsa force to the city of Multan. The city was surrounded, and the fort was besieged for many months. During the bombardment of the fort, one of the wheels of a cannon broke and many Akali Nihangs steadfastly supported the gun on their shoulders and died in the process. Akali Phula Singh and Sadhu Singh Nihang stormed the fort and won the day for the Sikh Empire. Peshawar was also taken in the same year, after which the rulers of Kabul had the Sikhs on their doorstep.

Further conquests and territorial gains included the Battle of Shopian (1819) and the Battle of Nowshera (1823) in the Khyber Pakhtunkhwa. These were successful campaigns, the latter witnessing one of the most important figures of the Khalsa, Akali Phula Singh, falling in battle. Ranjit Singh was most aggrieved and personally conducted his final rites.[24] In 1831, further treaties or 'terms of friendship' were evoked with the British: William Henry Cavendish-Bentinck (1774–1839), in the newly created post of Governor-General, negotiated the treaty, giving British access to the waters in Panjab.[25] This historic meeting took place at Ropar (the area of the Sikh Empire below the Sutlej), where a plaque recalling the event is still displayed. It was a lavish affair, demonstrating the pomp and ceremony of both the British and the Sikhs. Ropar was beneficial for the British as a trading route for goods and commodities to pass through Sikh territories. The event was described by Colonel James Skinner

22 Hari Singh Nalwa was responsible for conquering Afghan territories. Legends of his conquests continue today in Afghanistan, with misbehaving children being told the 'Nalwa' is coming to frighten them.

23 The battle was fought on the banks of the Indus under the leadership of General Dewan Mokham Chand (d.1814), who was commander of the Sikh forces in the early years of the Sikh Empire. He fought against Wazir Fatteh Khan and his brother, Dost Mohammad Khan, on behalf of Shah Mahmud of Kabul.

24 At the location of Pir Sabaq stands a dilapidated fort and the *smadh* of Phula Singh. It is unfortunate that nothing has been undertaken to preserve this important place for the Sikhs.

25 Later known as Lord Bentinck, he was the first Governor-General of India; prior to him they were governors of Bengal (Fort William). He also passed the Bengal Sati Regulation of 1829, abolishing the practice of *Sati* (immolation) practised by widows on the funeral pyre of their deceased husband. The influence of William Bentinck can be seen in London, with streets named Bentinck, and Portland Street is named after him and his family name.

(1778–1841) – creator of the cavalry regiments known as Skinner's Horse, from which the famous Bengal Lancers emerged – who stated that, "The meeting with Runjeet was very grand on his side, very poor, on ours."[26] A bridge of boats was created over the river, where elephants and horses crossed. Ranjit Singh was dressed extravagantly and wore the *Koh-i-Noor* diamond on his left arm:

> [He was] escorted by 1,000 horse-men, dressed in silk and velvet, and with rich armour. As he passed along, each corps saluted; the Company's colours only dropped. The Governor-General, with all his suite, received him about 100 yards from the Government tent. After going through the ceremony of talking and asking after each other's health … several double-barrelled guns and pistols, two horses, and two elephants … were all presented to the Maha Rajah.[27]

A review of troops took place and allowed each side to show their military strength.[28] The British had ordered from Meerut and Karnal two squadrons of British lancers (the 16th), a European regiment (the 31st Foot), two battalions of native infantry (the 14th and 32nd), eight guns of horse artillery and two squadrons of Colonel Skinner's irregular horse.[29]

The stability of Afghanistan was important to the British as they wanted to check the potential Russian advance in the region and bring it under their influence. It was political thinking like this and confrontations over control of Afghanistan which were part of the 'Great Game'. Maharajah Ranjit Singh continued his conquests in the region. The Battle of Jamrud (1837) saw the fort taken after the Sikhs despatched a strong army, with the Khalsa general, Hari Singh Nalwa, falling in the fight, a huge blow to the Sikh Empire.

In 1838, Governor-General George Eden, Lord Auckland (1784–1849) met with Ranjit Singh as well as despatching an embassy to the Panjab which looked to the Sikhs for help in Afghanistan.[30] This led to the Tripartite Treaty of 1838 between

---

26   Colonel E.B. Maunsell, 'An Historic Durbar', *Journal of the United Service Institution of India*, Vol. LXII, Jan to Oct 1932 (Lahore: Printed by E.A. Smedley at the Civil and Military Gazette Press, 1932), pp.252–57.

27   James Baillie Fraser, *Military Memoir of Lieut-Col. James Skinner, C.B.: For Many Years a Distinguished Officer* Vol. II, (London: Smith, Elder and Co., 1851), pp.209–10. Prinsep states: "Runjeet Singh made to cross before him, 3000 of his best Gorchur cavalry, dressed in new yellow silk quilted coats, also about 800 of Monsieur Allard's dragoons." Prinsep, *Origin of the Sikh Power*, p.163.

28   Skinner did not think much of the Sikh troops and did not agree with Allard's view that they were superior to those of the British. Fraser, *Military Memoir*, p.214.

29   Prinsep, *Origin of the Sikh Power*, p.161.

30   George Eden, 1st Earl of Auckland, was a Whig politician and First Lord of the Admiralty who served as Governor-General of India between 1836 and 1842. He met with Ranjit Singh at the start of 1838. The mission and negotiations were headed by William Hay MacNaghten (1793–1841), the secretary to the Governor-General.

Ropar: The meeting place of the Anglo-Sikh Treaty of 1831, on the banks of the River Sutlej.
(Photograph by Gurinder Singh Mann)

the Sikhs, the British and Shah Shuja (1785–1842) of the Durrani Empire. The idea behind the treaty was to depose Dost Muhammad Khan (1793–1863) and place Shah Shuja on the throne.[31] However, it can also be seen as a British attempt to limit Ranjit Singh's control of the Afghan and Sind regions. This would lead to the First Anglo–Afghan War (1839–42), which was a disaster for Lord Auckland and the British.

Military makeup

At the start of the 18th century, the Sikh army was composed of primarily infantry, lacking many of the military units such as artillery which were needed in modern warfare. The employment of Europeans in the army would benefit the Sikhs by ensuring that they improved on their drills and methods of warfare. There were also a number of British personnel and other mercenaries from around the world who

---

31   Dost Mohammed Khan was later reinstated to the throne of Afghanistan and helped the
     Sikhs during the Second Anglo–Sikh War.

joined the Sikh army.[32] These *firangis*, who were given senior command in the Khalsa army, included the Frenchmen Jean-Francois Allard (1785–1839) and Claude Auguste Court (1793–1880) and the Italians Paolo Di Avitable (1791–1850) and Jean-Baptiste Ventura (1794–1858).[33] The *Fauj-i-Khas*, the elite wing of the army raised by Generals Ventura and Allard, was strictly trained under the French pattern and had a separate emblem and flag consisting of the words *Degh-Tegh-Fateh* written in Persian. The commands and language used were in French, which showed the faith the Maharajah had put in the foreign generals. The artillery was reorganised by Court and Alexander Gardner (1785–1877),[34] but commanded by the Muslim Ilahi Baksh.[35] The artillery was mainly composed of Muslim recruits, and they served the Khalsa well.

The army's weapons and equipment (including clothing) were of the best kind. The *Fauj-i-Khas* was supplied with the best available ammunition and were very loyal to Ranjit Singh, whom they usually escorted. The *Fauj-I-Ain* (regularly army) was a well-drilled force composed of infantry, cavalry and artillery. The *Fauj-i-Be Qawaid* (*Jagirdari Fauj*), or irregular army, were horseman furnished by holders of large estates of the Misls. These were the feudal levies from the old Sikh landowners. The Akali Nihangs were part of the irregular army, but the best of them were promoted to the *Ghorchurahs* or *Fauj-i-Sowari* who were the cavalry army and formed part of Ranjit Singh's personal elite bodyguard and troops.[36]

The improvement in the artillery paid great dividends. Some designs and patterns of cannons were gifted by the British, including two 6-pdr horse artillery pieces given by William Bentinck at Ropar in 1831[37] and two specially commissioned gun howitzers from Governor-General Auckland at Ferozepur in 1838.[38] Another example

32 These included John Holmes (d. 1848), a trumpeter in the Bengal Horse Artillery; Dr Harvey, attached as a medical officer and a soldier named as Ratray or Lesli who was part of the infantry battalion of the Sikh army. For a list of other British officers at the Lahore court, see Devinder Kumar Verma, *Foreigners at the Court of Maharaja Ranjit Singh* (Patiala: Arun Publications, 2006).

33 Verma, *Foreigners at the Court.*

34 Gardner's work was published posthumously by Major Hugh Pearse as *Soldier and Traveller; Memoirs of Alexander Gardner, Colonel of Artillery in the service of Maharaja Ranjit Singh* (London: William Blackwood and Sons, 1898). The accounts by Gardner are considered untrustworthy.

35 He effectively commanded the artillery in the Sikh Wars, but after the Battle of Chillianwallah he went over the British side.

36 Sita Ram Kohli, *Catalogue Of Khalsa Darbar Records*, Volume 1 (Lahore: Printed by the Superintendent, Government Printing, 1919).

37 Brig R.C. Butalia, *The Evolution of the Artillery in India: From the Battle of Plassey 1757 to the Revolt of 1857* (New Delhi: Allied Publishers, 1998), p.280.

38 Khushwant Singh, *Ranjit Singh Maharaja Of The Punjab* (London: George Allen and Unwin Ltd, 1962), p.209. One of these cannons is in the Royal Armouries, Leeds. It was transferred from the Royal Arsenal, Woolwich. See object number XIX.247. See also my article 'The Maharajah's howitzer', Royal Armouries, https://royalarmouries.org/stories/our-collection/the-maharajahs-howitzer/ (accessed 9 September 2019).

of the modern armament employed is a pair of English percussion holster pistols which were highly decorated and embellished, possibly in Sialkot (see colour plate section).[39] Lehna Singh Majithia (d. 1854) was an amazing character in the court of Ranjit Singh: a scientist, inventor, astronomer and weapons expert who controlled the weapon foundries at Lahore and Amritsar. He introduced improvements in gun technology, the results of which proved most effective in the Sikh campaigns against the British in the Anglo–Sikh Wars. Captain William Humbly of the 9th Queens Lancers would later write of them: "The Sikhs fired their Guns in the ratio of thrice to our twice, which multiplies most fearfully the battering power of artillery, and raises the calibre of a six into a nine-pounder."[40] The Sikh guns were many and varied. Captain Ralph Smyth of the Bengal Artillery records 96 different types, with more than 50 different calibres, compared to about 15–20 types in EIC service.[41] The Sikhs used gun-howitzers in much the same proportion as the EIC, but they also used mortars as howitzers. Sikh cannon barrels were also marginally thicker than their British equivalents, which allowed them to double or even triple-shot them and use more powder. Consequently, they had somewhat greater range and hitting power than conventional field artillery of the period.[42]

The change in the composition of various parts of the army can be seen in the following table, covering from the beginnings of the Sikh Empire to the start of the Anglo–Sikh Wars.

Table 1 Composition of the Sikh Army during the Sikh Empire[43]

Service	1818–19	1838–39	1843–44
Infantry	7,748	26,617	37,791
Cavalry	750	4,090	5,381
Artillery	834	4,535	8,280
Total	9,332	35,242	51,452
Irregular army	3,577	10,795	14,383

39   These particular pistols were designed by the British manufacturer Wilkinson, with the barrels, locks and fittings finely gold-damascened in the Panjab. The pistol is dated *c.* 1835. Thanks to Sukhbinder Singh Paul for supplying me with this information.
40   William Wellington Waterloo Humbly, *Journal of a Cavalry Officer: Including the Memorable Sikh Campaign of 1845–46* (London: Longman, Brown, Green, and Longmans, 1854), p.116.
41   See *Inscriptions on the Seikh Guns Captured by the Army of the Sutledge 1845–46. Volume of 64 hand-coloured engravings by and after C. Gomeze* (Calcutta: publisher not known, 1846).
42   I would like to thank Neil Carleton of the Victoria and Albert Museum for supplying me with this information.
43   Sita Ram Kohli, *Sunset of the Sikh Empire* (New Delhi: Orient Blackswan Private Limited, 2012), p.87.

The end game

The Lahore Durbar was originally composed of the older guard and experienced Sirdars from the Misl period, many of whom were of Jat-peasant origin. These individuals either died in battle or were too old to participate in the latter years of the empire. The deaths of Akali Phula Singh and Hari Singh Nalwa proved of great consequence for the Khalsa Empire. As a result, the court's makeup was radically changed and replacements were not necessarily Sikhs, with an influx of European mercenaries (as described above), the Dogra Rajputs, Gaur Brahmins from Uttar Pradesh and Pandits of the Kashmiri Brahmin order, all of whom Ranjit Singh relied on. Sikh support also came from the Attariwalas, Sandhanwalias and the Majithias.[44] These different factions would create a split in the court, each vying for power and furthering their interests after Ranjit Singh's death, but the tensions, whilst simmering, were kept in check when he was Maharajah.

Upon the death of the Maharajah in 1839, the Lahore Durbar witnessed many intrigues, betrayals and assassinations. The Khalsa army turned in on itself and internal conflict threatened to destroy the Sikh state. Two strong factions – those of the Dogra brothers and the Sandhanwalia chiefs – vied for control. Those who were in power during this turbulent period were Maharajah Kharak Singh, Maharajah Nau Nihal Singh (1821–40), Maharajah Sher Singh (1807–1843) and Maharani Chand Kaur (1802–42).[45] One ruler after another was deposed of in rapid succession until 1843, when Duleep Singh, the youngest son of the late Maharaja, was crowned, with Maharani Jindan Kaur becoming the Queen-Regent.

Whilst after 1839 the Sikhs continued to help the British in various campaigns and provided resources to them, the instability offered an opportunity for the British to witness the internal conflict and take over the Panjab. The Sikh Army had become too powerful and started making unreasonable demands, and wages were not being paid. The increase in army numbers (see Table 1) led to the Khalsa Panchayats having greater control of the empire. This became a problem for Raja Lal Singh (d. 1866), commander of the Khalsa Army, Raja Tej Singh (1799–1862), his commander-in-chief, and Raja Gulab Singh (1792–1857), the Maharajah of Kashmir. One way to curtail the size of the army was by going to war with the British. Maharani Jindan Kaur has also been accused of instigating the fall of the Sikh Empire by some commentators, but there is no firm evidence to support this claim.

---

44   Sita Ram Kohli, *Sunset of the Sikh Empire* (New Delhi: Orient Blackswan Private Limited, 2012), p.9. First published in 1967.
45   See Gurmukh Singh Sandhu, *Maharaja Duleep Singh, the King in Exile* (Chandigarh: Institute of Sikh Studies, 2006), pp.1–4.

Maharani Jindan Kaur with Maharajah Duleep Singh, 'Our Enemies in India.'
(Illustration for *The Pictorial Times*, 14 March 1846)

7

The Charter Act of 1813: Green Light for Christian Missionaries

---

The British began their translation work in Calcutta (modern Kolkatta), Bengal, in Fort William.[1] This had already become the capital of their administration, as well as serving the purpose of holding administrative information in a central location. A short distance away at Serampore was a missionary centre set up by a group from Denmark. This mission became a centre for the dissemination of Christian scriptures and was already providing religious instructions from the *Bible*. The Danish had no issue with their subjects preaching religious affairs in India. There was, however, a tension between the policies of the EIC and those of Christian missionaries: both had ideas of how to gain a better understanding of the people, mannerisms and religious affairs of India, but chose different ways to pursue this.

At Fort William, a concerted effort had been made to set up a literary centre whose role was to translate the literary and religious texts of India into English. There were several key individuals based here, including Charles Wilkins (discussed earlier), William Jones (1746–94), a philologist and orientalist who created the Asiatic Society in 1784,[2] and Nathaniel Halhed (1751–1830). The publication of their work was not concerned with the translations of Christian scriptures; as a result, the British administration was favourable to the orientalists. The Asiastic Society, however, did not allow Christian Missionaries into their establishment.

The Danish Mission at Serampore allowed in missionaries regardless of their origins, and as a result, the British missionaries found a haven during their early period in India. Their objectives included translating the *Bible* and several parts of the New and Old Testament into the various languages of India. In the 1790s, several missionaries arrived in Serampore, namely Joshua Marshman (1768–1837), William

---

1 Kolkatta was originally named Calcutta. Fort William was named after King William III (1650–1702).
2 He also started the journal *Asiatick Researchers* with Henry Thomas Colebrooke.

Ward (1769–1823) and William Carey (1761–1834).[3] These individuals, sometimes referred to as the 'Serampore trio', were pioneering missionaries who set up Serampore College.[4] In 1801, the British authorities, after initial reluctance, allowed the trio into Fort William. The role played by William Carey, known as the 'father of modern missions', is instrumental in our understanding of how Christianity would be spread throughout India. A mission can be described as a centre where the teachings of Christianity are propagated. At the time of Carey, these missions were limited by the EIC. Carey wanted to spread the teachings of the *Bible* in foreign lands, especially where there was apathy to do so from the military or trading companies that were already there. In 1792, he wrote a book entitled *An Enquiry into the Obligations of Christians, to use means for the Conversion of the Heathens* which called for exactly that. However, the missionaries had a problem as the EIC did not want them interfering in their politics of trade and commerce, and thus thwarted any attempts by Christian ministers to bring religion to the masses. Professor Daniel Jeyaraj writes:

> According to the Church of England, they were dissenters and, moreover, they did not bring with them any ecclesiastical permission from the Archbishop of Canterbury or the Bishop of London. These Baptists were not trained in Cambridge or Oxford. Instead, they came from artisan families such as shoemakers, weavers, and printers.[5]

There were several other key individuals who wanted to push through reforms which would enable them to introduce the Christian gospel into India. William Wilberforce (1759–1833) was already famed for bringing an end to the slave trade in the British Empire. However, the same Christian faith that compelled him to oppose the slave trade also compelled him to want to spread the gospel and convert others.

Wilberforce called for changes in the Charter Act in 1793 and failed. In 1813, he created a mass movement to lobby Parliament to approve the introduction of missionary centres in India. He was able to get over 900 petitions sent to Parliament. On 22 June 1813, Wilberforce gave a resolute speech lasting three hours which influenced Parliament's decision to finally change the Charter Act.

---

3   William Carey had a ministry in Leicester. He lived and worked at the present Southgates underpass. Interestingly, there is a museum to William Carey at the Old Baptist Church, Leicester. I visited the museum in November 2012 and was given a guided tour by Roger Beeby (Deacon at Central Baptist Church) and the museum's archivist, Keith Harrison.
4   Originally set up to teach families, it grew to encompass education in arts and science and most notably to train people for ministry in the Church in India. The college is considered one of the oldest in India.
5   Lecture by Prof. Daniel Jayaraj, Liverpool Hope University, Henry Martyn Seminar with Tyndale House, 14 March 2012 at Tyndale House, Selwyn Gardens, Cambridge, 'Embodying Memories: Early Bible Translations in Tranquebar and Serampore.'

The Charter Act of 1813

The British had been using laws created in England to influence decisions in the subcontinent. This affected the lands they had subjugated and influenced the lives of millions. One of these laws was the Charter Act of 1813, which was an extension and renewal of earlier Acts of 1773, 1784 and 1793, which previously gave the EIC a monopoly in terms of Trade in India. The 1813 Act was different in several ways, and was essentially a means to end the EIC being the sole recipient of money and resources. This would lead the way for preachers to travel and set up in India.

How and in what way did the missionaries influence the Sikhs and Panjab as a whole?

The EIC's relationship with the Sikh Empire was just beginning, although they had already subdued much of India. Under the Treaty of Amritsar in 1809 with Maharajah Ranjit Singh, the British would not militarily cross the Sutlej River and vice-versa. This produced a stalemate from the British point of view, and it was only when the Maharajah died in 1839 that it became easier for the British to capture the Panjab (see next chapter). This was not achieved overnight and not without huge military intervention on the part of the British, with the Panjab annexed in 1849 after the Second Anglo–Sikh War.

The missionary movement was able to influence the population of Panjab in different ways to the EIC. William Carey remarked on the various places where the *Bible* should be translated, including the Panjab. Carey and his team of translators set up a printing press at Serampore to undertake the process of producing the Christian scriptures in native languages. The team was able to translate the *Bible* into Bengali, Oriya, Marathi, Hindi, Assamese and Sanskrit, with many parts of it also translated into other languages and dialects.[6] The translating centre managed to create the following texts in Panjabi between 1811 and 1826:

1. *The Holy Bible, Containing the Old and New Testaments, Translated from the Originals into the Punjabee Language* (1811).[7]
2. *The New Testament Shikh* (1814).[8]
3. *The Pentateuch in Punjabi* (1814).[9]

---

6   For a complete list of languages and translations, see 'Works/Bible Translations', William Carey University, https://www.wmcarey.edu/carey/bib/works_bible.htm (accessed 10 November 2018).

7   Carey, William, *et. Al.*, *The Holy Bible, Containing the Old and New Testaments, Translated from the Originals into the Punjabee Language*, Vol. V, Containing the New Testament (Serampore: Printed at the Mission Press, 1811).

8   William Carey *et. al.*, *New Testament Shikh* [on spine] (Serampore: publisher not known, 1814).

9   The Pentateuch is what Torah scholars usually refer to as the first five books of the Hebrew *Bible*. William Carey, *The Pentateuch in Punjabi* (Serampore: Mission Press, 1814).

4.   *The Old Testament* (1826) together with translations of Christian saints.[10]

A major effort was undertaken to ensure different variations of the *Bible* were trans-lated for Panjabi readers. The centre was able to cast fonts for different languages and dialects, and the script of *Gurmukhi* was established for the Panjabi language.[11] However, the translation centre caught fire and many of the drafts of the *Bibles* were lost. The Serampore Press also published the first grammar text of the Panjabi language. This was prepared by Carey in 1812, entitled *A Grammar of the Punjabee Language*, in the introduction of which he writes:

THE extensive territorial possessions, the political influence and the extended commerce of the British nation in the East, are constantly giving rise to a variety of circumstances which render a knowledge of the languages spoken in every part of India, and the countries contiguous thereto, highly important. Hence the necessity of elementary Works in these languages.

The language which this grammar is intended to teach is spoken by the Shikhs, that singular people, who inhabit the Punjab, or the country lying between the Sutledge and the Indus.

The following sheets are intended to furnish short and appropriate rules for the acquisition of this language, without attempting any remarks upon the nature of grammar in general.[12]

This would be useful to other translators in the future. Interestingly, Dr Leyden was able to produce his translations of the Sikh language without the aid of this. There are different estimates of the number of Panjabi *Bibles* that were printed, but it is thought to run into the thousands. The biographer of Carey explains the influence that was being asserted in the Panjab after they were translated:

The Punjabi Bible, nearly complete, issued first in 1815, had become so popular by 1820 as to lead Carey to report of the Sikhs that no one of the nations of India had discovered a stronger desire for the Scriptures than this hardy race. At Amritsar and Lahore "the book of Jesus is spoken of, is read, and has caused a considerable stir in the minds of the people."

10   For a complete list see 'Works/Bible Translations', William Carey University, https://www. wmcarey.edu/carey/bib/works_bible.htm (accessed 10 November 2018).
11   Thomas Roebuck, *The Annals of the College of Fort William* (Calcutta: Printed by Philip Pereira, at the Hindoostanee Press, 1819), p.292.
12   William Carey, *A Grammar of the Punjabee Language* (Serampore: Printed at the Mission-press, 1812), p.III.

A Thug, asked how he could have committed so many murders, pointed to it and said, 'If I had had this book I could not have done it.' [13]

The establishment of the *Bible* in the Panjab had begun to take shape, and was furthered by the American missionaries establishing themselves in the Panjab. In 1834, the same year as Carey's death, an American mission had set up in Ludhiana. The Presbyterian Church of USA established this centre on 5 November under the Rev. John C. Lowrie (1808–1900). It was initially established as an English language school and was set up with directions from Calcutta. The impact of the mission is narrated in Lowrie's book, *Travels in North India: Containing Notices of the Hindus; Journals of a Voyage on the Ganges*.[14] Lowrie spent some time researching the people and customs of Panjab, together with meeting Maharajah Ranjit Singh. Within his travel narrative, he writes that he presented the *Bible* to the Maharajah:

> After being seated on the floor like the rest, and after exchanging the usual compliments, I presented the English Bible and Gurmukhi Pentateuch I had brought with me for that purpose.[15]

The Maharajah was indeed intrigued, and dialogue took place on the nature of god and the intricacies of the *Bible*. Lowrie spent some time with Ranjit Singh.[16] A barrier to the propagation of the Christian ethos was the Akali Nihangs, who were the guardians of the Sikh scriptures and places of worship. Lowrie talks of them negatively, as did many British accounts in the 19th century. On his visit to the Harimandir Sahib and the *sarovar* (holy tank), he stressed they could be problematic: "[T]here was some danger attending the visit; as there are always present many of the Akalis, a kind of desperate fanatics, who fear not God nor man."[17] His view was simple: *only when the Akalis [Nihangs] are no more would the preaching of Christianity become more favourable* [author's emphasis]. He added:

> There is, perhaps, reason to hope that the very wickedness of these people [Akalis] will contribute much to cut short their sway, and to render men more willing to receive the teachers of our mild and pure religion.[18]

---

13   George Smith, *Life Of William Carey: Shoemaker & Missionary* (London: John Murray, 1909).
14   Rev. John C. Lowrie, *Travels in North India: Containing notices of the Hindus; journals of a voyage on the Ganges and a tour to Lahor; notes on the Himalaya mountains and the hill tribes, including a sketch of missionary undertakings* (Philadelphia: Presbyterian Board of Publication, 1842).
15   Lowrie, *Travels in North India*, p.149.
16   He was invited to see the Natch girls (dancing girls) of Lahore; Lowrie declined.
17   Lowrie, *Travels in North India*, p.141.
18   Lowrie, *Travels in North India*, p.175.

This was not a one-off attempt to make the Akalis subservient to the Christian way of thought. A remarkable description is made of a visit to the state of Nabha by another minister of the church"

> The books distributed were chiefly Gurmukhi. A large amount of the population of this city are Sikhs. Hence the demand for Gurmukhi books. We were visited this forenoon by a singular character, an Akalin, or female faqir of a peculiar sect [Akali Nihangs]. Like the class of mendicants to whom she belongs she was armed to the teeth. Over her shoulder was slung a sword, while her belt was graced with a large horse pistol, a dagger, and sundry other weapons of destruction. Another sword hung by her side. Her turban was ornamented with panji and five or six chakkars. The Panji is a horrid instrument made something in form of a tiger's claw, with five curved blades exceedingly sharp.[19] The chakkar is a steel discus, of six or eight inches diameter, very sharp also, and no doubt a destructive weapon where hurled with sufficient force. She was certainly the most dangerous looking lady I ever saw. We had her called into our tent and gave her a gospel or two in the Panjabi language, which she could read tolerably well. Not withstanding her formidabble appearance, she was quite civil, and appeared to possess a share of intelligence. It appeared by her own statement that she was a widow… and after his [her husband's] death she had joined the sect and had remained with them ever since. She has she stated, been on tour to the south of India, and had travelled a great deal since she had become a faqir. May she learn the religion of the meek and lowly Jesus, and exchange her carnal weapons for the armour of god.[20]

This description is unique in the representation of a female Akali Nihang or Akalin. She is described as being like her male counterparts, armed to the teeth, as well as being adept in reading the Gurmukhi language. The gospels were given to her with a view to converting the hardened Akali. There is no follow-up as to whether she did convert, but it must be assumed that there was no effect of the Christian scriptures on the Akalis. Speaking with the Akalis, it is clear they have kept oral stories of how the British had a policy of destroying the Nihang way of life.[21]

19 *Panji*: a reference to the number five. Also known as *Bagha Nakha*, which fits over the knuckles. Thanks to Dr Kamalroop Singh for shedding light on this weapon for me.
20 'Rev. J. Caldwell's Journal of a Missionary tour amongst Towns and villages in the neighbourhood of Lodhiana', *The Missionary Chronicle*, Volume 11 (New York: Mission House, 1843), p.304.
21 My discussion with many Nihangs points to the collective memory of how they view the Colonial period. The Nihangs were singled out for their defiance, as would be expected due to their sacrifices for the Sikh faith in the 19th century. The British were seen as another Imperial power out to destroy them, after the Mughals. These thoughts have been repeated to me by many Akalis on many occasions. The opposition to the British by Akali Phula Singh during the Ranjit Singh period is paramount in their thoughts.

Other missions were set up, with branches in the cities of Jalandhar, Ambala, Hoshiarpur, Ferozepur and Rawalpindi. Whilst Gurmukhi was the script in which the Sikhs read, there was also missionary literature published in Shahmukhi, the script which many Muslim Panjabis understood. The key aim of the missions was to understand the language, teach Panjabi to the English officers and convert the local people to Christianity.

The downward filtration theory and English Education Act, 1835

Thomas Babington Macaulay (1800–1859), an important historian, essayist and Whig politician, was appointed as the Law Member of William Bentinck's Council of India in 1834.[22] Macaulay was a great advocate of English education. He was of the opinion that support for English education in India would create "a class of persons Indian in blood and colour, but English in taste." It was presumed that this class would eventually become strong pillars of the British in India. It was expected that these Indians, trained through English education, would learn Western morality and ethics. When incorporated into the structure of colonial rule, these 'Indians' would help to strengthen the British domination of India. This was the 'downward filtration' theory.

Parliament wanted to push through reforms that made the Western curriculum more predominant, with English as the language of instruction, together with promoting it as the language of administration and that of the legal system (replacing Persian). The British built schools and colleges, with English being reinforced by the English Education Act of 1835. Essentially, with the annexation of the Panjab in 1849, this laid the foundation of a more radical Company policy in Panjab which would influence traditions and education in the Panjab. The reallocation of EIC funds ensured that Company policy began mirroring and converging with the views of the missionaries. Particularly in the Panjab, the administrators were more religious in their outlook than their predecessors. However, it was not until 1858 that Lord Palmerston (1784–1865), the British Prime Minister, initiated The Government of India Act 1858. This Act of Parliament called for the liquidation of the EIC (which had up to this point been ruling British India under the auspices of Parliament) and the transference of its functions to the British Crown. This was a direct result of the Indian Mutiny, and thus the justification required for enacting greater control over India was given the final push.

The alignment of EIC policy with that of the missionaries can be seen in the case of Maharajah Duleep Singh (1838–93), who was deposed by the British. The treaty dated 29 March 1849 (see appendices) essentially made Duleep Singh a ward of the British,

---

22   He had also been a cabinet minister and had served on the Board of Control in London before going to India.

the famous *Koh-i-Noor* diamond, or 'mountain of light', was surrendered to the Queen of England, and the costs of the Anglo–Sikh Wars were paid to the British. The young Duleep Singh was under the direction of Sir John Login, a staunch Christian, and Lord Dalhousie.[23] In 1853, the last Sikh sovereign, the 15 year old Maharajah Duleep Singh, adopted Christianity, becoming the first Indian prince to do so. Initially he was tutored by Fakir Azizuddin (d. 1845), but his assistance was not needed as moves were made for the conversion of the Maharajah.[24] He was then tended to by one Bhajan Lal (himself a Christian convert). The Maharajah's initiation into Christianity took place at Fatehgarh, Farrukhabad, in the state of Uttar Pradesh.[25] His conversion remains controversial, having been affected in unclear circumstances at an early age. The question arises whether he was forced to convert? And did he know what he was undertaking? He was also heavily, and continuously, exposed to Christian texts under the tutelage of the devout Login, the keeper of the *Toshkhana* (treasury) or revenue of the Panjab. His friends and other tutors were also Christian. After his conversion, he was sent to Britain in 1854. Interestingly, the parting gift by Lord Dalhousie was a *Bible*, the inscription of which reads:

> To his Highness Maharajah Duleep Singh.
> This Holy Book in which he has been led by God's Grace to find an inheritance, riches far (greater?) than all earthly kingdoms is presented. With sincere respect and regards by his faithful friend Dalhousie. April 18th 1854.[26]

Duleep Singh's conversion was a victory for the missionary movement, as they had converted a Maharajah to Christianity. Duleep did not find a wife in England, and on his trip back from India in 1864 he was to marry Bamba Muller (1848–87), a Christian missionary from the mission at Cairo in Egypt.[27] Whilst nurtured in the ways of the British and living as an English gentleman, Duleep still yearned for his deposed title and lands, and most importantly the money which was taken from his family at the time of annexation. He was administered back into the Sikh faith with the aid of his cousin, Thakar Singh Sandhanwalia.[28] This was undertaken at Aden, and was not the symbolic readmittance of a Maharajah looking to reclaim his kingdom.

---

23 James Andrew Broun-Ramsay, 1st Marquess of Dalhousie.
24 Fakir Azizuddin was a spokesman for the Sikh state under Ranjit Singh. Even after the fall of the Sikh Empire, he became part of the Regency Council which looked at the affairs of the Sikhs. See Fakir S. Aijazuddin, *The Resourceful Fakirs: Three Muslim Brothers at the Sikh Court of Lahore* (New Delhi: Three River Publishers, 2014).
25 I have been able to see the *Bible* that was presented to Duleep Singh. This is in a private collection in the UK.
26 The *Bible* in question is now kept at the Ancient House Museum of Thetford Life in Norfolk, England.
27 Princess Bamba was also part of the American Presbyterian Mission.
28 The other four Sikhs who undertook Duleep Singh's initiation were Aroor Singh, Jawan Singh and two Sikhs from a transport ship. See Peter Bance, *Sovereign, Squire and Rebel*

During this time his movements were watched by the British. Eventually he moved to Paris after a renegotiation of his pension was refused, and he died alone in France. His body was brought back to England by his family, and he was buried at Eleveden near Thetford in Norfolk. The burial to this day evokes contested views over whether this was the true wishes of the Maharajah.[29] (The graves of Maharajah Duleep Singh, Maharani Bamba Duleep Singh and Albert Edward Alexander Duleep Singh. See colour section.)

The idea of ushering in more conversions was discussed at the Missionary Conference in Lahore which took place in 1862–63 (see appendices). A report published afterwards focused

Bible of Maharajah Duleep Singh. (Norfolk Museums Service, Ancient House, Thetford)

on how the Sikh scriptures, and moreover the Sikh faith, could be dissected. The common religious theme was the goal which would make it more favourable for Sikhs to understand the 'Christian God'. The Rev. William Keene, considering the teachings of the Guru Granth Sahib and the Dasam Granth, stated:

> The question now arises – Has the teaching of Nanak in any way, prepared the Sikhs for the reception of Christianity? …

Maharajah Duleep Singh and the Heirs of a Lost Kingdom (Coronet House, London, 2009), p.84.

29   In his will he states that he wished to be buried where he died, but this was not the case. Duleep Singh is buried next to Princess Bamba. The final rites of a Sikh are by cremation, and there are regular calls for Duleep Singh's body to be returned to the Panjab. This demand has come about from many politicians in India. The town of Thetford, however, sees the Maharajah and his family as being great patrons of the area, and as a result his life is commemorated on a regular basis through exhibitions and events.

There is no doubt that Nanak's tenets, where understood and believed, must dispossess the mind of many gross errors, superstitions, and prejudices, which have taken firm hold of the Hindoo. His spirit of toleration, too cannot be without its good effect.

As the influence of Nanak's teachings was for good, so was that of Govind for evil. He abused the principle of Nanak, to lay the foundations of Sikh independence; in doing so, he roused the very worst passions of the soul; and his influence, on the whole, did but demoralize and corrupt the peaceful followers of Nanak.[30]

It was clear that the pacifist and peaceful nature of the Guru Nanak, as envisaged within Guru Granth Sahib, was to be promoted, to the detriment of the martial qualities of the Guru Gobind Singh and the Dasam Granth. The name of Guru Gobind Singh was to be tarnished, as the martial spirit of the Guru contained within his writings was not consistent with the Christian ethos of the missionaries. However, this martial spirit was wholly consistent with the motives and requirements of the military under the British Raj, a theme I take up in Chapter 13. The mission also looked at converting regiments of Sikhs into the Christian fold, including the 32nd Native Infantry of Mazhabi Sikhs.[31]

The missionary movement continued its course of conversions across Panjab and throughout India. They were met with opposition at the end of the 19th century with the formation of the Singh Sabha movements, who wanted to bring the Sikh faith back to its origins. The paradox was that the Singh Sabha movement was established by Sikhs educated or affiliated with British institutions.

30   Rev. William Keene, 'The Sikhs: All that can be said about them, from a Missionary Point of view', in *Report of the Punjab Missionary conference held at Lahore In December and January 1862–63* (Lodiana: American Presbyterian Mission Press, 1863), pp.261–68. Keene was part of the Church Missionary Society in Amritsar. See appendices for the full report.
31   Keene, '*The Sikhs*', pp.266–67.

8

The Anglo–Sikh Wars: Empires in the Balance

Whilst some people see the Anglo–Sikh Wars as simply a fight between the British and the Sikhs, it was far more than this. It was the East India Company – a company run from Leadenhall Street in London – that was protecting its business interests in India and Pakistan against a Sikh Empire whose leading generals had their own vested interests at heart. The Sikh Empire, whilst under the banner of the Khalsa, also constituted the population of Hindus and Muslims.

Cause of the First Anglo–Sikh War

Relations between the British and the Sikhs up until the Anglo–Sikh Wars had, on the face of it, been generally cordial. However, there were some key factors which brought matters to a head. These included some of the Lahore Durbar instigating a war to curtail the size of the Khalsa Army. Newly appointed Raja Lal Singh, the commander of the Khalsa army, Raja Tej Singh, its commander-in-chief, and Raja Gulab Singh had negotiated with the British over future Panjab rule. There was also an increase of British forces in the Panjab from 2,500 in 1836 to 14,000 in 1843.[1] Preparation of boats at Bombay which could be used for making pontoon bridges across the Sutlej was being viewed suspiciously by the Sikhs too.[2] The appointment of Major George Broadfoot (1807–45), the British Resident at Ludhiana, was also seen

---

1   V.C. Pandey and U.S. Khattri, *Modern India: Based on Dr. Ishwari Prasad, Dr. Tarachand, Majumdar, Raychaudhuri, Datta, and H. H. Dodwell, Etc* (Lucknow: Prakashan Kendra, 1978), p.258.
2   Kohli, *Sunset of the Sikh Empire*, p.105, "In September 1845, sixty large boats were delivered at Ferozepore, which would serve either as a flotilla or a bridge … designed in Bombay, each fitted with a gun and two grappling irons with strong chains, and the capacity to carry 100 men. With them came a special detachment of soldiers to serve as guards."

as a catalyst of the war, in light of him declaring certain areas of the Panjab as British territory as well as confronting Sikh soldiers.[3]

First Anglo–Sikh War: The Battles

The Sikhs fought the following battles with the British in what was known as the First Anglo–Sikh War or the Sutlej Campaign:

1.   Battle of Mudki – 18 December 1845
2.   Battle of Ferozeshah – 21 December 1845
3.   Battle of Buddowal – 21 January 1846[4]
4.   Battle of Aliwal – 28 January 1846
5.   Battle of Sobraon – 10 February 1846

The British, having witnessed the drama and intrigues at the Lahore court, gathered intelligence on any impact on their territories. The Sikh army crossed the Sutlej border on 11 December 1845 near Ferozepore, where the British cantonment was based. The *Fauj I Khas* was previously stationed in Sikh enclaves across the river, as discussed in Chapter 6. As part of the Treaty of Amritsar, several territories below the Sutlej were designated as Sikh areas. The British viewed the crossing of the river as a contravention of the treaty, and war was declared by Governor-General Henry Hardinge (1785–1856) on 13 December.

The first encounter which took place on 18 December 1845, the Battle of Mudki, resulted in both sides suffering many causalities. The British Commander-in-Chief in India, General Hugh Gough (1779–1869), led the British forces.[5] A few days later the fate of the British Empire was said to have hung in the balance during the hard-fought two-day encounter at Ferozeshah, with the anxious Governor-General Hardinge burning state papers and sending away important items for safekeeping.[6] Robert Crust (1821–1909) wrote about the events of 22 December, the day after the battle opened:

---

3   Kohli, *Sunset of the Sikh Empire*, pp.105–06. The author had studied the Khalsa Durbar Records, which go into incredible detail on the structure of the Khalsa Army, to write his book. He believes Major Broadfoot was the chief instigator of the First Anglo–Sikh War.
4   This battle is sometimes overlooked as it was more a skirmish than a full-scale battle.
5   Christopher Brice, *Brave As A Lion: The Life And Times Of Field Marshal Hugh Gough, 1st Viscount Gough* (Solihull: Helion & Company, 2017).
6   Hardinge had sent away a sword for safekeeping which was presented to him by the Duke of Wellington. The sword was originally owned by Napoleon Bonaparte and taken at the Battle of Waterloo in 1815. It was sold by the auction house Christie's on 17 December 2015 for £74,500. The sword was recreated in 3D by Taranjit Singh (Taran3d) for the Sikh Museum Initiative exhibition 'Anglo Sikh Wars: Battles, Treaties and Relics' at Newarke Houses Museum, Leicester, in 2017.

> News came from the Governor-General that our attack of yesterday had failed; that affairs were desperate, that all state papers were to be destroyed, and that if the morning attack failed, all would be over; this was kept secret by Mr. Currie and we were concerting measures to make our unconditional surrender to save the wounded, the part of the news that grieved me the most.[7]

After the first day of the battle, the British feared they were facing defeat, but during the night Lal Singh abandoned the battlefield.[8] The following morning, Tej Singh brought up his forces but withdrew at the last moment. The British took their opportunity and overpowered the Sikhs.

At Buddowal, the baggage train of General Harry Smith (1787–1860) was attacked by Ranjodh Singh Majithia (d. 1872), together with Ajit Singh from the British Protectorate state of Ladwa. Whilst this attack was successful, they missed an opportunity to cut off the British and march further into the Cis-Sutlej areas.

This gave an opportunity to the British at Aliwal, where the Sikh squares were broken up by the 16th (The Queen's) Lancers. The Sikh forces under General Avitable were constantly charged at, and Harry Smith was commended for his actions during the battle. The final battle of the campaign took place at Sobroan in March 1846, and was known as the 'Indian Waterloo.' Many Akali Nihangs fought to the death, including General Sham Singh Attariwala (1790–1846), a veteran of the Maharajah Ranjit Singh's army who was called upon to help during the war, who was commended for his gallantry by General Gough.

The British victory led to further treaties being enacted. However, the Panjab was not annexed at this stage; this brought into play the role of the Queen-Regent, Maharani Jindan Kaur, and her young son, Maharaja Duleep Singh. She was awarded a pension as per clause X in the Treaty of Bhyroval. However, she was viewed with suspicion and attempts were made to silence her. She was described in derogatory terms by the British, including being labelled as the 'Messalina of Panjab.'[9] She was also accused of trying to assassinate Henry Lawrence (1806–57) and Raja Tej Singh through a conspiracy known as the Prema plot. Whilst her role in the conspiracy could not be proved, she was strongly suspected of being involved.[10] As a result, her

---

7   Robert Needham Crust, *Linguistic and Oriental Essays. Written from the year 1840 to 1901*, Sixth Series (London: Luzac & Co., 1901), p.48.
8   General Harry Smith was commended for his actions by the Duke of Wellington and was created a baronet. He would later name a part of Africa where he was to serve as Aliwal.
9   Messalina, a reference to the wife of Roman Emperor Claudius Augustus (10 BC–AD 54).
10   The plot centred on a person named Prema, a soldier in the service of Gulab Singh, sent to kill Henry Lawrence, the agent in Lahore, and Raja Tej Singh. The idea was to abduct Maharajah Duleep Singh. Together with his co-conspirators, Prema did not go ahead with the plan and was later arrested. Bhai Maharaj was considered central to this plot. See letter No. 9, 'The Governor-General to the Secret Committee', dated 5 September 1847, *Papers Relating to the Punjab. 1847–1849* (London: Printed by Harrison and Son, 1849), p.34., M.L. Ahluwalia, *Bhai Maharaj Singh* (Patiala: Punjab University), pp.50–51

East India Company Officials. From R. Montgomery Martin, *The British Colonies: their History, Extent, Condition, and Resources*, vol. v. (London and New York: The London Printing and Publishing Company, not dated).

influence was eroded by Lawrence, who had her imprisoned and then exiled from the Panjab to Chunar Fort. She subsequently escaped and was given haven in Nepal by the ruler, Jung Bahadur Kunwar (1817–77).[11] Governor- General Dalhousie, describing the Maharani, stated, "She has the only manly understanding in the Panjab; and her restoration would furnish the only thing which is wanting to render the present movement truly formidable, namely, an object and a head. Trust me this is no time for going back or giving back or winking an eyelid."[12] From his vantage point, her removal from the Panjab was a clear victory for the British: "The thing in itself is of no great importance now. I have confiscated her 9 lacs worth of jewels, and she has no money of her own, so that she can't do much harm. If she flies to Nepal and keeps quiet there, it will be a clear gain, for she will lose her pension, of course."[13]

Second Anglo–Sikh War

The Second Anglo Sikh War consisted of the following battles:

1. Siege of Multan – 19 April 1848–22 January 1849.
2. Battle of Ramnuggar – 22 November 1848.
3. Battle of Sadullapur – 3 December 1848.
4. Battle of Chillianwallah – 13 January 1849.
5. Battle of Gujarat – 21 February 1849.

In 1848, an encounter took place between officers of the Lahore Durbar and the Government of Multan. The area was controlled and led by the Hindu ruler Diwan Mulraj (1814–51), whose soldiers set off a series of events that culminated in the Second Anglo–Sikh War.[14] The murder of British officers Patrick Vans Agnew (Bengal Civil Service) and Lieutenant William Anderson (Bombay Fusilier Regiment) led to

---

11 Jindan Kaur was moved to a fortress in Sheikhupura as well as receiving a pension of 48,000 rupees. She was given refuge in Nepal, but was unable to see her son Duleep Singh until she was given permission to travel to England in 1861. She died at Abingdon House, Kensington. A plaque commemorates her internment at Dissenters' Chapel in Kensal Green Cemetery, and her broken headstone (found in 2009) can be seen at Ancient House Museum, Thetford. Her ashes were eventually moved to Lahore to be next to the remains of her husband Maharajah Ranjit Singh in 1924.
12 Letter to Brig. Mountain, 31 January 1849, in Ganda Singh (ed.), *Maharajah Duleep Singh Correspondence* (Patiala: Punjabi University, 1977), pp.32–33.
13 Letter to George Couper on 2 May 1849, in Singh, *Maharajah Duleep Singh Correspondence*, p.78. She would later be reacquainted with her jewellery after she was given permission to visit Duleep Singh in England.
14 Mulraj was the son of Diwan Sawan Mal Chopra (d. 1844), a commander in Ranjit Singh's army and from Gujaranwala. Together with Hari Singh Nalwa he had wrestled control of Multan from the Afghans, after which time he was made governor of the region.

the siege of Multan, which lasted for several months. Until this time, the affair was considered a local issue, and it was not until Chattar Singh (d. 1855) and Raja Sher Singh Attariwala rebelled against the Lahore Durbar that the British became directly involved.

Ramnuggar was the setting of the first direct engagement between the EIC and the Sikh Empire in the Second Anglo–Sikh War. More of a skirmish than a full-blown battle, the Sikhs repulsed the British attack. Diwan Mulraj and Raja Sher Singh both invoked the name of Maharani Jindan Kaur, citing her treatment as the cause of them taking up arms against the British (see proclamation issued by the Multan Government in the appendices). The Battle of Chillianwallah was a more serious encounter, with many British and Sikh losses, and led to the Government calling for General Gough to be replaced. The battle, with neither side able to claim a decisive victory, was a major embarrassment for the British. (See the painting of the 3rd King's Own Light Dragoons clashing with the Khalsa Army at Chillianwallah in the colour section).

The final and decisive battle of the campaign took place at Gujarat and was known as the Battle of Guns (the siege of Multan had ended), leading to Gough repairing his battered reputation. Several days later, at Rawalpindi, the Sikhs laid down their arms to Major-General Walter Raleigh Gilbert (1753–1853), under the eyes of Raja Sher Singh. This scene was depicted on the Sutlej Campaign medals. Each Sikh soldier was given two rupees given in exchange.[15] There were still pockets of resistance, but the British quickly eliminated the threats.

The Treaty of Lahore, dated 29 March 1849 (see appendices) effectively made the young Maharaja Duleep Singh a ward of the British. The Lahore Durbar paid the cost of the war, as well as relinquishing the famous *Koh-i-Noor* diamond. This diamond still plays on the sentiments of the Sikhs, as well as other interested parties. Much of the Lahore treasury was taken by the British, with many priceless items of the Sikhs sold off or brought back to Britain. The next Governor-General of India, Lord Dalhousie, was instrumental in this process.

With Duleep Singh being exiled to Britain, the whole affair is a sad tale of a once mighty empire losing its kingdom. The Sikhs fought with pride in both campaigns, and it was clear to the British they were not fighting a 'native' army. The British were involved in several hard-fought encounters which might have seen them defeated, notably at Ferozeshah and Chillianwallah. However, the tenacity of generals such as Hugh Gough was clear for all to see, and despite some criticism of his actions he won the wars for the British.

15   1st Baronet Sir Walter Gilbert, Colonel of the 1st Bengal European Fusiliers, fought in both Sikh Wars. A descendant of the famed Sir Walter Raleigh (d. 1618) of the Elizabethan era, he is buried at Kensal Green Cemetery, London. His descendants live at Compton Castle, Devon, where there is a trophy with a battle scene from the Sikh Wars depicted on it.

Treachery and expansionist desires

The wars have since provided much information for analysis and reflection. The Sikhs have felt that the British wished to annexe the Panjab as it was the last major Indian state left for them to subjugate, a view seen in several accounts. The defeat of the Sikhs in the First Anglo–Sikh War has been viewed in the narrative of the British colluding with the commanders from the Lahore Durbar who were out to destroy the Sikh army for their own personal and territorial gain, namely Raja Lal Singh and Tej Singh. According to J.D. Cunningham, "It was generally held by the English in India that Major Broadfoot's appointment as Agent in Oct., 1844 greatly increased the probabilities of a war with the Sikhs, and the impression was equally strong, that had Mr. Clerk, for instance, remained as agent, there would have been no war."[16] Captain Peter Nicholson (d. 1845), the Political Assistant at Ferozepore, addressed exactly that sentiment to Major Broadfoot on 23 November 1845: "Knowing that the [Lahore] Durbar and our Government were in friendly relation … at least, that I had never been told the contrary … and in spite of that relation finding the head of the Durbar [Prime Minister Lal Singh] consenting to a hostile march against its allies and those [Tej Singh and Gulab Singh] supposed to be friendly to us the most active in bringing that march about, the doubt did occur to one whether the Durbar might not be consenting to the march of the army against us with your knowledge."[17]

The actual crossing of the Sutlej River on which the First Anglo–Sikh War centred can also be questioned and subjected to scrutiny. At the time of the Treaty of Amritsar, the British had confirmed many areas across the Sutlej as Sikh territory, and according to Major G. Carmichael Smyth of the North Western Agency:

> Regarding the Punjab war, I am neither of the opinion that the Sikhs made an unprovoked attack, nor that we have acted towards them with great forbearance. If the Sikhs were to be considered entirely an independent state in no way answerable to us, we should not have provoked them – for to assert that the bridge of boats brought from Bombay, was not a causa belli, but merely a defensive measure, is absurd; besides the Sikhs had a translation of Sir Charles Napier's speech (as it appeared in the Delhi Gazette) stating that we were going to war with them; and as all European powers would have done under such

---

16   J.D. Cunningham and H.L.O. Garret (eds), *A History of the Sikhs* (Delhi: S. Chand and Co., 1955), p.255. Cunningham was present in the First Anglo–Sikh War and was reprimanded for writing about the Sikhs in a positive light. He was removed from his political appointment and sent back to regimental duty.
17   Cunningham, *A History of the Sikhs*, p.70; Captain Nicholson of the 28th Native Infantry was a surgeon who died at the Battle of Ferozeshah. His name is recorded at St Andrew's Church, Ferozepore.

circumstances, the Sikhs thought it as well to be first in the field ... Moreover they were not encamped in our territory, but their own.[18]

Carmichael Smyth further states, "The year before the war broke out, we kept the island between Ferozepore and the Punjaub, though it belonged to the Seiks, owing to the deep water being between us and the island."[19] These were not isolated comments, but were widely held. Sir George Campbell, a district Magistrate who was posted at Kaithal, wrote:

> It is recorded in the annals of history, or what is called history, which will go down to posterity, that the Sikh army invaded British Territory in pursuance of a determination to attack us. And most people will be very much surprised to hear that they did nothing of the kind. They made no attack on our outlying canton-ments nor set foot in our territory. What they did do was to cross the river and to entrench themselves in their own territory.[20]

Even when hostilities broke out, Henry Hardinge was questioning the situation that was to arise. According to Robert N. Crust, on 11 December 1845, "I rode behind the Governor General and we sat under a tree to await the infantry. The Governor General remarked will the people of England consider this an actual invasion of our frontier and a justification of war?"[21]

The role of Tej Singh and Lal Singh had been questionable from the start of the campaign. Their part in the Sikh campaign was politically damaging to the Lahore state, aided by Major Broadfoot and his assistant, Captain Nicholson. Cunningham comments on this, "These men considered that their own chance of retaining power was to have the army removed by inducing it to engage in a contest which they believed would end in its dispersion, and pave the way for their recognition as ministers."[22] He adds that their strategy at the Battle of Mudki was "not to compromise them-selves with the English by destroying an isolated division but to get their own troops dispersed by the converging forces of their opponents".[23] This is also the reasoning of William Edwards, commenting on the Battle of Ferozeshah, "Subsequently at Lahore, however, I was informed that their leaders had restrained the men on the pretext that the day was inauspicious for a battle, it by no means being the inten-tion of the regency that their troops should be successful, but, on the contrary, be

---

18   G.C. Smyth, *The History of the Reigning Family Of Lahore: with Some Account of the Jummoo Rajahs, the Seik Soldiers and their Sirdars* (Calcutta: W. Thacker and Co., 1847), p.xxii.
19   Smyth, *The History of the Reigning Family*, p.xxii.
20   George Campbell, *Memoirs of my Indian Career* (London: Macmillan and Co., 1893), p.78
21   Crust, *Linguistic and Oriental Essays*, pp.46–47.
22   Cunningham, *A History of the Sikhs*, p.257.
23   Cunningham, *A History of the Sikhs*, p.263.

destroyed by the British, so as to get rid of them for ever."[24] The final act of Rajas Lal Singh and Tej Singh was at the Battle of Sobroan, where, Edwards continues, "emissaries from Rajah Lall Singh arrived, and gave us valuable information Respecting the enemy's position. From the intelligence thus received, it was determined to attack the entrenchment on its extreme right, where Lall Singh reported the defences to be low and weak."[25] This weakened the position of the Sikhs:

> The Sikhs made a gallant and desperate resistance, but were driven towards the river and their bridge of boats, which, as soon as the action had become general, their leaders, Rajah Lall Singh and Tej Singh, had, by previous consent, broken down, taking the precaution first to retire across it themselves, their object being to effect, as far as possible, the annihilation of the feared and detested army. They fully succeeded in their purpose, for the retreating masses, finding the bridge broken, and having no means of escape, were driven into the river, and shot down or drowned.[26]

Gulab Singh was also negotiating with the British and assuring them of non-interference in the wars and to work with the British towards the state's destruction.[27] He was to garrison his men and send out Lahore troops to the Sutlej, assuring the troops that he would eventually join them, which was not the case.[28] He was looking for favours from the British once the Sikhs were defeated, and was rewarded with the state of Kashmir and Jammu as part of the Treaty of Lahore, drawn up on 9 March 1846, for his services to them and invested as a Maharaja of these regions on 15 March. The treaty was endorsed by Lal and Tej Singh, who also wanted him removed from Panjab politics.[29] Gulab Singh was the single winner from the Sikh Empire in terms of acquiring vast amounts of territory without lifting a finger.

---

24 William Edwards, *Reminiscences of A Bengal Civilian* (London: Smith, Elder And Co., 1866), p.97.
25 Edwards, *Reminiscences Of A Bengal Civilian*, p.99.
26 Smyth, *The History of Reigning Family*, pp.183–84; Tej Singh "ordered up eight or ten guns and had them pointed on the bridge as if ready to beat it to pieces or to oppose the passage of the defeated army".
27 Sir Charles Gough and Arthur Donald Innes, *The Sikhs and the Sikh Wars: The Rise, Conquest, and Annexation of the Punjab State* (London: A.D. Innes & Company, 1897), p.59. "Gholab Singh judiciously persuaded the soldiers to allow him to return to Jammu, from whence he sent offers to the British of co-operation to enable them to march on Lahore, if they would guarantee him the North Eastern Provinces as an independent ruler." This idea was originally refused but his efforts to collude with the British persevered; "Gholab Singh sent a messenger affirming positively that the Sikhs were determined on war, and offering to throw in his own lot with the British", pp.60–61.
28 Edwards, *Reminiscences Of A Bengal Civilian*, p.104.
29 This did not work out well for Raja Lal Singh, who would go on to to oppose Raja Gulab Singh's position, at which point the British had him tried in court and exiled to Agra and then Dehradun, where he died in 1866.

The Anglo–Sikh Wars have been neglected by both the British and the Sikhs. Whilst the British created memorials to the battles, the Sikhs have been rather slow to commemorate the importance of the campaigns.[30] It appears that for the Sikhs, the loss of the empire plays into those emotions whilst for the British, it could have been a different story; as a result, the wars were indeed a balancing act between winning and losing. In recent times there has been renewed interest in the wars, highlighted by the publication of books and staging of exhibitions. However, this story, like other British conflicts, has been erased from both mainstream British and Sikh history.[31]

---

30 The British created memorials at many of the battle locations. It is only recently that a Sikh memorial has been created at Aliwal (2015). On my request, the area around the British memorial was cleared up in 2018. The British memorials from both campaigns require urgent restoration.

31 The two books by Amarpal Singh Sidhu started a renewal of interest in the Anglo–Sikh Wars, together with the 'Anglo Sikh Wars: Battles, Treaties and Relics' exhibition in 2017.

9

The Relics and Loot from the Anglo–Sikh Wars

In every religion, the sanctity which is accorded to relics and artefacts is an important aspect which gives the believer something tangible to relate to. This reverence of arte-facts can be seen in the same light as having sight of the leader of the faith himself. Elements of the Christian religion have been obsessed with the search for the Holy Grail, the cup from which Jesus Christ drank. This search for over a millennium has seen many conspiracy theories, and the role of the Knights Templar – the archetypal warriors of Christianity – has been highlighted in recent years.[1]

In various parts of India and Pakistan, where the Sikh Gurus resided and gave their religious instructions, there are numerous artefacts related to them. This includes the Sikh scriptures, the handwritten instructions such as the *hukamnamas* or 'letters of command' which are sources of historical importance as they give us an insight into the life of the Gurus. The minting of coins was another symbol of sovereignty which started under General Banda Singh Bahadur, and *degh-tegh-fateh* became a popular slogan from the writings of Guru Gobind Singh which later became a standard imprint on coins. These artefeacts can be seen in numerous Gurdwaras, and many Sikhs venerate such objects as if the Gurus were present themselves. Just like the Holy Grail, there has been one artefact which many Sikhs claim they either possess or know the whereabouts of. This artefact is referred to as the Guru's *Kalgi*, or plume. Historically, this plume is said to have been worn by the 10th Guru of the Sikhs, Guru Gobind Singh. Hence there are references to the Guru as *Kalgidhar* ('wearer of the plume').

As there is relatively little written on this subject, the search has been based on hearsay and speculation. The therorists are unable to say what the plume looks like or what form it takes. This problem can also be compounded by whether there is more

---

1   A religious and military order set up by a group of knights who originally grouped
    together to protect pilgrims. It had the permission of the Patriarch of Jerusalem. These
    saintly soldiers played an important part in the Crusades in the Middle Ages. There are
    parallels between these and the Khalsa warriors, namely the Akali Nihangs.

than one *Kalgi*. Indeed, Sikh history tells us that there was more than one *Kalgi* worn by the Guru. Recently, a *Kalgi* has been retrieved by researchers and is kept at the Akal Takht; however, the matter does not rest there.[2] This plume, which was in the *Toshkhana* of Ranjit Singh, has not been seen since the annexation of Panjab and the cataloguing of Sikh relics. The search for lost relics is thus seen as an important quest to reclaim heritage which brings devotees of a faith closer to their religious leaders.

The tracking of relics in the UK has led to many important finds which do not appear in catalogues and other papers noted by the EIC. I recently came across a handwritten list of Sikh relics which includes some known relics, including the Chair of Maharajah Ranjit Singh, the *Koh-i-Noor* diamond and the swords of Holkar and Rustrum. However, there is also mention of relics which have never been seen or known about in the UK:

Table 2: Typed up list of Sikh relics lying in the UK

List of Relics lying in England
1. Ranjit Singh's throne   Lying in Museum, East India House, London
2. Ranjit Singh's Chair   Lying in Westminster Abbey Church in London
3. Koh-i-Noor   Lying in the Tower of London

Relics lying in Museum of London
4. Kalgee Plume of the last Guru (Govind).
5. Ranjit Singh's Silver Summer House, gold and silver, poled, tents, and Camp equipage or rich Cashmeres, arms and armour, very magnificent.
6. The Armour worn by the Warriors and Sardars of note including Sardar Nalva and Akali Phula Singh, stained with their blood removed after their death.
7. The wedding garment of S. Maha Singh father of Ranjit Singh.
8. Relics of the Prophets: his shoes, walking stick, shirt, cap, and Pyjamas, his book of prayers in kufic character, several locks of hair.[3]
9. The Sword of Holkar (an old Spanish blade).
10. The sword of the Persian hero Roostum taken from Shah Sooja by Ranjeet Singh.

Much of these relics bear a mark – JSL – [for] John Spencer Login, who collected these from the Toshkhana of Ranjit Singh and despatched these to England.
    Most confidential (handwritten).[4]

---

2   Harpreet Singh Sidhu, Kamaljit Singh Boparai and others recently claimed they had found the *Kalgi* belonging to Guru Gobind Singh. This was not correct. It was later established to be of a different origin. It once belonged to the late Dr Chanan Singh Sandhu. The son of Dr Sandhu stated he had never claimed the artefact belonged to the 10th Guru.
3   Reference to the Prophet Mohammed of the Muslim faith.
4   Mss Eur F236/216. In the collection of W.G. Archer papers, British Library.

जेसा सीध राम गड़ीया

Jassa Singh Ramgharia. 19th Century. (© The Trustees of the British Museum)

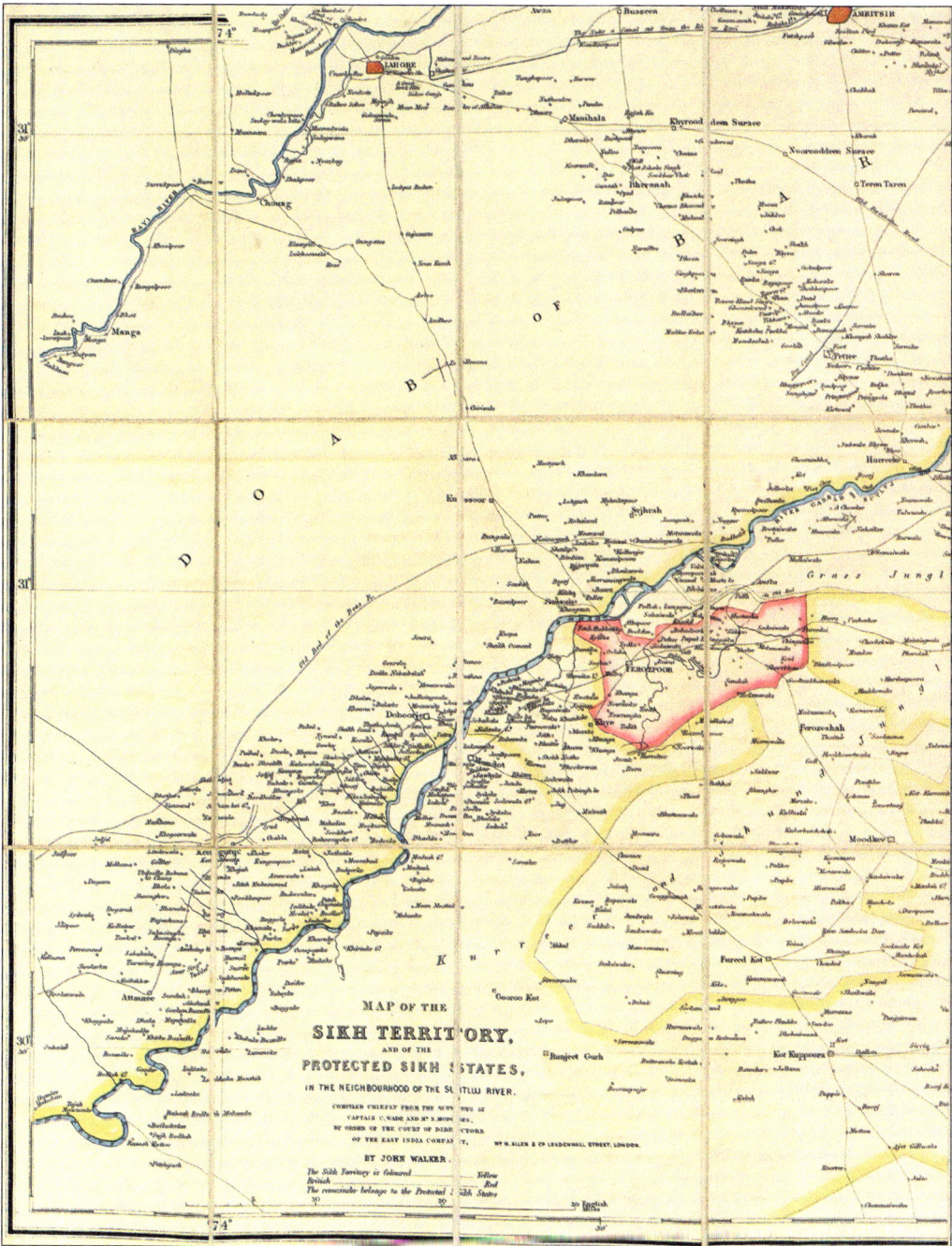

Map of the Sikh Territory and of the protected Sikh States, in the neighbourhood of the
Sutluj River, 1846. Walker, John, 1786-1873, J. & C. Walker (Firm), W.H. Allen & Co.,

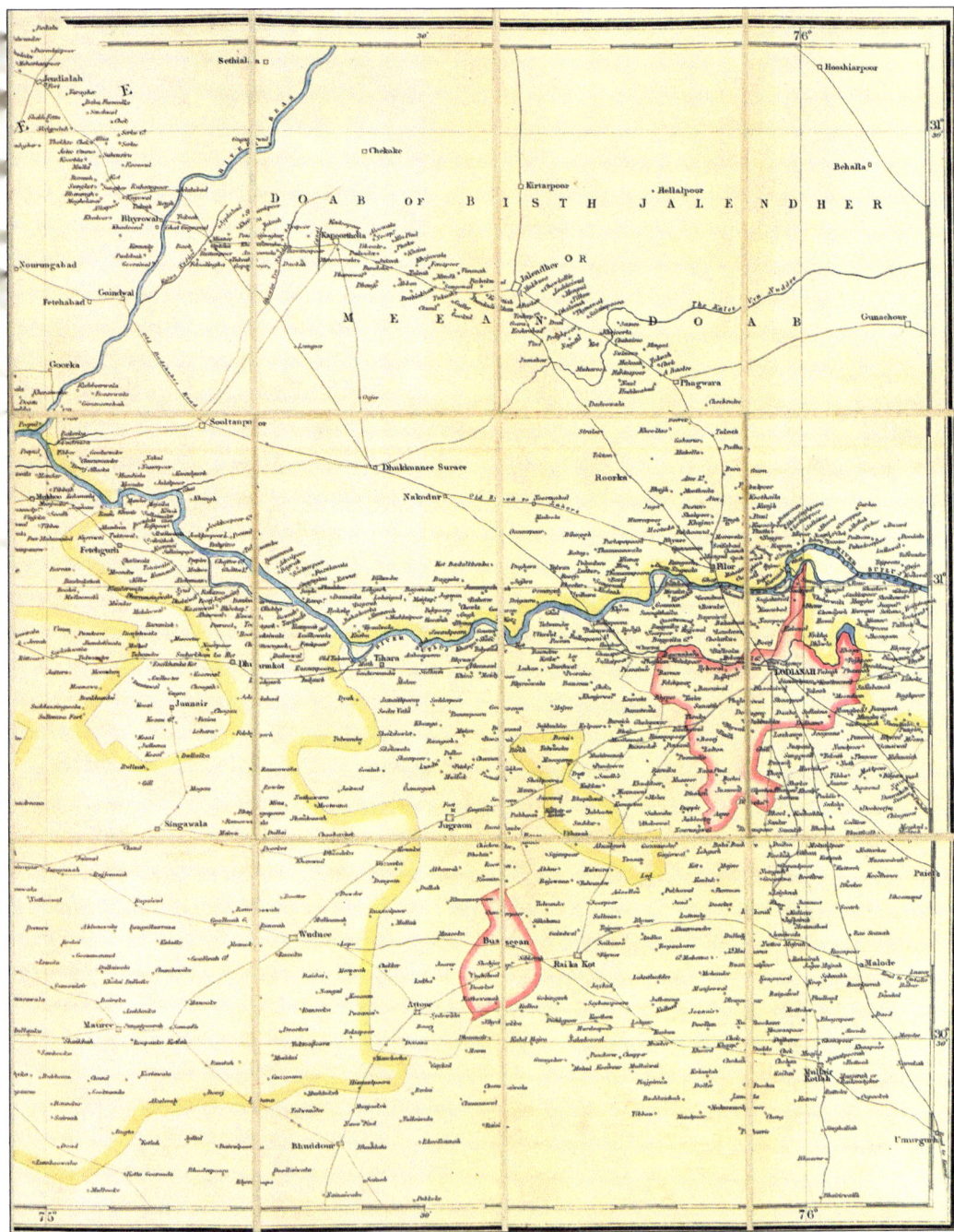

East India Company. (University of Minnesota Libraries, John R. Borchert Map Library, umedia.lib.umn.edu/item/p16022coll246:265)

Ranjit Singh sitting with Guru Nanak offering him a flower, 1828.
(VS 1885 © The Trustees of the British Museum)

Governor Generals: 'Lieut. General Lord W.C. Bentinck. 1834-35' and
'The Marquis of Dalhousie K.T. 1848-56.' (George Arents Collection,
New York Public Library Digital Collections)

Maharajah Ranjit Singh.
(Wellcome Collection. CC-BY)

Akali Phula Singh.
(Wellcome Collection. CC-BY)

Maharajah of Patiala Talwar.
(Royal Collection Trust/©
Her Majesty Queen
Elizabeth II 2019)

3rd King's Own Light Dragoons clashing with the Khalsa Army at Chillianwallah. (The Queen's Hussars Museum)

The graves of Maharajah Duleep Singh, Maharani Bamba Duleep Singh and Albert Edward Alexander Duleep Singh, St Andrew & St Patrick's Church, Elveden, Thetford. (Photograph by Gurinder Singh Mann)

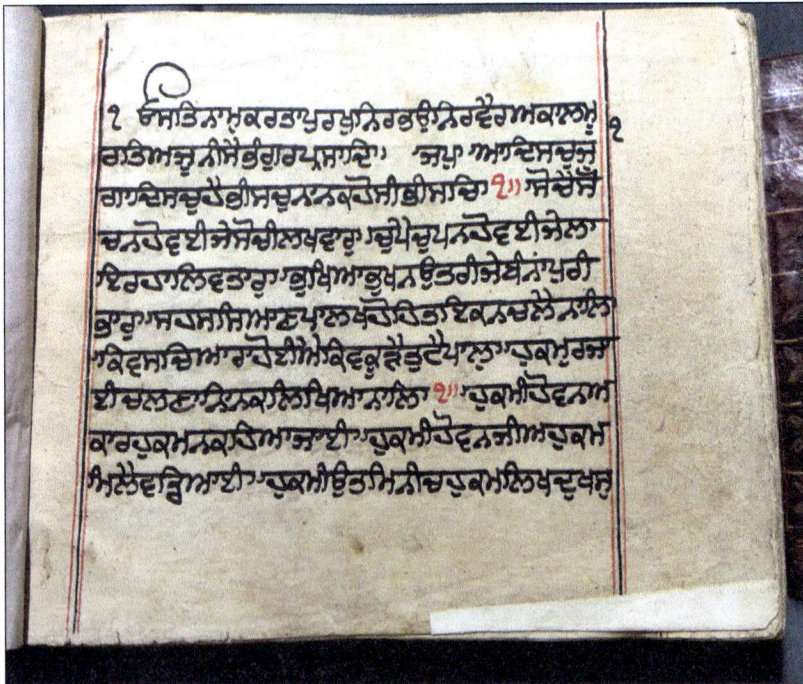

Sikh manuscript from the Battle of Ferozeshah, MS early 1800s. (University of Leicester Library, MS 241)

Drawing of the 'Koh-I-Noor Diamond', 1851. R.S. Garrard & Co. (The Elisha Whittelsey Collection, The Elisha Whittelsey Fund, 1966. Metropolitan Museum of Art)

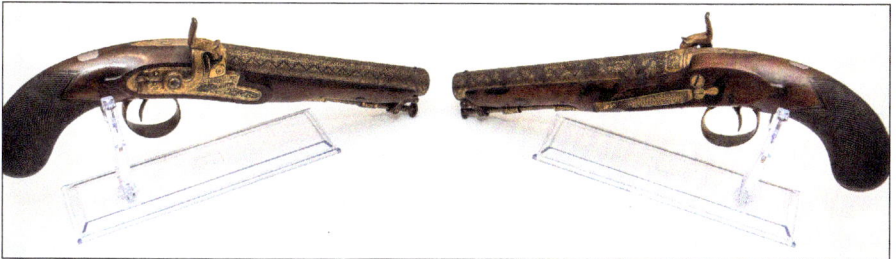

19th-century Sialkot pistols. (Sukhbinder Singh Paul Collection)

Maharajah of Jind Talwar sword.
(Royal Collection Trust/© Her Majesty Queen Elizabeth II 2019)

The significant relics are numbers 1, 6 and 7, notably the armour related to the Sikh warriors. The list also seems to suggest that relics were not limited to just Akali Phula Singh and Hari Singh Nalwa, but also other important Sikhs. The throne of Ranjit Singh is also interesting; whilst the chair is known about, the throne is something new. As this list is typed up, there needs to be some caution, but it points to a strong possibility of these items being in the UK. Whilst I discovered this document in the papers belonging to G.W. Archer, it is not clear if he had compiled the list.

The scriptures of the Sikhs are fundamental to the faith, especially in light of the battalions carrying the complete scriptures and some individual warriors having smaller *pothis* or breviaries. These small manuscripts would contain selections from the Sikh scriptures and were referred to as *Safari birs* (small breviaries). During the reign of Maharajah Ranjit Singh, the Sikh scriptures were carried on elephants accompanied by *Granthis*, or reciters of the scriptures. One eyewitness reports the following:

> The Maharaja maintained an elaborate establishment of Bhais (Sikh priests), one or two of whom held the charge of every Sikh shrine in the Punjab. There was a separate estate attached to every shrine, the produce of which was enjoyed by the incumbent. He was always attended on his tours by a priest with a volume of each of the two chief scriptures [Adi Granth and Dasam Granth]. They were wrapped up in rich pieces of silk, placed in a cot under a big canopy, and thus borne from one place to another. A special military escort was provided, each member of which carried a Sikh banner. The procession was often followed by a number of priests on elephants. Besides this, every regiment had its own volumes of the Granths and religious insignia. Even the ministers of state carried separate copies of the Granths on their journeys.[5]

During the Anglo–Sikh Wars, when the battlefields were surveyed, the British and Sikhs were keen to pick up any objects. For British soldiers, it was nothing more than opportunistic looting as these items could be sold for money.[6] This included attire such as turbans, weapons and Sikhs manuscripts. It is beyond the scope of this section to list every artefact which was found on the battlefields; however, we can consider some important finds which are pertinent to our understanding of Anglo–Sikh relations. There are numerous manuscripts in UK collections which were taken during these wars. British army personnel have listed dates on some manuscripts, which helps with our inquiries. One early and very significant recension of a Guru Granth Sahib manuscript has recently been identified by the Panjab Cultural Association as being worthy

---

5   *Ibratnama*, by Mufti 'Ali ud-Din', in Gulshan Lall Chopra, *The Punjab as a Sovereign State (1799–1839)* (Lahore: Uttar Chand Kapur & Sons, 1928), p.204.
6   Sikhs would have also picked up many British items from the battlefields, but British weapons from the Anglo–Sikh Wars are limited at best within Panjab museums. This is an area which requires further research.

of restoration,[7] labelled as 'Adi Granth Guru Granth Sahib Panjabi MS. 5.' It can be dated to the time of Guru Gobind Singh and hence is one of the earliest complete Guru Granth Sahib manuscripts in the UK. Recovered by the British after the Battle of Gujarat, it was alleged to have been taken from a "Sikh priest by an officer of the 52nd Bengal Native Infantry at the Battle of Guzerat (Gujrat) on 21 February 1849."[8] Another Sikh manuscript picked up at the same battle can be found at Edinburgh University Library.[9]

Whilst in 1849 many Sikhs gave up their arms in Rawalpindi, there were still pockets of resistance faced by the British. Bhai Maharaj Singh (d. 1856), who fought at Multan, was one of those who continued the revolt. Henry Lawrence noted, "Bhai Maharaj Singh, a Sikh priest of reputed sanctity, and of great influence, the first man who raised the standards of rebellion beyond the confines of Multan in 1848, and the only leader of note who did not lay down his arms to Sir Walter Gilbert at Rawalpindi." The manuscript noted as 'MSS. Panj. A4.' kept at the British Library is a case in point, containing compositions from Guru Granth Sahib and the Dasam Granth. Inscribed on the manuscript, which belonged to Maharaj Singh, are the following words:

> Holy Book of Maharaj Singh Gooroo Captured by H Vanstittart Esq CS Dy Commissioner Julandhar Dec 28th 1849.

It was later recorded on the manuscript "Never to leave England".[10] This poses some interesting questions. The manuscript was a prize catch and was seen as a great spoil of Empire as it was attached to such a revered figure, and as a result his possessions were viewed as a continuation of the cult. When Maharaj was captured, Henry Vansittart wrote, "The Guru is no ordinary man. He is to the natives what Jesus is to the most zealous of Christians."[11] The British government, not wishing to take any risks, deported him far away from his native Panjab to Singapore, along with one of his followers, Kharak Singh. Governor-General Dalhousie undertook this measure

---

7   The Panjab Cultural Association of the UK had been in discussion with John Rylands Library, Manchester, to get this manuscript restored.

8   This manuscript was acquired for the John Rylands Library by Enriqueta Rylands in 1901 as part of the manuscript collection of the Earls of Crawford. Lord Crawford purchased the manuscript from Bernard Quaritch in 1862. See also F. Taylor, 'The Oriental Manuscript Collections in the John Rylands Library', *Bulletin of the John Rylands Library*, vol. 54 (1971–72), pp.449–78.

9   Gurumukhi script. Incomplete at end. About .3in tall by 12in wide. Red leather decorated binding with gold appliqué; upper cover detached. The note on the flyleaf reads "Picked up on the field at Goojerat – battle fought 21st February 1849. Charles James Imlach."

10   The manuscript is kept at the British Library, MSS. Panj. A4.507 ff, bound in two volumes. See C. Shackle, *Catalogue of The Panjabi and Sindhi Manuscripts*, pp.12–13.

11   See Richard Gott, *Britain's Empire: Resistance, Repression and Revolt* (London: Verso Books, 2011), p.353.

without any trial. Maharaj was considered a state prisoner, and even when he was being transferred he was kept in chains. After several years of solitary confinement, he died on 5 July 1856.[12] His relics, in a similar fashion, were also far removed and no Sikh would see them until the 20th century.[13]

Another significant manuscript picked up at the Battle of Ferozeshah which is now in the archives of the University of Leicester was brought to the public's attention by the author in 2017. (See the image of the Ferozeshah MSS in the colour section). The flyleaf reads, "Sikh 'Granth' taken from a tent in the Entrenchment of Ferozsheheir, Dec 24, 1845." The manuscript contains verses from both the Guru Granth Sahib and Dasam Granth Sahib. This manuscript was also on display at the exhibition 'Anglo–Sikh Wars: Battles, Treaties and Relics' in 2017.[14] In the same manner, the British took their Bibles to the battlefield and writings within them provide details of the battles; one belonging to Colonel Robert Brookes of the 24th Regiment of Foot was retrieved by the British at the Battle of Chillianwallah.[15]

The battle standards of all armies are objects of veneration, and it is also a strategic win to secure the flags of opposing armies. Ten Sikh flags were brought over to Britain by Lord Dalhousie, described as crimson silk battle standards. These had "block printed gilt motifs comprising a floral sprig with a central burst medallion."[16] The other side had the goddess Durga on her tiger flanked by Hanuman and Kartikeya.[17] These flags were taken at the Battle of Gujarat. A number of these were later sold at a Sotheby's auction in 1990 and now regularly do the rounds, being resold from private collection to private collection.[18] Two similar flags captured by the 80th (Staffordshire) Regiment are at Litchfield Cathedral in Staffordshire, together with

12   There was a permanent guard keeping watch over Maharaj and Kharak Singh. To make matters worse, his cell was reduced in size, which led to further complications with Maharaj's health. He was also refused exercise. Ahluwalia, *Bhai Maharaj Singh*, pp.67–76. Interestingly, Diwan Mulraj was also deported with them but was imprisoned in Calcutta.
13   There are other relics of Bhai Maharaj in the British Library labelled as F.5009, F.5010, F.5011, F.5012 F.5013 and Panj.A.7.
14   I came across this manuscript some years earlier and brought this to the archives' attention. I undertook an analysis of the manuscript and decoded the verses within it. I worked with Dr Simon Dixon (Head of Archives and Special Collections) at the University of Leicester to ensure that the manuscript was displayed according to Sikh tenets and in keeping with the sentiments of the Sikh community at the exhibition. I would like to thank Jasmohan Singh Obhi for his assistance during the work on the manuscript.
15   Colonel Brookes was killed at this battle, near where the Sikh guns were positioned. The *Bible*, which is heavily annotated with descriptions from the battle, is now kept at the Regimental Museum of The Royal Welsh at Brecon. Exhibited at the 'Anglo Sikh Wars: Battles, Treaties and Relics' exhibition at Newarke Houses Museum, Leicester, in 2017.
16   Description taken from *Sotheby's Coulston Auction Catalogue*, 21–22 May 1990.
17   Kartikeya (aka Skanda), who is the leader of the Armies of the Gods.
18   These were listed as Lot 63 in *Sotheby's Coulston Auction Catalogue*, pp.28–29.

an Akali Nihang battle standard.[19] Interestingly, a whole narrative had been created on how the Sikh flag was captured, but it appears that that the account of Colour Sergeant Matthew Kirkland taking the flag is an embellished one.[20] This has led to a fictitious portrayal of how the standard was captured.[21] The memorial at the cathedral records, "The Sikh colours on this memorial were taken by 80th Regiment at the Battles of Ferozeshah and Sobraon. The capture of the Black Standard at Ferozeshah cost the lives of some of those commemorated."[22] A damaged crimson standard also can be found at Maidstone Museum, Kent, together with what appears to be a flag of the French-trained forces of the Khalsa.

Weapons from the battles became sought-after items, and each side had interesting tales of how they employed their military arsenal. We start our assessment of weapons by considering a Sikh sword which belonged to an artilleryman and was found at the Battle of Aliwal. Cornet George Bigoe Williams of the 16th (Queen's) Lancers was involved in a struggle with a Sikh during the battle, and both died in the action. This sword was taken from the hands of a dead Sikh who was found lying close to the body of Cornet Williams by Lieutenant Arnold Knight of the 16th Lancers immediately after the battle on 28 January 1846. An etching on the sword describes what took place: "It is supposed that the Sikh and Cornet Williams had struggled together, as their bodies lay side by side, and at some distance from the rest."[23] The sword is still in

19   These battle standards are in need of urgent repair. The flags were removed in 2017 and were due to be conserved; however, it was not clear who was doing the work or how long this would take.

20   Kirkland has been credited with taking this from an Akali Nihang, but the account by John Cumming has been questioned. He describes the event as follows, "I saw with surprise a large body of Sikhs all clad in chain armour, rise from the ground and attack our people hand to hand. Captain Sceberras seized the (Sikh) Standard and immediately fell. Captain Best next rushed to it, but was also cut down. Sergeant Browne, a young married man next took it and shared a similar fate. The touch of that standard seemed fatal but no sooner was it down, that [sic] another seized it. Finally, Sergeant Kirkland of the Grenadier Company got it and kept it, although severely wounded." This account was in a set of letters sent by John Cumming and were sold at auction at an Islamic And Indian Art sale at Bonhams on 24 April 2012. See https://www.bonhams.com/auctions/19960/lot/295/ (accessed 10 November 2018). The whole story has been revealed as a myth by Brigadier J.K. Tanner in the article 'Immortal Fame – The 80th (Staffordshire Volunteers) at Ferozeshah', in *Soldiers of the Queen, Journal of the Victorian Military Society*, Issue 130, September 2007. The problem here is that Cumming claims he was at the battle when there are no other records of this story. There is no testimony found from Kirkland or any other soldiers said to have captured the standard. There is a memorial to Captain Sceberras at Valetta, Malta, which I visited in 2017.

21   The Leicestershire-based artist Peter Archer depicted the battle in 1996, based on Cummings' account. I discussed this with Peter in 2017 and he agreed his painting was more of an amalgamation of events as opposed to a portrayal of fact.

22   I have visited the cathedral several times.

23   The etching is very easy to read, even now. Cornet Williams is named on the 16th Lancers' memorial at Canterbury Cathedral, Kent. The sword was shown at the 'Anglo Sikh Wars: Battles, Treaties and Relics' exhibition at Newarke Houses Museum, Leicester, in 2017.

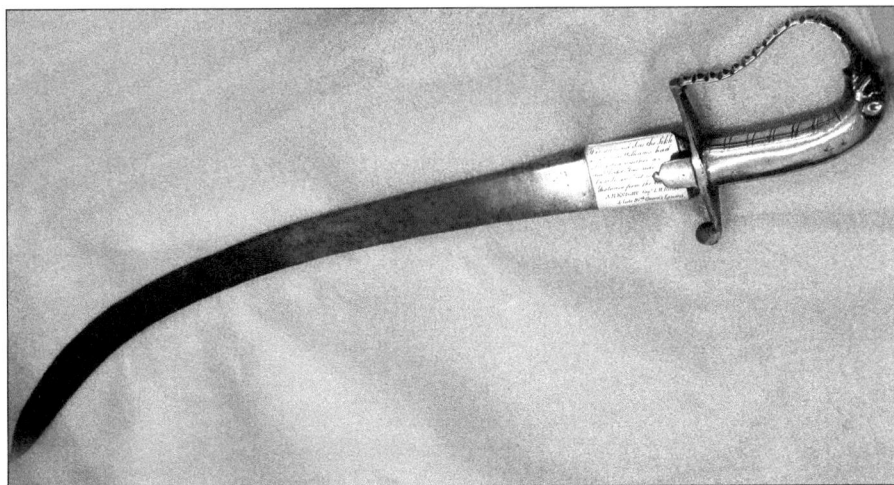

Sikh sword found lying close to the body of Cornet George Bigoe Williams. (Photograph by Gurinder Singh Mann. Reproduced by kind permission of The Royal Lancers & Nottinghamshire Yeomanry Museum)

remarkably good condition and is now kept at The Royal Lancers & Nottinghamshire Yeomanry Museum.

After the Anglo–Sikh Wars, various relics of the Sikhs made their way to Britain, including *Shastars* (arms), manuscripts and other objects. Some of these can be seen in various museums and libraries in the UK, including the British Library, the Wellcome Trust, the Victoria and Albert Museum and others. Many universities in the UK also possess manuscripts and treasures of the Sikhs. Lord Dalhousie, the Governor-General of India, was instrumental in bringing many of these items to the UK. He also became the guardian of Maharajah Duleep Singh after the Panjab was annexed by the British. It was Dalhousie who made the Lahore Government pay the expenses of the Anglo–Sikh Wars, after which the property of the Panjab was confiscated. As a result, the Royal Treasury of Lahore, or *Toshkhana*, became the property of the British (see appendices). Some items were sent directly to Queen Victoria, including the *Koh-i-Noor* diamond, which was later cut down and placed into the crown of Queen Elizabeth for her coronation as Queen Consort in 1937.[24] The Royal Collection Sikh relics are discussed in Chapter 12.

John Login was appointed by Lord Dalhousie as the keeper of the treasury. He was familiar with Sikh items of interest as he was present during the Second Anglo–Sikh War, where he tended to injured soldiers from both sides. He picked up several items,

---

24   The *Koh-i-Noor* has an illustrious history, with several rulers having possession of the diamond through the ages.

including a copy of a Sikh scripture, the Akali quoits and a musket ball.[25] He made an inventory of the *Toshkhana* of Ranjit Singh after the annexation of the Panjab. The treasury deserves further consideration, as does the role played by Lord Dalhousie and John Login. According to letters we understand that:

> On the 6th April he [Lord Login] was installed by Henry Lawrence, with the Governor-General's sanction, as Governor of the Citadel and its contents, including all the political prisoners and harems of the late Maharajahs, the *Toshkhana*, or Treasury, with its jewels and valuables, amongst which was the Koh-i-Noor, kept always under a special guard, and also as Governor to the young dethroned king, Duleep Singh, a very lovable, intelligent and handsome boy.[26]

Login started assessing the wealth in the treasury, "His first rough estimate of the jewels in the *Toshkhana*, exclusive of the *Koh-i-Noor*, was little short of a million pounds."[27] The *Koh-i-Noor* at the time of Maharajah Ranjit Singh was kept in a special case with a military guard and was carried on a camel, the location only known to the key-holder Misr Makraj.[28] The astonishment of the marvels of the treasury was noted by Login when listing its contents:

> I wish you could walk through that same Toshkhana and see its wonders ; the vast quantities of gold and silver ; the jewels not to be valued, so many, and so rich; the Koh-i-noor, far beyond what I had imagined; Runjeet's golden chair of State; silver pavilion; Shah Soojah's ditto; Relics of the Prophet; Kulgee plume of the last Sikh Guru; sword of the Persian hero Rustum (taken from Shah Soojah); sword of Holkar, etc.; and, perhaps above all, the immense collection of magnificent Cashmere shawls, rooms full of them, laid out on shelves and heaped up in bales it is not to be described! … And all this without any list or public document of any sort; all put in his hands to set in order, value, sell, etc.[29]

25 Lady Login, *Sir John Login and Duleep Singh, with an introduction by Colonel G.B. Malleson, C.S.I.* (London: W.H. Allen & co., 1890), pp.144–45: "A good copy of the Grunt'h was found here, and as no one else attaches value to it, I shall take it. I have also, as a relic of the fight, my friend the Akali's 'quoits', as sharp as a razor; he had them in his turban when I picked him up in the ditch, also a jingall ball, which passed close by me." A jingal (pronounced gingall; Hindi *janjal*) is a type of gun, usually a light piece mounted on a swivel; it sometimes takes the form of a heavy musket fired from a rest.
26 E. Dalhousie Login, *Lady Login's Recollections: Court Life and Camp Life 1820–1904* (London: Smith, Elder & Co, 1916), p.73.
27 Login, *Lady Login's Recollections*, p.75.
28 Makraj was Ranjit Singh's treasurer and was employed to continue his role to handle and look after the diamond.
29 Login, *Lady Login's Recollections*, p.80.

By the end of 1849, the treasury had been catalogued and Dalhousie had made the decision on the fate of the relics. This included bringing much of the treasury to the UK; other artefacts he kept himself, while a series of sales in Lahore would dispose of the rest. It is maintained that there were seven auctions/sales, with only two catalogues available.[30]

This was conducted in a very hasty manner, and within weeks many Sikh relics had been sold. Subsequently, Maharajah Duleep Singh researched the whereabouts of relics of the Sikh Empire whilst trying to understand what wealth was taken by the British. He was able to track down two of the sales catalogues from 1850–51. According to him, the Treaty of Lahore did not differentiate between state property and personal property. As a result, he felt he was due recompense in terms of a larger pension.[31]

According to one writer, "The Dalhousie auctions remain one of the most egregious acts of cultural malevolence in Sikh history."[32] Many of the items were shipped to the Indian Museum on the first floor of the EIC headquarters in Leadenhall Street, London. In 1879, many objects and relics from these offices – including Ranjit Singh's Golden Throne and the turban which may be attributed to Akali Phula Singh – were moved to the South Kensington Museum, later renamed the Victoria and Albert Museum. Whilst many of the larger UK museums and universities are aware of the Sikh relics in question, there are others who are oblivious due to lack of enquiries about these items and lack of expertise in Sikh objects. This is more acute if relics are mislabelled as 'Indian', and so remain away from the Sikh public.

---

30 None of these catalogues survived. Maharajah Duleep Singh had two of these reprinted in 1885 after rediscovering them. Thy were published as *A Reprint of two sale Catalogues of jewels & other confiscated property belonging to his highness the Maharajah Duleep Singh (1837–1893): which were put up to auction and sold at Lahore, in the years 1850 and 1851 by the government of India. With introductory remarks* (privately printed, 1885). See also Susan Stronge, 'Sikh Treasury', in Kerry Brown (ed.), *Sikh Art and Literature* (London: Routledge, 1999), p.80.

31 This request was refused by the British authorities.

32 Amandeep Madra, *Punjab Heritage News*, 'A glimpse inside the Royal treasury: Ranjit Singh's Golden Throne', 13 October 2009, (accessed 10 February 2014).

10

The British Attack the Akal Takht and Capture the Nihangs

The Khalsa, or 'fraternity of the pure', was the spiritual and military goal of the 10 Gurus, together with consecrating the Sikh scriptures. Whilst the Sikh religion initiated by Guru Nanak followed a saintly path, it was the change in spirit and direction after the martyrdom of the fifth preceptor, Guru Arjun Dev, that ushered in a new policy for the Sikhs. The sixth preceptor, Guru Hargobind, was guided by the spirited and ageless Baba Buddha. The Sikhs embarked on a policy of combing the saintliness with the martial. The Sikh martial art, *Shastarvidia*, was introduced and the Sikhs wore weapons and were initiated for battle.

Under the tenure of Guru Gobind Singh in 1699, the traditional date of the Khalsa initiation, the Sikhs were reborn after undertaking *Khande ki pahul*, initiation with the double-edged sword. Verses from the Sikh scriptures Guru Granth Sahib and Dasam Granth Sahib were recited, and the vessel of water was stirred with a *Khanda*, (the sword which consecrated the holy water). All initiates drank the water and wore the emblems of the Khalsa. Whilst tradition refers to them as the '5Ks', the Khalsa were heavily armed and continued to be so until after the annexation of the Panjab. Further use of weapons was restricted under the Indian Arms Act initiated by the British in 1878 (which we discuss later). Whilst there were some appeasement between the Akalis and the British, much of the time the Akalis were defiant.

Lieutenant Colonel Malcolm, whom we considered in Chapter 5, describes the Akali Nihangs – the vanguard army of the Sikhs – in an interesting way and sheds light on their practices. Looking at his *Sketch of the Sikhs*, he describes the Akalis as the "never-dying (the most remarkable class of devotees)."[1] He describes their attire and physical makeup by writing, "The disciples of Govind were required to devote themselves to arms, always to have steel about them in some shape or other; to wear a blue dress."[2] The term 'Akal' is a reference to God and is central to their thoughts, and they

1   Malcolm, *Sketch*, p.50.
2   Malcolm, *Sketch*, p.48.

"wear blue chequered clothes, and bangles or bracelets of steel, round their wrists."[3] As a result, they recite verses in praise of steel, namely from the *Akal Ustati* (Praise of the Timeless) from the Dasam Granth.[4] The Akali Nihangs were not only the warrior vanguard but also the priestly class, they have "sole direction of the religious ceremonies at Amritsar" and are "leading men in a council which is held at that sacred place, and which deliberates under all the influence of religious enthusiasm."[5] It was seen that Maharajah Ranjit Singh, who held the Akali Nihangs in great esteem, was also to some extent subject to their directions and even punishments.[6] The Nihangs under Akali Phula Singh had several skirmishes with the British during the Ranjit Singh period.[7] Interestingly, even after the annexation of the Panjab and up until partition, the Nihangs were consistently in opposition to the British as colonial powers. There have been several movements and personalities credited with the beginnings of a 'free India movement', but the contribution of the Akali Nihangs has remained relatively unnoticed despite them being, at the start of the 19th century, the only Sikhs who were a military barrier against any foreign presence.[8]

After the reign of Ranjit Singh, the Nihangs were called into action in the Anglo–Sikh Wars. Maharani Jindan Kaur had asked for the involvement of General Sham Singh Attariwala and Akali Hanuman Singh (d. 1846) to face the British at the Battle of Sobroan.[9] Many Akalis perished at Sobroan, and Hanuman Singh retreated to the area around Patiala. It was envisaged that the Patiala forces would give sanctuary to the Akalis. Several more skirmishes took place, and again many Akalis died at the hands of the British, but this time aided by the Patiala forces who fired their cannons on the Khalsa army. The remaining Akalis retreated to Sohana near Chandigarh, and Akali Hanuman Singh met his death in battle.[10]

After the First Anglo–Sikh War, the British turned their attention to the institutions of the Sikhs, including the Golden Temple and the Akal Takht. The British

3   Malcolm, *Sketch*, p.117.
4   Malcolm quotes lines from the composition *Akal Ustati* from the Dasam Granth.
5   Malcolm, *Sketch*, pp.116–17.
6   The famous anecdote given in Sikh history is that of Ranjit Singh marring a dancing girl named Moran. Because of this act, the Maharajah was subjected to lashings by Akali Phula Singh. It should also be noted that Akali Phula Singh, as well as being the deliverer of justice, was also one of the finest battlefield commanders. The Maharajah on numerous occasions turned to the Akali Nihangs to further his campaigns.
7   There are several paintings of the Akali Nihangs at the British Library; see Add.Or.1351 and Add.Or.1350.
8   Whilst many modern Sikh sources have marginalised the role of the Akalis, many British sources keep referring to them as fanatical and a constant threat throughout the colonial period in India.
9   He was custodian of the Akal Takht as per Khalsa tradition. S.J.S. Pall, *The Beloved Forces of the Guru* (Amritsar: B. Chattar Singh Jiwan Singh, 2007), p.66.
10   Gurdwara Shaheedan in Sohana near Chandigarh was created as a reminder of the sacrifices made by Akali Hanuman Singh and his Akali forces. I visited the Gurdwara in September 2018.

brought in their own officers to control the affairs of the Golden Temple. However, some of the remaining Akalis at the Akal Takht were still defiant. Whilst a treaty was made with the Lahore Durbar, the Akalis did not pay heed to this. As a result, the British, after taking over the affairs of the Harimandir, had to clear the dissenting Nihangs.

The Akali Nihangs had spent many years watching the British depleting their forces and making a mockery of their traditions. As a result, they continued to congregate at the Akal Takht. Anti-British resentment had been brewing after the First Anglo–Sikh War, and some months before the second war, the Akalis again challenged British authority. It was reported that one Ganda Singh had taken over the 'minaret' at the Harimandir complex. An initial report stated he should be captured, with a major force employed and the tower blown up if necessary to extract the Nihang:

> The Acting Resident at Lahore to the Secretary to the Government of India. Lahore, January 31, 1848.
>
> I have further to report that a fanatic Akalee, with four or five followers well armed, has taken possession of one of the towers which surround the sacred tank and temple at Umritsur, and has, for the last three days, defied all attempts to seize him. A portion of the regiment in Govindgurh was called out against him; but I am sorry to add that, on the first day, he wounded the colonel and a sepoy; and, on the second, killed a subadar, and wounded three sepoys. Partly, from the difficulty of assailing the post, and partly, I conceive, from a certain awe which the Sikhs entertain for such characters, he has not yet been captured. I hear that the party have got provisions; but how they manage for water, I do not comprehend; it is evident that they must have an understanding with some one below. The Durbar have sent a select party from Lahore, with instructions to give the Akalee and his men half an hour to surrender, and, on their refusal, to attack them; but, if this cannot be done without the chance of losing many lives, *to undermine the tower, and blow it up* [author's emphasis].[11]

One of the Subedar commanders was killed by the Nihangs and many officers were wounded. As a result, Nihang Ganda Singh and two Akalis were sentenced to death by hanging, with several others sentenced to seven years' imprisonment. The following details give more information on the incident:

11   *The Sessional Papers of the House of Lords*, Session 1849, (12 & 13 Victoria) Vol. XV (London: Harrison and Sons, 1849), p.106. This also appears in *The Sikh Review*, Volume 31, Issues 355–360 (Calcutta: Sikh Cultural Centre, 1983). All the following quotes are taken from these texts.

From John Lawrence, Esquire, Offg. Resident of Lahore.
To H.M. Elliot Esquire, Secretary to the Government of India,
Foreign Department, Fort William
Lahore, 19th February, 1848.

Sir, In paragraph 7 of my letter No. 18 dated First ultmo, I had the honour to report, for the information of the Right Honourable the Governor General in Council, that an Akali, with some followers, had taken post in one of the buildings – Akal Bunga or Akal Takhat – adjoining the Temple at Umritsur; and in resisting the troops who were endeavouring to capture them, had, killed a Subedar and wounded an officer and several men. Before dispatching my letter, I had the satisfaction of adding that these Akalees had surrendered to the party dispatched from Lahore against them.

The culprits were brought to Lahore and the case investigated before the Darbar. Ganda Singh the leader of the party and his associates, all Akalees, were arraigned for the murder of the Subedar and wounding the Commandant of the Corps and some of his men, with intent to kill, the guilt of the prisoners being fully proven, and there being no extenuating circumstances pleaded in defence, the leader Ganda Singh, and two of his associates, were sentenced to be hanged; and the remaining 6 prisoners to "confinement with labour and irons for 7 years.

These sentences I confirmed on the 14th instant; and accordingly this morning the 3 Akalees, sentenced to death were hanged. As this was the first instance in which Akalees have been sentenced to death, I requested the Brigadier Commanding at Lahore to have the 18th Regiment of Native Infantry whose Parade ground is within 100 yards of the spot where the executions take place, drawn up as a precautionary measure. The ground was guarded by the Seikh troops, and the sentence of the law was carried out under the directions of Mr Cocks, Lieutenant Pollock and Sardar Kahan Singh, Udaluttee of Lahore.

I consider that the execution of these Akalis will have most beneficial effect on this turbulent race, and thoroughly convince them that the days have gone by when they could murder with impunity [author's emphasis]. Ganda Singh Akali was a man of some note; he had been engaged, at different times, in various desperate affairs and was at feud with Sardar Lehna Singh Majithia, the late Governor of the Manjha country, whose property, on one occasion, he plundered.

As these Akalees are looked up to with respect and even reverence by the Sikh population of the Punjab, it is not improbable that the 6 prisoners, noted in the margin, who have been sentenced to 7 years' imprisonment, may hereafter make their escape with the connivance of their guards; I therefore beg to recommend that the Right Honourable the Govenor General in Council may be pleased to direct the issue of warrant, allowing them to be confined, for the period for which they have been sentenced, in one of the jails in the Regulation Provinces. The exile of such desperate characters will, I am satisfied, have a most beneficial effect.

I have the Honour to be, Sir
Your most obedt servant,
Sd/- John Lawrence
Officiating Resident[12]

The letter drew the following response:

No 50: Fort William, Foreign Department,
10th March, 1848
To Officiating Resident, Lahore.

Sir,
I have the honor to acknowledge the receipt of your letter dated the 19th eltimo, No. 33 reporting the proceedings of the Durbar against Ganda Singh and other Akalees, who had killed a Subadar and wounded officer and several men.

With reference to the 5th para, of your letter, the G.G. in C [Governor-General in Council] is pleased to direct that the prisoners noted in the margin who have been sentenced by the Durbar to seven years imprisonment, be confined in the jail at Bareilly to which place you are requested to forward them under proper guard, a warrant has been sent to the Magistrate of Bareilly, through the Secy. to Govt., N.W Provinces, to carry the order into effect.

I have & C.,Sd/

As a result, a warrant and attachments were sent to the Magistrate and he was advised to "deal with them in conformity to orders of the Governor General in Council and the provisions of Regulation III of 1848."

A message needed to be sent to the public showing them that the Nihangs could not continue their war with the British, and the proposed execution of the Ganda Singh would be that signal – or they thought. However, it appears that the Akalis were eventually just put in solitary confinement. The matter was reported in the *Indian News and Chronicle of Eastern Affaires* as follows, "Those who were capitally punished were sentenced to death by the durbar, and are the first Akalees who have ever been so condemned. The execution of their sentence will doubtless have a good effect on this turbulent race."[13] Baba Lachman Singh oversaw the Golden Temple at the time of the incident. He was hesitant to have Ganda Singh arrested, which was not to the liking of the British Resident. As a result, the British took steps to install Jodh Singh as *Sabrah* (caretaker) of the Temple, which was opposed by Bhai Parduman Singh and his faction. The British Resident not only wanted to clear the "rebel influence", but

12   *The Sessional Papers*, p.110.
13   *The Indian News and Chronicle of Eastern Affaires*, London, 24 April 1848.

Group portrait of Sikh Soldiers. Willoughby Wallace Hooper (1837–1912), India, 1873.
(Digital image courtesy of Getty's Open Content Program)

also their supporters.[14] They were later to create a *dastur-al-amal* (governing document) in 1859 giving the *Sabrah* powers of administration of the Golden Temple. The Akal Takht was never cleared of the Akalis, although there were fewer clashes with the British after this event. The Arms Act of 1878 also ensured that the traditional Jathedar of the Akal Takht and the leader of the Buddha Dal, Baba Giana Singh, took his warriors to the Takht at Hazur Sahib, as British policy towards the Akalis was one of non-appeasement. It was also seen that many Akalis had taken employment around the area, especially with the Nizam of Hyderabad.

Another version, published some year later, appears to describe the same event. In this, the Akalis were surrounded by the British when they barricaded themselves in the "Akalis Tower." This was noted in the *Illustrated London News* of 20 November 1858 (p.472), in a depiction of what appears to be the Baba Atal Gurdwara, Harimandir Sahib, as opposed to the Akal Takht:

> The Akalis Tower, Umritzir. For whatever purpose this elegant and fanciful building was erected, its present name is derived from the circumstance in the war of the Sikhs, when a band of Akalis (those furious fanatics, in their blue dresses and bands and chains of steel, who had constituted themselves the guardians of the tank and temple) were persued here after the city was taken, and

14   See Navtej Singh, 'British efforts to gain control of the Golden Temple, 1844–63', in P. Singh *et. al.* (eds), *Golden Temple* (Patiala: Punjabi University, 1999), pp.71–75.

driven from floor to floor till the remnant finally precipitated themselves from the summit rather than yield and confess themselves vanquished.

This description seems to suggest that the Akalis jumped from the tower rather than submitting to the British. A reference to the threat of blowing up the tower is also made by Arnold (1862).[15] It would be some years before the Indian Arms Act (1878) was instituted by Lord Lytton curtailing the use of arms by the Indian populace. The Indian Mutiny of 1857 would be a catalyst for this act.

The Akalis were armed to the teeth day and night, and they practised the use of weapons known as *Shastarvidia*. The Indian Arms Act would also curtail the right of the Akalis to practice their art. However, a defiant message was sent from the Akal Takht, the edict or *hukamnama*, in the same year, showing their defiance. The edict refers to the compositions that should be recited by Sikhs and goes on to state, "To practice *Shastravidia* and keep a Shastra in a gatra."[16] Essentially, the Sikh martial arts should thus continue, and the *Shastra* or weapon should be kept in the cummerbund. It does not appear that the British took any action regarding this edict, presumably because that they were not aware made of it. The Akali Nihangs are the only state-sanctioned religious group that can bear arms in India to this day.

15   Edwin Arnold, *The Marquis of Dalhousie's administration of British India*, Volume the First (London: Saunders, Otley and Co., 1862), pp.62–63: "Thus Ganda Singh, an Akalee with some followers seized a building near the tank at Umritsur, and held it against a company for three days. The threat to blow the tower up enforced his submission."
16   This edict is kept in a private collection of Navjot and Preeti Randhawa of Delhi. For a copy, see T.S. Randhawa, *The Sikhs. Images of a Heritage* (New Delhi: Prakash Book Depot, 2007).

11

Translating the Sikh Scriptures: Guru Granth Sahib and Dasam Granth

We now consider the project to translate the Sikh scriptures by the philologist Ernest Trumpp (1828–85). Most Sikhs consider Trumpp as the chief architect of the first Sikh translations, and in some respects, this is true in relation to the scripture the Guru Granth Sahib. Dr Trumpp spent several years translating the Granth, but his results were marred by his disrespect for the Sikh scriptures, not only in his writings but by his actions; for example, on one occasion he smoked his pipe over the Granth.[1] However, the recent discovery of the works of Dr Leyden, which we discussed earlier, leads us to a different conclusion as to when the British started translating early Sikh sources.

Whilst Trumpp was German, the project was initiated by the British to understand more about the Sikh institutions and mannerism. Trumpp was born on 13 March 1828 at Ilsfeld in Wurttemberg (now Baden-Wurttemberg), Germany. He migrated to London after 1849 and was employed as an assistant librarian at East India House (later known as India Office), headquarters of British East India Company. The lack of oriental literature, especially on the Sikhs, was commented on by Professor H.H. Wilson, Director of the Royal Asiatic Society. In his lecture in 1852, he stated, "Although not altogether idle, European Scholars in India have not of late done much for Oriental literature, yet there is much to do, especially in consequence of the recent ascensions to our territories; and grammars and dictionaries of the dialects of the Punjab and frontier districts are essential to the due discharge of public duty."[2]

However, some work was undertaken on the translations of the Sikh scriptures. The major project in this field was commenced by Trumpp from 1869–75.[3] Much emphasis

1   There are various restrictions for Sikhs known as *Kurehats* (conduct from which to refrain from), tobacco being one of them. It is considered abhorrent for someone to smoke over the Sikh scriptures.
2   'Lecture on the Present State of the Cultivation of Oriental Literature', H.H. Wilson, *The Journal of the Royal Asiatic Society of Great Britain and Ireland*, Vol. 13 (1852), pp.191–215.
3   The evidence of translating the Dasam Granth comes from the foreign proceedings papers which are now kept in the National Archives of India (NAI) office in Delhi. These papers

has been given to his translation of the Guru Granth Sahib only. The original project, however, was envisaged to translate both Sikh scriptures, the Guru Granth Sahib and the Dasam Granth. The idea came in 1857 from Robert N. Crust, who was already familiar with the Khalsa due to his participation in the Sikh Wars; together with a call by another administrator, Donald Friell McLeod (1810–72), who in 1859 requested the Granths be translated into English.[4] The translation project was precipitated by the Indian Mutiny. The work was originally due to take place in Britain. McLeod looked upon the *Dasven Patishah Ka Granth* as the work created by Guru Gobind Singh, hence its reason to be translated. McLeod was given two manuscripts, which he sent to England, after an original manuscript from the time of Guru Arjan known as the *Kartapuri Bir* was returned to Sadhu Sodhi Singh.[5] McLeod wrote:

> I have now in my possession, an authentic copy of all the 'Grunths' made to me by 'Guru' Sadhu Singh Sodhi of Kartarpur, the chief of the Sodhi priesthood; the representatives of Guru Gobind all the natives with whom I consulted, indicated him as a proper party to supply a copy as he possessed the originals, written or signed by the Gurus themselves and could at once have them faithfully transcribed and on my applying to him he promised to have this done …
>
> I would now suggest that these two volumes which I have had filled into a suitable box, be sent to England for deposit in the Oriental Library belonging to Her Majesty, and it would in my opinion be most appropriate that Sir John Lawrence should present them on their reaching England.[6]

These two manuscripts are now in the British Library and bear inscriptions made by the Deputy Commissioner in 1859 confirming receipt of the scriptures. The Guru Granth Sahib is identified as 'MSS Panj. E2' and contains the inscription, "Transcribed from the original copy, said to bear the signatures of the Guru themselves, in the possession of Guru Sadho Singh of Kartarpur and by him presented. Dy. Comr. Lahore. June/59."[7] However, the description of this Granth is erroneous. This was not a copy of the so-called *Kartarpuri bir*, as this manuscript is a Damdama recension originating from the time of Guru Gobind Singh.

reveal the extent to which the British wanted to translate the Dasam Granth.

4   Sir Donald McLeod was Lieutenant-Governor of Panjab from 1865 until 1870. He was responsible for the development of roads, railways and canals during his term in office. He also founded Lahore Oriental College.

5   Sadhu Sodhi Singh was a descendant of the Guru's and was a custodian of several Sikh manuscripts. The manuscript in question was procured by Maharajah Ranjit Singh from Sodhi Singh and kept at Lahore.

6   Letter from Donald McLeod to R.H. Davies (Secretary to Government, Punjab and its dependencies). Proceedings Foreign Dept., 8 April 1859, no. 142. (NAI). Dr Nazer Singh, *Guru Granth Sahib Over to the West, Idea of Sikh Scriptures translations: 1810–1909* (New Delhi: Commonwealth, 2005), pp.97–98.

7   MSS Panj. E2, British Library.

The Dasam Granth manuscript is identified as 'MSS Panj. E1', with the transcription "Daswan Padshah Ka Grunth or book of the Tenth King. Being a collection of writings & precepts of the last Guru of the Sikhs, taken from the original copy, said to bear the signatures of the Guru himself."[8] The manuscripts were presented with a stool and cushions to the British.[9]

Trumpp was tasked with translating the Guru Granth Sahib as well as the Dasam Granth, but for several reasons this was later dropped. It seems that Trumpp had numerous observations regarding the scripture: firstly, that the Dasam Granth was the work of Guru Gobind Singh; secondly, that it was worthy of translation but was a difficult text to understand. Trumpp had in 1871 stated that he needed more money to translate the Dasam Granth, a matter that was accepted by the British. However, it was clear that Dr Trumpp was not overly excited at the prospect of having to see the project through. In 1872, several pronouncements and demands were made by Trumpp regarding the translation project. He stated he wanted more time to undertake the endeavour – again this was accepted, and he was given another seven-and-a-half years and an increase in salary. However, in the same year he reported that "the translation of the whole Granth [Dasam Granth] would be a useless undertaking, for Govind Singh was only acknowledged by a very small portion of the Sikh community."[10] This meant the scripture, in his opinion, was not a significant one.

Even more bizarrely, he seemed to emphasise the importance of the *rahitnama*s over the Granth: "He considered the Rahitnamas of Govind Singh which contains the constitution of the Sikh Khalsa, of far greater importance and offered to translate them observing 'if Her Majesty's Government should wish the whole Granth be translated, I would beg that this work be entrusted to someone else, as I would see no end of my labours.'"[11]

Trumpp was effectively abandoning the project in 1872, and his thoughts on the Dasam Granth were mirrored by one Sardar Attar Singh of Bhadour (1833–96).[12] T.H. Thornton, Secretary to the Government of Panjab and its dependencies, canvassed the opinions in 1873 of both Trumpp and Attar Singh, as well as the *Granthis* of Lahore and Amritsar. The *Granthis* determined that the Dasam Granth was of far more importance than the *rahitnamas*:

---

8   Mss Panj. E1, f.3a, British Library. Again, this manuscript is not a copy of any original Dasam Granth manuscripts from the 17th or early 18th century and does bear any signatures of Guru Gobind Singh.
9   Mss Panj. E1, f.4a, British Library.
10 Singh, *Guru Granth Sahib Over to the West*, pp.106–07.
11 Singh, *Guru Granth Sahib Over to the West*, pp.106–07.
12 Attar Singh was a strong British loyalist. As a result of Trumpp's inability to translate the Granth he was commissioned to produce the following portions: *Jaap Sahib*, *Akal Ustati*, *Bachitar Natak*, *Zafarnamah* and the *Hikayat* section in Persian and Panjabi in March 1874. He also translated into English *Rahitnamas* of Prahlad Singh and Bhai Nand Lal. In January 1876, he published his English translation of *Malva Des Ratan di Sakhi Pothi*, or *The Travels of Guru Tegh Bahadur and Guru Gobind Singh*.

From these documents it will be perceived that the General opinion of the Lahore, and Amritsar Granthis, as well of the late Sardar Sir Nehal Singh, Chacchi, K.C.s.9, is that of the two works the Granth [Dasam] is more important, and should be preferentially translated; while Pandit Radha Kishan and Bhai Budh Singh assert that the rules of Rahitnamas are far more strictly observed by the Sikhs of the present day. On other hand, Sadar Attar Singh, Bhadour, entirely concurs in the views of Dr. Trumpp.[13]

The project was eventually abandoned by the British authorities in 1873, which meant that no complete translation of the Sikh scriptures was carried out. Robert Crust, commenting on the translation project, wrote in 1878:

Trumpp was employed by the Government of India at my suggestion, made in 1858, to translate the Adi Grunth, or Holy Scriptures of the Sikhs, compiled by Nanuk and his immediate successors. It is not often in India, that we get at the Language spoken by the people three hundred years ago. Trumpp examined the Grunth of Guru Govind Singh of a later date, and it will be a surprise to some to know, upon so high a linguistic authority, that this last volume is written in pure Hindi of that period, and that the first volume is written in a Hindi Dialect.[14]

The published work of Sikh translations of Trumpp was seen in 1877 in his *Adi Granth or the Holy Scriptures of the Sikhs, Translated from the original Gurmukhi, with introductory essays*.[15] It was not a complete translation, but a translation of one-third of Guru Granth Sahib.[16] The work was not only a translation of the scripture, but also contained some deliberations on the *Janamsakhis*. He stated"

I am also drawing out a life of Guru Nanak from original Sikh sources which could be added as an introduction to the translation of the Granth, together with remarks on the compositions of the Granth.[17]

In 1872, Trumpp was sent a copy of the so-called 'Colebrooke *Janamsakhi*' in Germany. However, he also had other manuscripts in his possession, including commentaries on Guru Granth Sahib, *Prem Sumarag Granth*, a *Pothi* of the Dasam Granth and

13   Progds. For-Gen., A, Sept 1873, no. 6, (NAI).
14   Robert N. Crust, *A Sketch of the Modern Languages of the East Indies* (London: Trubner & Co., Ludgate Hill, 1878), pp.38–39.
15   Ernest Trumpp, *Adi Granth or the Holy Scriptures of the Sikhs, Translated from the Original Gurmukhi, with Introductory Essays* (London: W.H. Allen, 1877).
16   W.H. Mcleod, *The A–Z of Sikhism* (Plymouth: The Scarecrow Press, 2009), p.207.
17   Progds. For-Gen., A, Sept 1873, no. 35, (NAI).

another *Pothi* of *Sakhis*, as well as other texts.[18] He discussed the *Janamsakhi* in a lecture he gave in Munich. The lecture was subsequently published in 1876 as a text entitled *Nanak, Der Stifter der Sikh-Religion*, or *Nanak – the pacifier of Sikh-Religion*. The consideration of the *Janamsakhis* was not a part of Trumpp's commission. Whilst the translation of Guru Granth may be significant as being the first attempt at Sikh scripture translation, his work on the 'Colebrooke Translation' is also worthy of note.

This *Janamsakhi* was named after Henry Colebrooke, whom we considered in Chapter 5. He was the orientalist who was symbolic in combining the Asiatic Society and Fort William College. This collaboration was symbolised in 1807 when Colebrooke became President of the College Council as well as President of the Asiatic Society. In 1808, Colebrooke, as President of the College, transferred a section of the Fort William College Library to the Asiatic Society. Dr Leyden, as mentioned earlier, was also based at Fort William, yet he is silent on the *Janamsakhi* tradition and does not appear to have commented on these works.

Trumpp, commenting on the *Sakhis* or accounts of Guru Nanak, suggested that the accounts were not very authentic and made some crude observations on the text. He also poured scorn on Colebrooke, whom he considered might have been igno-rant of the contents of the text.[19] This is not, however, borne out by the facts, as Malcolm (1812) records that Colebrooke had procured "not only the Adi Granth but also the Dasima Padshah Ka Granth; and that, consequently, he is in possession of the two most sacred books of the Sikhs."[20] Hence he must have been aware of Sikh manuscripts.[21] After all, Colebrooke was versed in many languages and dialects of the Indian system.

However, this particular *Janamsakhi* was more authentic than the others he had studied. He states:

> After a lengthened examination and comparison of this manuscript with the later Janam-sakhis, I am satisfied that this is the fountain, from which all the others have drawn largely: for the stories, as far as they are common to both relations, very frequently agree verbally, with the only difference, that the later Janam-sakhis have substituted more modern forms for old words, which with the progress of time had become unintelligible. This old Janam-sakhi, as hinted already, belongs, according to all external and internal marks, to the latter end of the time of Guru Arjun or to that of his immediate successor. The Granth, which

---

18   My lecture 'Translating the Sikh: An assessment of the works of Leyden, Trumpp and Macauliffe', at the Second Max Arthur Macauliffe Conference, University College Cork, Ireland, 22 March 2014. The Sikh manuscripts in question are presently kept in Munich, Germany.

19   Trumpp, *Adi Granth*, p.ii.

20   Malcolm, *Sketch of the Sikhs*, p.8.

21   The British Library records 'MSS Panj. D.5', a manuscript of the Dasam Granth, being brought over by H. Colebrooke.

Guru Arjun compiled of the writings of his four predecessors and the old famous Bhagats, as well as of his own numerous poetical effusions, is cited throughout, without any paraphrase, whereas the later Janam-sakhis have deemed it already necessary to add to every quotation from the Granth a paraphrase in the modern idiom.[22]

What may have appeared as a minor description in his book, however, provoked much interest in the Panjab. In 1883, a group of Sikhs from Amritsar petitioned the Lieutenant Governor of the Panjab, Charles Aitchison (1832–96), to have the *Janamsakhi* sent to India for inspection. Aitchison agreed and, having perceived the interest aroused by the manuscript, arranged to have it reproduced. A facsimile was issued in 1885.[23] To distinguish it from other *Janamsakhi*, this manuscript is now known as the Colebrooke *Janamsakhi* or the *Vilayat Wali Janamsakhi*, a reference to the manuscript having British connotations. It is labelled as 'Panj. B.6' and kept at the British Library. Shackle (1977) made some observations regarding this manuscript in his *Catalogue of the Panjabi and Sindhi Manuscripts in the India Office Library*.[24]

Later commentators started appreciating the teachings of the Guru and the importance of the educational context laid down by Guru Gobind Singh. One of these was G.W. Leitner (1840–99), a linguist who was responsible for promoting the educational system in Lahore:

> What greater proof, again can be afforded of the importance of Gurmukhi literature and poetry, than the reference to the fact that the court of Guru Govind Singh, the warrior-poet and reformer of the Sikhs, was composed of the '52 immortals', the great gurmukhi poets of all denominations, including even the hated mussalman, who wrote on theology, moral philosophy, history and state economy (sisasat mudan), in verse which was only surpassed by the 'unsurpassable', Guru Govind himself, who corrected their manuscripts with his own hand? One of these manuscripts extending to 4000 pages still exists at Anandpur, in the Hushiarpur District, and is corrected throughout in the very handwriting of the second founder of the Sikh faith.[25]

22   Trumpp, *Adi Granth*.
23   Meanwhile, in 1884, the Lahore Singh Sabha, part of a Sikh reformation movement in Panjab, had a lithographed version of the text produced.
24   Christopher Shackle, *Catalogue of The Panjabi and Sindhi Manuscripts in the India Office Library* (1977), p.19.
25   G.W. Leitner, *History of indigenous Education in Punjab Since Annexation and in 1882* (Calcutta: Printed by the Superintendent of Government printing, India, 1883), p.30. Leitner was following Sikh tradition in noting the Guru had a retinue of 52 poets; modern research points to the court having over 100 poets. See also my 'The Kavi Durbar of Guru Gobind Singh', Bhai Nand Lal, http://www.bhainandlal.com/website/ebooks/kavidurbar.pdf (accessed December 2018).

The Granth he is referring to is likely to be the *Vidyasagar Granth* (Ocean of Knowledge), parts of which can still be located scattered in various libraries.[26] This manuscript does not appear to have been taken to the UK, unlike other Sikh manuscripts in the 19th century. Grierson (1889) would later add numerous Sikh texts to his list of oriental literature, including the *Prem Sumarag Granth* and *Sarabaloh Granth*.[27]

What we discover from the project is that Trumpp produced various incomplete translations and brought to the fore several pertinent manuscripts. It also shows how the knowledge of Sikh texts had been eroded during the 19th century. We have analysed the work undertaken by Dr Leyden and even the Christian missionaries who had created grammar books on the Panjabi language. Trumpp seems to have had no information on the previous works, or overlooked them, and as a result his own limitations were his undoing. The British did not approach the educational centres, or *Taksals*, and so the translation project was always going to be a half-hearted attempt. Some years later, Max Arthur Macauliffe (1841–1913) was commissioned to bring out a history of the Sikhs with many translations, the idea being for the incorrect work of Trumpp to be superseded with some accurate works.

26   I have seen a copy of the *Asvedh Parva*, or the ritual of horse sacrifice, written by Takhan, a court poet of Guru Gobind Singh, where in the colophon it states it is part of the *Vidyasagar Granth*.

27   G.A. Grierson, *The Modern Vernacular literature of Hindustan* (Calcutta: Asiatic Society, 1889), p.128. The *Sarabloh Granth* is a religious text attributed to Guru Gobind Singh, verses of which are recited by Sikhs.

12

The Gifts of Friendship from the Sikh Maharajahs

The Treaty of Amritsar in 1809 had technically created a two-tier Panjab. This assertion counters a major fallacy that all the Panjab was subjugated in 1849. Parts of India conquered by the Sikhs Misls also came under a so-called British protectorate. As a result, many of the places referred to as the Cis-Sutlej States, such as Patiala, Nabha, Jind, Kalsia and Kapurthala, would be neutral states or be loyal to the British as part of the Amritsar treaty. This also included territories of the Kararosinghia Misl (Baghel Singh's) successors in the areas which form part of present-day Haryana.

After the Anglo–Sikh Wars, the friendship of the Rajas from these states continued and as a result, they continued their patronage under the British. The British were also keen on receiving 'spoils of Empire' from around the world. After the annexation of the Panjab, a number of the items found their way to Queen Victoria or other British collections, as discussed in the previous chapter. Some items were sent to the Tower of London and others were kept at Windsor Castle. Many were also sent to the Indian Museum, which was later disbanded. A new Indian Museum in Kensington took many of these items. Some also went to Osborne House on the Isle of Wight, Queen Victoria's private residence.[1]

Queen's Collection and exhibitions

Queen Victoria had requested that some Sikh relics be considered for herself or her estates, a permanent reminder of her conquest and annexation of the Panjab:

---

1   The Durbar Room was made to represent a Sikh court. It was designed by Panjab's foremost architect, Bhai Ram Singh, who had designed the Khalsa College in Amritsar. He had received a Royal Commission from Queen Victoria in 1890 and worked with John Lockwood Kipling (1837–1911), father of Rudyard Kipling. Maharajah Duleep Singh also visited Queen Victoria at Osborne House. His portrait can be seen here, painted by Franz Xaver Winterhalter (1805–73). See RCIN 403843 in the Royal Collection Trust for a bust of Duleep Singh.

Queen Victoria declared her wish to place in the armoury at Windsor Castle specimens of arms and armour of the Sikhs and Afghans worn in the late battles of the Punjab and captured by British troops. Selected from the Lahore *Toshkhana*, Lord Dalhousie sent the queen two complete sets of arms and armour and portions of other sets remarkable for their beauty or history. Specifically included was a sword presented to Ranjit Singh by Holkar, Maharajah of Indore when the two met at Amritsar.[2]

The British had also captured many guns during the Anglo–Sikh Wars, which were received with great fanfare at Indian House, Calcutta. Various depictions show the vast number of cannons that were captured, with some being melted down and others shipped to England.[3] The first display of such guns was at Windsor Castle; these were the Sutlej guns, most likely from the Battle of Aliwal. These were originally intended for display outside Buckingham Palace. The cannons were decorated with presentation plaques and embellishments by the EIC at the Cossipore foundry. The *Illustrated London News* described the guns in elaborate detail in 1848.[4] The cannons were later moved to various places, and one was on display at Maidstone Museum and Art Gallery, Kent, in 2019.[5]

The *Koh-i-Noor* was by far the most famous and expensive diamond that was taken from the *Toshkhana* and received by Queen Victoria (see the image of the *Koh-i-Noor* Diamond in the colour pages). It was referred to in the Treaty of Lahore in 1849,

---

2   Caspar Purdon Clarke (Intro. Robert Elgood), *Arms and Armour at Sandringham: The Indian Collection Presented By The Princes, Chiefs And Nobles Of India … In 1875–1876* (Cambridge: Ken Trotman Publishing, 2008; reprint of the original from 1898). The sword of Holkar had been listed by John Login in his inventory of the *Toshkhana*; see E. Dalhousie Login, *Lord Login's Recollections*, p.80. C. Purdon Clarke (Intro. Robert Elgood), *Indian Art in Marlborough House: A Catalogue of Indian Arm and Objects of Art presented by the Princes and Nobles of India to H.R.H. the Prince on Occasion of His Visit to India in 1875–1876* (Cambridge: Ken Trotman Publishing, 2008, reprint of the original from 1910), p.xxii.

3   Interestingly, there is some suggestion that the statue of Hugh Gough originally in Phoenix Park, Dublin, but now at Chillingham Castle, Northumberland, may have been composed of gun metal from one of the captured guns from the Sikh Wars. See Brice, *Brave As A Lion*, pp.544–45. For a depiction of the guns, see The *ILN*, 'Triumphal return of the Guns at Calcutta. With Henry Hardinge and Harry Smith looking on.'

4   The *ILN*, 14 October 1848, p.233. "Taken from the Battle of Aliwal (First Anglo Sikh War), 6 pounder Guns. Presented by Lord Hardinge (Governor General) to Queen Victoria. The two beautiful brass Guns representations of which by permission of her Majesty … are striking and beautiful specimens of Oriental art … the carriages are elaborately inlaid with mother-of-pearl, brass and steel and the Guns have been thoroughly cleaned and put in order at Woolwich."

5   Other places include Derby Sikh Holocaust Museum, which has several guns loaned from the Royal Artillery Museum; Belvoir Castle in Leicestershire; the Royal Armouries Museum, Leeds; and at the Chillianwallah Memorial in the Royal Hospital grounds in Chelsea.

"The gem called the Koh-i-Noor, which was taken from Shah Sooja-ool-moolk by Maharaja Runjeet Singh, shall be surrendered by the Maharaja of Lahore to the Queen of England" (see appendices for the full treaty). Many myths and interesting stories have circulated regarding its origins and ownership. After the annexation of the Panjab, the diamond was kept under guard and brought to Britain under Lord Dalhousie's direction.[6] It was exhibited at the Great Exhibition of the Works of Industry of All Nations (1 May to 15 October 1851) at the Crystal Palace in Hyde Park, London. The public response was muted, and the diamond was later recut and now forms part of the Queen Mother's Crown kept at the Tower of London. The original amulet which it was housed in is kept within the Royal Collection.[7]

The notion of gifting between Indian Maharajahs and the British had commenced since the EIC visited the shores of India. Even during the reign of Maharajah Ranjit Singh, many Sikh items were given to the British and reciprocated. After annexation, many Maharajahs pledging allegiance to the British sought to gift artefacts of importance, including two swords known as the *Toshkhana* and *Raikot* swords which are attributed to Guru Gobind Singh. The *Raikot* sword is said to have belonged to the family of Rai Kalah of Raekote.[8] It had been kept with them as a family heirloom for generations. It was said to have been given to Rai Shabazz Khan and his brother-in-law, Rai Fateh Khan, by Guru Gobind Singh in 1705. The sword was highly sought-after by many in the Panjab, including the Maharajah of Patiala, who had at different times offered very large sums for its possession: "All temptations have been however indignantly repelled by the late Rani and [the] offer by Rae Imam Bux is I think a graceful act on his part and deserves acknowledgement."[9] Henry Bretton, Deputy Commissioner of Ludhiana, referred to the owner Rae Imam Bux as expressing the wish to gift the sword to the British so that it could be presented to Queen Victoria.

The importance of Guru Gobind Singh's sword was noted by R.C. Temple in 1854: "He was emphatically the warrior Priest and his memory is reverentially cherished by the remnant of what was one of the strongest and most vigorous sects that ever arose

---

6   The *Koh-i-Noor* was originally guarded by the 53rd Regiment (later the King's Shropshire Light Infantry). The Shropshire Regimental Museum notes this information and has a replica of the *Koh-i-Noor* on display. Exhibited at 'Anglo Sikh Wars: Battles, Treaties and Relics', Newarke Houses Museum, Leicester, in 2017.

7   Bhai Nahar Singh and Bhai Kirpal Singh, *Two Swords of Guru Gobind Singh (1666–1708 AD)* (Delhi: Atlantic Publishers and Distributors, 1989), pp.8–9.

8   The sword bears inscriptions from Guru Gobind Singh's composition the *Akal Ustati*, Dasam Granth.

9   Bhai Nahar Singh and Bhai Kirpal Singh, *Two Swords of Guru Gobind Singh*, p.8. The owners of the sword were Rae Imam Bux and Ahmed Buksh, distant relatives of the late Rani, who received the sword after her death. As there was no direct descendant, the estates would fall into British hands (known as the Doctrine of Lapse). The custodians wanted to ensure they received some share of the estate.

Weapons of Guru Gobind Singh displayed at India House, 1966.
(Courtesy of Peter Bance © www.duleepsingh.com)

in India. The sword of such a man … is doubtless a relic of much historical interest."[10] It was also stated by Lord Dalhousie that it was "impolitic to permit any Sikh institution to obtain possession, either by gift or by means [of] sale, of these sacred and warlike symbols of a warlike faith."[11] The understanding here is that these relics were intrinsic to the Sikh faith and as a result were considered to be part of the conquest and fitted in with general ideas of colonial rule. In essence, separating the Sikhs from their sacred relics would make them weaker;[12] consequently, they should not remain in the hands of the Sikhs. Various attempts were made to locate the *Raekote* and *Toshkhana* swords after they had made their way to Britain, but unfortunately they can no longer be traced.[13] It would indeed be something to behold if they were to be found.

10   Bhai Nahar Singh and Bhai Kirpal Singh, *Two Swords of Guru Gobind Singh*, p.18. Letter dated 18 September 1854 by R.C. Temple (Secretary to the Chief Commissioner of Panjab) to the Secretary to the Government of India.
11   Bhai Nahar Singh and Bhai Kirpal Singh, *Two Swords of Guru Gobind Singh*, p.v.
12   The worship of weapons at that time would have been more paramount. This tradition appears to have been lost on modern Sikhs.
13   Bhai Nahar Singh and Bhai Kirpal Singh, *Two Swords of Guru Gobind Singh*, p.40. According to L.D. Wakely (Political Secretary of the Government of India) writing

However, in December 1966, some Sikh swords and other weapons from the family of Lord Dalhousie's residence were returned to the Indian Government.[14]

The wedding gifts for the Prince and Princess of Wales, 1865

The *Illustrated London News* published a story, as well as a detailed drawing, of the many gifts given by the Maharajahs of the Panjab for the occasion of the marriage of Prince Albert Edward (later King Edward VII from 1901–10), the Prince of Wales and the eldest son of Queen Victoria, in 1865. One of the presents was a shield which may have belonged to Maharajah Ranjit Singh. The donor is not listed, but it was described as a "Shield of very handsome workmanship, with four large diamond bosses in the centre … It was considered that a shield would be a fit emblem of the Punjaub, as the Punjaub is a frontier province and it's [*sic*] army holds the gates of India."[15] Another gift was a sword belonging to the Maharajah of Kapurthala, Randhir Singh, described as "set with diamonds, rubies, and emeralds and furnished with gold trappings studded with diamonds."[16]

Prince of Wales' tour of India, 1875

In October 1875, the Prince Albert Edward embarked on an extensive tour of the Indian subcontinent. Travelling on HMS *Serapis*, he visited more than 20 towns and cities before returning to England in May 1876.[17] The Prince of Wales' tour of India was envisaged as a way of forging diplomatic links between Indian rulers and the British Crown. The Prince exchanged gifts with each ruler he met, and some of the most significant Indian works of art in the Royal Collection today were acquired during this tour. As part of the correspondence sent in advance, it was advised that the Indian rulers should only present "curiosities, ancient arms and specimens of local manufacture" to the Prince.[18]

in 1922, the swords could not be traced at Windsor, Buckingham Palace, the Tower Armouries, British Museum or Victoria and Albert Museum.

14   The weapons had been in the Broun-Lyndsay family, who agreed to return them to the Indian Government. The weapons were received with great fanfare in Delhi in 1966 by Prime Minister Lal Bahadur Shastri and are now kept at Takht Keshgarh Sahib, Anandpur Sahib.

15   The *ILN*, 6 May 1865, pp.431–32.

16   Randhir Singh led Sikh forces against British protagonists in Awadh at the time of the Indian Mutiny. He was rewarded with the Order of the Star of India by John Lawrence in Lahore.

17   Kajal Meghani, *Splendours of the Subcontinent: A Prince's Tour of India 1875–76* (London: Royal Collection Trust, 2017), p.5.

18   Meghani, *Splendours of the Subcontinent*, p.12.

Gifts of the Princes of the Punjaub to the Prince and Princess of Wales.
(*The Illustrated London News*, 6 May 1865)

He visited the main areas of Panjab, namely Lahore and Amritsar, and while he did visit the Golden Temple Complex, he did not enter it. He also visited the Museum of Lahore, where he saw items related to the Sikh Empire, and that of Maharajah Ranjit Singh. Curiously, there was a replica of the *Koh-i-Noor* on display which attracted his attention.[19] His visit to Panjab took place between 18 and 24 January 1876 and included an extravagant banquet with 120 Indian chiefs.

He met the following Panjab Maharajahs: Maharajah Mahendra Singh (1852–76) of Patiala; Maharajah Raghbir Singh (1834–87) of Jind; Maharajah Bikram Singh (1842–98) of Faridkot; Maharajah Hira Singh (1843–1911) of Nabha; and Maharajah Kharrak Singh (1850–77) of Kapurthala. These Rajas had much at stake to ensure they maintained their hegemony and status quo. The gifting of treasures to the 'Empress of India' via Prince Edward thus became a lavish affair. The treasures given to the British would be the finest that many had ever seen; not just from the Panjab, but from the whole of India. Some relics that were gifted during this tour now form part of the Royal Collection Trust.

Maharajah Mahendra Singh presented a number of items, including a talwar (RCIN 11303) with "curved blade and an iron hilt with knuckle guard and circular pommel gilded and inlaid with diamonds and rubies around the edge of the pommel (see the image of the Maharajah of Patiala Talwar in the colour section). The black velvet covered wooden scabbard embroidered with seed pearls and silver-gilt mounts set with diamonds."[20] He also gave a rhinoceros hide shield, or *dhal*, with four large and two smaller enamelled and diamond-inlaid bosses in the form of curled-up cheetahs. It had an enamelled and diamond crescent-shaped mount fixed to the top of the shield, and in the centre a diamond-shaped openwork ornament inlaid with emeralds and diamonds. The edge of the shield was embellished with a gold textile border embroidered with pearls in floral motifs. This one shield demonstrates the magnitude of elaborate design and workmanship on the items.

A highly decorated sword and scabbard (RCIN 11258) was gifted by Maharajah Raghbir Singh, referred to as a "talwar with a European steel blade and a gold hilt, knuckle guard and circular pommel inlaid with diamonds, rubies and emeralds. The red velvet covered wooden scabbard embellished with gold openwork mounts inset with rubies, emeralds and diamonds arranged in a floral pattern."[21] (See the Maharajah of Jind Talwar in the colour section). The Prince invested the Raja of Jind with the Order of the Star of India for his services during his visit.

Another type of weapon which was used predominantly by the Sikhs was the *chakkar* (chakram), or quoit. The quoits associated with the Akalis or Nihangs as

---

19   George Wheeler, *India in 1875–76: the Visit of the Prince of Wales* (London: Chapman and Hall, 1876), p.275.

20   The edge section of the blade near the bottom is overlaid with gold to represent a *Makara*, a dragon-like mythological creature associated with Hindu iconography. See the description at https://www.rct.uk/collection/11303/sword-and-scabbard (accessed 24 June 2019).

21   See the description at https://www.rct.uk/collection/11258/sword-and-scabbard (accessed 24 June 2019).

The arrival of the Prince of Wales at Lahore. (*The Illustrated London News*, 19 February 1876)

described earlier were worn around the tall conical turbans called the *Dastar Bungas*.[22] We can see several *chakkars* in the Royal Collection. The one labelled RCIN 11397 has a sharpened outer edge and is overlaid in gold, with a chevron pattern on one side and a trail of flowers on the other. Another (RCIN 11396) has a sharpened outer edge and is overlaid in gold with chevron and lozenge motifs. There is also a pair of *chakkars* (RCIN 11298) that are sharpened on the outer edge and overlaid in gold with trefoils and scrolling foliage. These can all be dated from the 19th century.

Some years earlier, at the Paris Exhibition of 1867, a pair of golden quoits were exhibited and formed part of the collection of HRH the Duke of Edinburgh, Prince Alfred Edward. They were later described as:

A pair of Sikh War quoits, with gold ornamentation of Koft Garhi work. The usual type of war quoit, as hurled by the practising hands of the Akali, is of polished steel, with a very sharp edge. Specimens are in the East India Museum, and in the fine collection of Oriental Arms belonging to HRH, the Duke of Edinburgh.[23]

22   Two fine examples of the *Dastar Bunga* can be seen at the Victoria and Albert Museum. One is on display and other is in the museum archives, which I inspected in 2018. Another can be seen at the Royal Armouries, Leeds. See also my discussion on Sikh weaponry on *Celebrity Antiques Road Trip*, aired on BBC TV in December 2017.
23   Second son of Queen Victoria. *The Archaeological Journal*, Volume xxx (London: Royal Archaeological Institute, 1873), p.96.

In 1872, an obscure publication named *The Building News and Engineering Journal* contained a reference to relics that were in the collection of Prince Alfred. The objects that he had collected on his travels were noted as follows: "The Duke of Edinburgh, during a five years' cruise, which carried him round the world, collected the materials of a, small, but most magnificent museum, the principal riches of which are now displayed to the public at South Kensington." A note is given regarding the Indian collection and there is no surprise that the Akalis weapons are described: "There are the 'War quoits', called 'of Akali', an apparatus of fighting nowhere else employed; double-pronged spear-heads, resembling some of the savage implements stored up in the Tower of London."[24]

There are also several pieces of armour in the collection, including what is referred to as a cuirass, or sometimes *Chariana* (Persian for four mirrors), essentially body armour worn by warriors. There is a breastplate too (RCIN: 38130), comprising a floral gold-damascened steel breastplate and two side-plates, slightly curved and connected by hinges with draw-pins, lined with purple velvet. It was manufactured in Gujarat, Panjab, a principle Sikh arms-making location and where the final battle of the Second Anglo–Sikh Wars took place.[25]

The magnificent arms acquired by Prince Edward were put on display at the Indian Museum, Kensington (later the Victoria and Albert Museum) in 1876, leading to a tour of the exhibits in the UK and abroad. By the time the exhibition was over, more than 1.2 million people had viewed the relics. They were exhibited in places including Nottingham in 1881 and 1882. After the exhibition, arms and armour were displayed at Marlborough House and Sandringham, as well as Buckingham Palace. The admission fees generated extensive funds to broaden the collection. As a result, Caspar Purdon Clarke (1846–1911) was sent to search for and obtain more items, and he sent over 3,000 additional pieces back to the UK.[26] In 1878 at the Paris Exhibition, many objects were on display from the collections of Patiala, Nabha and Jind. These were intended to be sold and many items were purchased by the Nottingham Museum Service. These items mirror the quality in many respects of those Sikh objects in the Royal Collection Trust.[27]

---

24   *The Building News and Engineering Journal*, Volume The Twenty Second, January to June 1872 (London: Office for Publication and Advertisements), 1872, pp.167–68. There is also a reference to several Indian chain mail 'shirts'. For more information on the Sikh relics which were sent to the Tower of London by the EIC, see Thom. Richardson (ed.), *East Meets West: Diplomatic Gifts of Arms and Armour between Europe and Asia* (2013), pp.112–38.
25   Clarke, *Arms and Armour at Sandringham*, Intro.
26   Meghani, *Splendours of the Subcontinent*, p.27.
27   I was able to view and interpret some of these exhibits on my visit to the collection at Nottingham Museum Service. Searching through various texts, I was to establish the sales of these items. The items included an interesting Khanda/pistol (NCM 1879-105), decorated with an elephant and bird sculpted on the handle, together with a bullet

Following the annexation of the Panjab, many of the craftsmen practising various types of this technique began to work commercially and decorated objects for presentation such as address caskets and shields.[28] Indian craftsmanship was heralded as being some of the finest around the world. As a result, their style of work was copied and emulated by many companies in the UK which started the production of such items. Among those jumping on the bandwagon were Birmingham's Elkington and Co., who in 1872 produced Indian silver replicas, whilst Liberty of London and Proctor and Co. began developing elaborate tea sets based on designs of swords from India.[29]

Future

With Sikhs moving to Britain, the modern era has witnessed gifting to the Royal Family, with several Gurdwaras creating ceremonial special swords for Queen Elizabeth II. They include a sword given by Gurdwara Sri Guru Singh Sabha of Hounslow on the 400th anniversary of the first installation of the Sikh scripture, Guru Granth Sahib, and a 'Curved sword and scabbard of chased white metal' presented by Guru Nanak Gurdwara, in Leicester in 1999.

We can see that there is a large treasure trove which the Sikhs possessed. The *Toshkhana*, or treasury, under Maharajah Ranjit Singh was rich in artefacts of immense value. Queen Victoria sought several items from the Sikhs, starting with objects after the Anglo–Sikh Wars through to several Maharajahs gifting many pieces of arms and armour. These now reside in various locations, from Sandringham to Windsor Castle. This challenges the myth that everything in the Queen's Collection was taken and seems to suggest that many items were gifted and even bought from the Maharajahs. Some work is still required as to the exact location of all these items, and hopefully, by working closely with various institutions, we can learn more. In recent times, the Royal Collection has opened its collections to the public, giving access to items that have not been seen for hundreds of years.[30]

compartment within the hilt. The research was part of the project to create the Anglo–Sikh Virtual Museum incorporating the digitisation of objects in 3D.

28 Some of these were exhibited in 'Splendours of the Subcontinent: A Prince's Tour of India 1875–76' at the New Walk Museum and Art Gallery, Leicester, in 2017. The exhibition narrated the story of the Prince's grand tour of India through some of the finest Indian treasures from the Royal Collection, which were presented to the Prince during his visit.

29 Meghani, *Splendours of the Subcontinent*, p.30.

30 In 2017, the Royal Collection at Buckingham Palace also put on display several paintings and objects related to the Sikhs.

13

Sikhs in the British Indian Army

Another area which deserves our attention is Sikh employment in the British Indian Army. The Anglo–Sikh Wars were one of the most heavily contested in the 19th century, so employing Sikhs in the British Indian Army was an intriguing prospect. This policy therefore had to be carefully tested. There were differing views on enlisting Sikhs into the army, considering they had been very close in defeating the British. Yet the military prowess of the Sikhs was something that the British could exploit, while at the same time creating employment opportunities.

Various regiments were formed in the Panjab. These included, in 1846, the Regiment of Ferozepore, later to be known as the 14th King George's Own Ferozepore Sikhs (14th Sikhs), and the 15th Ludhiana Sikhs. These units were composed of soldiers who fought against the Sikh Empire. Captain Thomas Rattray formed the Bengal Military Police Battalion at Lahore in the Panjab in 1856. This unit later became known as the 45th Rattray's Sikhs. It was Sir John Lawrence (1811–79)[1] who first mooted the idea that the Sikhs should be enlisted in small numbers to undertake law and order within certain areas of Panjab. However, the so-called Indian Mutiny (the Sepoy Uprising of 1857, also known as the First War of Indian Independence),[2] put the British in a difficult position. Interestingly, they turned to the Sikhs to become the military backbone of their forces; the prospect of volunteering would also place them favourably in any new order set up by the British. It was also at this time that Hodson's Horse, an irregular cavalry regiment, was founded (see the photograph of soldiers of Hodson's Horse, 1858–59).[3] This resulted in a number of troops being raised by Sirdar

---

1   Later Baron Lawrence of the Panjab and Grateley, Southampton.
2   The first war of independence implies that there were no previous encounters against British rule prior to the Mutiny and is essentially erroneous. As Panjab was the last state to fall to the British, it was the Sikhs who would make the last stand against the British.
3   Hodson's Horse was raised by William Stephen Raikes Hodson (19 March 1821 – 11 March 1858), who fought and was injured in the First Sikh War. He is credited with capturing the Mughal ruler Bahadur Shah Zafar (1775–1862) during the Mutiny. However, the killing of the emperor's sons was criticised, and *Khooni Darwaza* (or 'Bloody

Man Singh (d. 1892), a veteran of Maharajah Ranjit's Singh's army and who fought against the British in the First Anglo–Sikh War.[4] The 34th Sikh Pioneers, originally Panjab sappers, were also raised to quash the Mutiny. The Sikhs' loyalty during this time was well received and praised.

What motivated the Sikhs to enlist into a foreign sovereign army? In the eyes of many British officers, the answer was that "money, revenge and opportunism were the operative motives and [they] essentially sided with the power of the day". Yet there were still some dangers posed with this course of action, according to Sir John Lawrence, who said, "of course there is a risk, but the balance is far on the side of advantage."[5] In truth, joining the British Indian Army provided discipline for Sikh youth in the villages of Panjab; it offered them employment opportunities in Panjab, in the rest of the Indian sub-continent and abroad, first in the army, then the police and, over the years, in other services and professions. Sikh soldiers received a basic education themselves, and in turn they could educate their children. However, this education was predominantly in the English system, which would influence their thinking and overall outlook.

During the suppression of the revolt of 1857, the aid of Sikh chiefs and soldiers had contributed immensely in ensuring British victory and helped saved the British Empire from defeat:

> The genius of Sir John Lawrence, the Chief Commissioner of the Punjab, warded off the danger. That eminent man, the saviour of India, issued a proclamation calling on the Sikhs to aid us in our trouble. They came at once in hundreds – nay, thousands – to enlist on our side. Veterans of Runjeet Singh's Khalsa army, the men who had withstood us on equal terms in many sanguinary battles, animated by intense hatred of the Poorbeah sepoy, enrolled themselves in the ranks of the British army, and fought faithfully for us to the end of the war. Their help was our safety; without these soldiers, and the assistance rendered by their chieftains, Delhi could never have been taken; while, on the other hand, had they risen and cast in their lot with the mutinous sepoys, no power on earth could have saved us from total annihilation.[6]

Gate') in Delgi marks the spot of this incident. In the photo taken in the aftermath of the Mutiny, where Hodson was killed during the assault, we see individuals indentified as (standing) Lieutenant Clifford Henry Mecham (1831–65), from Loughborough, Leicestershire, and Assistant Surgeon Thomas Anderson (sitting), with Jai Singh (seated) facing him, and on the far left, Man Singh.

4   A cavalry officer who served the Sikh Empire and fought in the First Sikh War. He received the Order of Merit 1st Class and the Order of British India 1st Class. He was appointed the first Risaldar Major of the 9th Bengal Cavalry.

5   Heather Streets, *Martial Races: The Military, Race and Masculinity in British Imperial Culture, 1857–1914* (Manchester: Manchester University Press, 2005).

6   Charles John Griffiths, *A Narrative of The Siege Of Delhi with an Account of The Mutiny at Ferozepore in 1857* (London: John Murray, 1910), pp.34–35.

The British Indian Cavalry on the road to Cairo, during the Anglo-Egyptian War, 1882. From a sketch by R. Caton Woodville. (*The Illustrated London News*, 30 September 1882)

There have been suggestions that one of the main reasons that the Sikhs helped the British during the Mutiny was their hatred of the *Purbias*,[7] the Rajput-led mercenaries who formed a majority in the Bengal Army and fought against the Sikhs in the Anglo–Sikh Wars. However, as we have seen, many of the Sikh states who sent soldiers to aid the Mutiny did not take part in the Anglo–Sikh Wars. It was earlier campaigns such as the Santhal rebellion in the Ganga Valley, which they contributed to in 1853–54, that highlighted the Sikhs' military importance. This campaign has largely been overlooked in the face of the Mutiny. The 15th Ludhiana Regiment of Sikhs was part of the contingent which was sent to Shanghai to quell the Taiping Rebellion in 1860–61. Overseas campaigns witnessed Sikh soldiers taking on duties in a more global context, either as part of Sikh regiments or other British Indian regiments. This included campaigns in Abyssinia (1867–68), Malta (1878–80), Afghanistan (1878–80) and Burma (1885). There were several campaigns in Africa comprising the Anglo–Egyptian War of 1882, in which the 20th Panjab Infantry, partly composed of Sikhs, took part. The 15th Ludhiana Sikhs also took part in the

7   Sometimes spelt Purbiya.

Soldiers of Hodson's Horse, 1858–1859. Albumen silver print, Felice Beato.
(Partial gift from the Wilson Centre for Photography. Digital image
courtesy of Getty's Open Content Program)

Suakin expedition in 1884–85 as part of the overall Gordon Relief Expedition.[8] An expedition to Tibet took place in 1903–04, with the 23rd and 32nd Sikh Pioneers taking part. Sikhs also helped suppress revolts by the Pathans and in policing the North-West Frontier Province for half a century.

It is important to be aware of these campaigns, as many people believe the Sikhs only became prominent within the British Indian Army during the World Wars of the 20th century. Sikhs had been deployed around the world many decades earlier, and were indeed 'Soldiers of the Queen'. Trust issues tended to have subsided by the time of the Indian Mutiny, and the *ILN* reported in 1857 that the Sikhs could now be trusted and were not as 'barbaric' as once thought. The paper published a picture of an Akali Nihang and claimed that they had been tamed.[9]

8   Also referred to as the Nile expedition to relieve Khartoum in Sudan.
9   *ILN*, November 1857.

Gooroo Swearing in a Sikh Recruit (from *The Illustrated London News*, 17 January 1891).
(Courtesy of Avtar S. Bahra Collection)

In 1887, the 35th Sikhs and 36th Sikhs were formed, the latter demonstrating Sikh loyalty and bravery at the Battle of Saragarhi (part of the Tirah campaign).[10] On 12 September 1897, a contingent of 21 soldiers from the 36th Sikhs led by Havildar Ishar Singh held off an attack by thousands of Afghans for several hours.[11] All 21 Sikh soldiers chose to fight to the death instead of surrendering. In recognition of their sacrifice the British Parliament paid their respects, each one of them being awarded the Indian Order of Merit, the highest award given to Indian soldiers at that time (the Victoria Cross was only conferred on them after 1911). It was influential actions like these which really made the British take note of Sikh sacrifices and contributions in warfare.[12]

10 A treaty had been initiated between the British and the Amir of Afghanistan, Abdur Rahman Khan (d. 1901), but the tribesmen of the Afridi and Orakzai ordered a Jihad, or holy war, with the British.
11 Overall command of the 36th Sikhs was held by Lieutenant Colonel John Haughton, who was stationed at Fort Lockhart. Whilst born in India, he came to the United Kingdom and was educated at Uppingham School, Leicestershire, where there is a plaque commemorating his service.
12 For examples of Sikhs who received gallantry medals, see Narindar Singh Dhesi, *Sikh Soldier – Gallantry Awards*, Vol. 2 (Uckfield, East Sussex: Naval & Military Press, 2016).

In 1900, the Sikh regiments, including the 14th Sikhs under the command of Colonel Hogge, took part in the quashing of the Boxer Rebellion (1900–02) in China alongside forces from Austro-Hungary, France, Germany, Italy, Japan, Russia, Britain and the United States.

Defining the identity

Field Marshal Frederick Sleigh Roberts (1832–1914), Commander-in-Chief of the Indian Army from 1885–93, was a principal proponent of the 'Martial race' theory. This theory implied that the Sikhs should be employed and their military prowess should be encouraged, but within the confines of a distinct identity. The martial race was a designation created by Army officials of British India, whereby they classified each ethnic group into two categories, martial and non-martial. A martial race was typically thought to be brave and well-built for fighting, while the non-martial races were those whom the British believed to be unfit for battle. This theme, however, was extended to groups who were against the British in the Indian Mutiny.[13] The martial races included, but were not limited to, the Sikhs, Gurkhas, Rajputs, Dogras, Marathas and Jats.

According to Roy (2012), the British felt that peasants made good soldiers, and most of the martial races were of peasant stock.[14] The British had also learnt from the Indian Mutiny never to rely too heavily on one religion, culture or caste for its supply of Indian soldiers. Muslims, for example, were generally limited to about a third of the British Indian Army. While some regiments drew from just one ethnicity, culture or religion, it was common for Indians of different faiths and backgrounds to also serve within the same regiment. This was a means of maintaining British control, since the diversity of backgrounds made it more difficult to spread seditious ideas (such as that of Indian independence). This has led to the idea that the British created these groups to divide and conquer India for their own political ends.

Lord Horatio Herbert Kitchener (1850–1916)[15] carried Roberts' policy of martial races selection to its conclusion. This would later result in separate kitchens created for the different martial races, based on religious dietary requirements.[16] This was most notable in the First World War. As a result, handbooks were written for army officers

---

13 High-caste Hindus were described as treacherous, faithless etc. Whilst Muslim sepoys were against the British, Panjabi Muslims were welcomed into the army. See Streets, *Martial Races.*
14 Kaushik Roy, 'Race and Recruitment in the Indian Army: 1880–1918', in *Modern Asian Studies*, Volume 47, Issue 4, July 2013, pp.1310–47.
15 The Commander-in-Chief of the Indian Army from 1902–09.
16 This included having separate kitchens for Muslims, Hindus and Sikhs. Muslims kitchens would have meat prepared according to the Halal or Islamic traditions, whilst Hindus abstained from eating beef.

setting out the rules and regulations that the Sikhs should adhere to, as well as the rules that British officers should enforce upon them. These included P.D. Bonarjee's *A Handbook of the Fighting Races of India* (1899) and Captain R.W. Falcon's *Handbook on Sikhs for the use of Regimental Officers* (1896). Once the Sikhs were established in the British Indian Army, a number of codes of conduct were created which enforced a distinct Sikh identity. According to Barstow:

> Sikh soldiers too are required to adhere rigidly to Sikh customs and ceremonial and every effort has been made to preserve them from the contagion of Hinduism. Sikhs in the Indian Army have been studiously 'notionalised' or encouraged to regard themselves as a totally distinct and separate nation; their national pride has been fostered by every available means, and their 'Granth Sahib', or Sikh scriptures are saluted by British officers of Indian regiments.[17]

Sentiments like these defined the difference between the Sikh and Hindu religions. These statements were further compounded by the Sikhs themselves, as the reformist Singh Sabha movement[18] felt that Gurdwaras were becoming infiltrated with 'Hindu' views and subsequently Sikhism was under threat.

We can assess this again by considering the downward filtration theory. This states that once certain ideas have been adopted by an elite, they will filter down to the masses and changes will begin to take root within the community. This is a fundamental point and should be elaborated on. The British were keen to recruit personnel from villages where there was a 'good stock' of warriors and those who held empathetic views towards them. This resulted in whole villages sending personnel to the British Indian Army. When the soldiers returned to these villages, they brought back a 'customised' version of Sikhism which began to filter back to the villages (see Mann, 2013).[19] According to Fox (1985), "The British Indian army nurtured an orthodox, separatist, and martial Singh identity among Sikh rural recruits to its regiments and companies. They served as the 'Lions of British India'."[20] Some would also argue that the British Indian Army ensured that the Sikhs maintained their identity of the '5Ks' by the wearing of the turban and keeping the beard. The fixed Sikh identity which was being promoted was at odds with the traditional Sikhs or Akali Nihangs. Their

---

17   Major A.E. Barstow, *A Handbook for the Indian Army: Sikhs* (Calcutta: Govt of India, Central Publications Dept, 1928). p.21.
18   The Singh Sabha movement sought to distinguish the Sikhs from the Hindu faith. There were views that the Sikh faith was infiltrated with Hindu doctrines and that Gurdwaras were prone to worshipping of Hindu deities within their confines. The Singh Sabha movement would lead to the setting up of the religious apex body the Sikh Gurdwara Prabhandak Committee (SGPC) in 1920 and the political party the Akali Dal.
19   My lecture 'The Impact and Legacy of Colonial Dominance in the Punjab', Punjab Research Group, University of Wolverhampton, 2012.
20   Richard G. Fox, *Lions of the Punjab: Culture in the Making*, 1st Edition (Berkeley: University of California Press, 1985), p.10.

defiance against the British we have previously discussed; they did not undertake British jobs and were armed to the teeth. So to suggest that there should be prescriptions limiting the weapons they could carry was not something they would adhere to. An Act tried to curtail the weapons that Indian subjects could carry, so the only way that that Sikhs could carry their weapons would be to sign up to the British Indian Army.

To this end, the colonial government under Lord Lytton as Viceroy (1876–80) brought into existence the Indian Arms Act in 1878, which exempted Europeans but ensured that no Indian could possess a weapon of any description unless the British 'masters' considered him a 'loyal' subject of the British Empire. This Act restricted the number of guns that were licenced: disarmament was the key factor in all of this.

This dual policy is interesting to note. Sikhs who enlisted as part of the British Army could carry weapons within reason. The Akalis, who were the most militarised, were to be sanctioned. The idea that the British banned *Shastarvidia* or any other act was not a direct policy decision, but was rather to deal with the 'lawless Indian subjects' and to ensure there was no repeat of the Mutiny.

Fostering pride

This engineering in a sense worked wonders for the British Indian Army, and as a result, the military became a profession in which the Sikhs could take pride. This was precipitated with the Order of the Merit and eventually the Victoria Cross medals conferred onto them. The once-proud independent Sikh state had thus been absorbed within the military boundaries of the British Indian Army. This tradition would continue after the partition of India. To this day, the Sikhs comprise a large ratio of recruits to the army in relation to their population in India. This pride of Sikhs in the British Indian Army has been felt throughout the world with the construction of memorials highlighting Sikh sacrifices, together with the celebration of notable conflicts in the form of Saragarhi Day through to later conflicts such as the two World Wars.[21]

---

21   There are numerous memorials to the Sikhs in the UK, including one at the National Arboretum in Staffordshire and at Smethwick, Birmingham. There are also plans to have a National Sikh Memorial in London. Saragarhi Day is celebrated by the British Army and Sikh groups in September each year.

14

Discussion

The history of the relationship between the British and the Sikhs is a chequered one. Early interactions did take place from the start of the 18th century, but these were limited at best. The Sikhs were an independent religion, and writings by the British described their modes of warfare as well as religious practices. The Sikh faith was grounded in the principles of the Sikh Gurus, and the Khalsa became a name synonymous with the word 'protector'. These saintly soldiers became most fearsome in the Indian subcontinent not because they were vying for power, but because their battles were 'battles of righteousness', a concept breathed into them by Guru Gobind Singh.

The EIC was set up to trade in various types of commodities, and as a result it obtained *firmans* granting them trading rights. This led to the rise of the Company, and trade and their interests were supported with native armies together with British troops. The embassy of John Surman, whose role was to receive a *firman* from the Mughal Empire, described the Sikhs as people of resolve and steadfast in unbearable tortures. Banda Bahadur being executed by the Mughal Emperor was not just an indicator of what was to come from religious intolerance, but also what was to become of the Sikhs if they wanted to survive. With the EIC based on the eastern side of India, they only heard about these conflicts. The Sikhs by the mid-18th century were fighting for survival, with the onslaughts of Shah Abdali leading to the two holocausts known as the *Choota* and *Vadhha Ghallugharas*. These attempts at annihilating the Sikhs were not successful. The Sikhs grouped together under their leader Jassa Singh Ahluwalia and the Sikh Misls; whilst they were independent, they would come together for the common cause. This, however, did not stop the inter-Misl rivalry, with battles taking places amongst them and the usurping of territories from one another on a regular basis.

Clive of India was aware that the Sikhs acted as a barrier between the Afghans and the British. From 1783 we start seeing the British taking notice of the Sikhs more seriously. As discussed in Chapter 4, the Afghans were becoming less of a threat for the Governor-General of the Presidency of Fort William (Bengal), Warren Hastings: it was the Sikhs the British needed to watch out for. In March 1783, the Sikh conquest of the Red Fort was a resounding success for the Khalsa as it had brought under

submission the Mughal Empire of Shah Alam II, if only temporarily. However, 'depredations' on the suburbs of Delhi were being noted, and Karorasinghia Misl leader General Baghel Singh was instrumental in instigating a plan to take over Delhi as well as receiving *Rakhy* from the Mughals, Afghans and other states. Allowing Baghel Singh to build seven Gurdwaras around Delhi defined Sikh sovereignty. If Sikhs had taken full control of Delhi, this would have resulted in a different set of outcomes and the concept of 'Raj Kharega Khalsa' would have been seen.

Channels were opened to seek friendship between the British and the Sikhs, but this did not lead to any agreements or treaties. In fact, the Sikhs began to enter British protectorate areas such as Oudh, which they plundered. Despite British officers, including Colonel Stuart, being abducted, this still did not result any military engagement between the British and the Sikhs. These Sikhs aligned with the Marathas in the Anglo–Maratha Wars and tried to prevent the British taking over Delhi, but the might of the EIC was too strong and Delhi became theirs in 1803.

The reign of Maharajah Ranjit Singh brought the Sikh Misls under his control, leading to the creation of the Sikh Empire. This ushered in a period of glory for the Sikhs, with the minting of coins, development of infrastructure and building of an army which would match and even surpass that of the Europeans. This expansionism was not able to unite all Sikh territories, however, as the remnants of the Karorasinghia Misl, Shaheedi Misl, Ahluwalia Misl and Bhangi Misl, together with the areas of Patiala, Nabha and Jind, would not side territorially with the Maharajah. The Sikh Empire was taking over the Cis-Sutlej territories with impunity and some Sikhs looked to the British for protection. This allowed the British to issue a declaration bringing these Sikh states under a British Protectorate. The Treaty of Amritsar of 1809 was initiated with the British under Governor-General Charles T. Metcalfe.[1] The idea that the Sikhs across the Sutlej were traitors for siding with the British doesn't fully explain the complex relationships that existed. In fact, the Cis-Sutlej states prospered without the resources of the Sikh Empire, and they saw themselves as just as a royal as Ranjit Singh. The Misls of Jassa Singh Ahluwalia and Baghel Singh – the two Sikh leaders of the 18th-century territories – both signed the treaty with the British in 1809, which shows that the Misls still wanted to maintain their independence from the Sikh Empire.[2] This did not mean these Sikh states did not want any further relations with Ranjit Singh; they just wanted their territories to be left intact. The Karorasinghia Misl and other Misls had pushed Sikh expansionism all the way towards the River Ganges, and Ranjit Singh's Sikh Empire brought the

1   Charles Metcalfe was also briefly the Governor-General of India between 1835 and 1836.
2   After the death of Baghel Singh, his widow's territories were taken by Ranjit Singh but later returned by British intervention. The state of Kalsia was a Karorasinghia Misl domain, and the rulers maintained the state up until recently. Jodh Singh of the Karorasinghia Misl had cordial relations with Ranjit Singh, as did Fateh Singh Ahluwalia of Kapurthala. Fateh Singh also signed a treaty of friendship in1806 and took part in some of his military campaigns.

border to the Sutlej. This may have been a product of the vision of Sikh Misls in creating Sikh sovereignty in 1783, but this was not the same expansionism that Ranjit Singh envisaged in 1809. The chance to create a unified Panjab was missed, although some may argue the Sikh Empire was a unification of sorts and did introduce much-needed stability.

This did not prevent the Sikh Empire from receiving their tributes from the Cis-Sutlej areas: there were numerous conclaves and villages that Ranjit Singh had access to across the River Sutlej. British administrators such as Major General David Ochterlony, and other political agents like Captain Murray, kept records of these areas, which were mapped out, but both sides seemed to have some difficulty in understanding the borders. Captains Wade and Murray were continuously arguing over jurisdiction in the Cis-Sutlej states, Captain Wade taking a stringent line whilst Murray, due to his connections and understanding of the Lahore court, was more pragmatic. Contentious decisions were sent to Delhi for arbitration on numerous occasions, and within three years of the 1809 proclamation the British had to send out another directive which was in effect a warning to the Cis-Sutlej states. This served notice that territories that weren't being controlled would fall into British hands. This was also clearly seen with British inheritance laws, namely the doctrine of lapse, under which where there was no male heir, estates would become British areas. This law essentially allowed the British to take over parts of India without lifting a finger. Whilst this was common knowledge at the time, it seems a lack of understanding in modern times has clouded the realities of the 1809 Treaty of Amritsar.

The treaty did, however, allow the Maharajah to push up towards Afghanistan, this move being undertaken by two of his most renowned warriors, Hari Singh Nalwa and Akali Phula Singh. Numerous interactions between the British and the Sikhs took place during this time, with the exchange of gifts as well as cannons being given by the British to the Sikhs. This included pompous gatherings like the one leading to the treaty of friendship in 1831, where William Bentinck managed to obtain water rights in the Panjab. The Europeanisation of the army, with the employment of French, Italian and other nationalitie,s proved a very strategic move on the part of Ranjit Singh. This would lead to elite units (the *Fauj-i-Khas*) being formed. It was well known there was no love lost between the British and the French, especially with the narrative of the Napoleonic Wars and the French support for the Marathas during the Battle of Delhi. This created a situation where the movements of French personnel were restricted, which was also extended to the Cis-Sutlej states in not allowing passage of these mercenaries through their areas.

Relations between the British and the Sikhs remained cordial during the time of the Maharajah, and further treaties were initiated. It was also during this time that the Charter Act allowed Christian missionaries to receive money from the British government towards the spread of the faith in India. This was not seen as favourable by the EIC as funds would be diverted from them. However, this did result in the translation of the *Bible* in Gurmukhi script and as well as other Indian languages. The development of churches in the Panjab and the conversion of Maharajah Duleep

Singh have been viewed as contributing towards the annihilation of the Sikh Empire in body and spirit. The missionaries viewed the Akali Nihangs as the chief group who needed to be converted, but it was an ambition they were unable to achieve. This defiance by the Nihangs to anything foreign led to them being targeted in the Anglo–Sikh Wars and afterwards.[3]

It was the death of Ranjit Singh in 1839 that set in motion numerous events, with the Sikh court imploding and there being assassination after assasination. This alarmed the British, as stability was needed for effective management of the rivers of the Panjab which were being used for transporting resources. With communications broken down between the Sikh Empire and the EIC, the Sikh army crossed the River Sutlej in 1845 into their own conclaves in a move seen by the British as a provocation, and a declaration of war was issued by Governor-General Henry Hardinge. Most of the Cis-Sutlej states remained neutral during the First Anglo–Sikh War, which witnessed several bloody battles between the British and the Sikhs with many lives lost on both sides. The battlegrounds of Mudki, Ferozeshah, Aliwal and Sobraon would be imprinted in British military history. Winning the war was not an easy undertaking for the British, and the Sikhs blamed what they saw as their treacherous commanders, namely Lal Singh and Tej Singh, for their failings. However, the Lahore Durbar did not send all its forces to participate in the war, Gulab Singh Dogra also stayed aloof from the clash and the Durbar did not reach out to the Cis-Sutlej states for support.[4] The tactical decisions and mistakes made by both sides can be questioned.

Success for the British in the war allowed the Sikh Durbar to continue functioning, but reporting to the British, under a Resident. However, the signing of treaties by the minor Maharajah Duleep Singh and banishment of his mother, Maharani Jindan Kaur, did little to preserve the peace in the Panjab. The killings of Patrick Vans Agnew and Lieutenant Anderson in Multan embroiled the Sikh Durbar in supressing a revolt, but this turned into a Sikh uprising by Diwan Mulraj and Rajah Sher Singh Attariwala. Multan was attacked several times by the EIC in an onslaught lasting nearly eight months. This also saw the Commander-in-Chief of the British forces in India, Hugh Gough, come face-to-face with the Sikhs for a second time. This resulted in the Second Anglo–Sikh War and in Ramnuggar, Chillianwallah and Gujarat becoming the final battle grounds. The losses at Chillianwallah would lead

3   "The power of the Akalees culminated after the death of Runjeet Singh, and on the bloody fields of Feroze Sherer and Soobraon the warlike fury, as it were, of the sect was spent and broken"; J. Forbes Watson and John William Kaye (eds), *The People of India: A series of photographic illustrations, with descriptive letterpress, of the races and tribes of Hindustan, originally prepared under the authority of the government of India, and reproduced by order of the secretary of state for India in council*, Vol. 4, (London: W.H. Allen and Co., 1869), Description 225.

4   It is not known whether the Cis-Sutlej states would have sided with the Sikh protagonists of the wars. Protecting their hegemony would have been their major goal.

to calls for Hugh Gough to be replaced, but by the time a replacement could be sent, the British were victorious in the campaign. These wars showed the Khalsa as being a resilient and effective fighting force pitched against a British force largely made up of native regiments. The eventual annexation of the Panjab resulted in the Sikhs laying down their arms at Rawalpindi. In similar vein to the first war, if this second uprising had been supported by most of the Durbar and/ or the Cis-Sutlej states, then the outcome could have been different. Those who took part in the campaigns and did not surrender to the Lahore Durbar or the EIC, like Diwan Mulraj and Bhai Maharaj, were taken out of Panjab and languished in jails in faraway places like Calcutta and Singapore.

The annexation of the Panjab in 1849 resulted in numerous Sikh relics and artefacts being catalogued, sold off and taken to Britain. The treasures of the Sikhs, some of the finest developed in the Indian subcontinent, whilst seen as 'Spoils of Empire', do not fit well with some members of the Sikh diaspora, especially where some of the items are related to the founder of the Khalsa, Guru Gobind Singh. Governor-General Dalhousie picked the items he wanted for himself, Queen Victoria and the East India Company Museum, all catalogued by John Login. This process was not subject to any scrutiny. Some of these items have since disappeared, such as the case of the *Kalgi*, whilst some were returned to the Indian Government in 1966 by the Dalhousie family.[5] I have also located a note in the Archer papers which points to the possibility that several unknown relics may still reside in the UK.

Queen Victoria also sought items for herself after the wars, and during the Prince of Wales' trip to the Panjab he was showered with gifts and objects of various types. The gifts by the Panjab Maharajahs – such as those of Patiala, Kapurthala and Jind – reveal a high quality of workmanship in their creation. Maharajah Duleep investigated the amount of wealth taken by the British. He was only young when he signed the treaties between 1845 and 1849, a child who most likely did not understand the importance of what he was doing. Unlike other deposed Indian rulers, who were allowed to rule under tribute to the British, he was separated from his mother and eventually taken to Britain. Duleep was brought up by John Login with a Christan ethos and this would have influenced his conversion to Christianity, something which is considered controversial to this day. Duleep Singh was taken into the British Empire and grew up as an aristocrat, and therefore initially did embrace a partly Western lifestyle, with Queen Victoria and the Prince of Wales being regarded as his close friends.

However, he was in dispute with the British Government for 30 years over his inadequate pension, the revenues of his personal property and the loss of his property during the Indian Mutiny.[6] Interestingly, he was also the owner of salt mines in

5   Many of the items in the family collection have also been sold off in several auctions in the UK, effectively putting them into private hands.
6   Bance, *Sovereign, Squire and Rebel*, p.83.

India, which were a large revenue earner.[7] He later researched the ramifications of the treaties as well as discovering sales catalogues of Sikh relics. He clearly felt that the Anglo–Sikh Treaties did not differentiate between Sikh Empire property and that of his family, i.e. that of the Sukerchakia Misl, something for which he felt he was not adequately compensated. He set out his case in his privately printed *Maharajah Duleep Singh and Government*, which was circulated amongst the elite, as well as writing in *The Times*.[8] After all attempts with the British for adequate compensation were refused, he left for India in 1886 after selling the majority of his possessions. However, he was prevented from ever reaching the Panjab as there were suggestions that he would solicit a reclaiming of his kingdom.[9] Broken and tired, he left for France, where he died. His burial at Thetford in Norfolk – based on his family's wishes – continues to create ripples amongst some in the Sikh community.[10]

There is also continued debate with regards to ownership not only of Sikh items, but many others taken by the British across numerous campaigns in the name of empire and colonial control. The *Koh-i-Noor*, whilst a focus of these debates, blurs the lines when we consider the different types of relics that are in the UK. Others have not fared any better, and there has never been any clear proposal as to why Sikh relics should be returned to India or even Pakistan. Many relics have been preserved effectively in the UK by museum curators and frequent some of the largest museums in the country. Some organisations have taken on the task to see where these items are kept and how to bring them to the public domain through exhibitions and projects. The Sikh Museum Initiative and other groups have been working with museums and private collectors to help make these objects accessible. The advent of new technologies has increased the possibilities in terms of creating objects through 3D modelling and 3D printing, as well as virtual reality and touchscreen technologies.[11]

It is quite clear there was no continuity of thought from the early descriptions of the Sikhs to the time of the Anglo–Sikh Wars.[12] The works of George Forster were used by the cartographer James Renell in constructing a map of India, highlighting Sikh territories, as well as by William Francklin in his work. However, in the 19th century

---

7   These are the Pind Dadun Khan salt mines. Duleep Singh estimated a revenue loss of £400,000 a year. Bance, *Sovereign, Squire and Rebel*, p.82.
8   He also set out his case by writing in *The Times* on 31 August and 8 September 1882. An anonymous Editorial on 31 August 1882 in *The Times* dismissed his claims and referred to the "metamorphosis of his social and cultural identity".
9   A plaque commemorating the Maharaja's final voyage from England was unveiled in July 2018 at Gravesend.
10   An interesting portrait created by the Singh Twins potrays the different aspects of the Maharajah's life. 'CASUALTY OF WAR: Portrait of Maharajah Duleep Singh', created in 2013, is on display at National Museums Scotland.
11   This includes the Anglo–Sikh Virtual Museum, where objects can be seen in 3D. See www.anglosikhmuseum.com.
12   An exception to this is the work by J.D. Cunningham, who incorporates descriptions from the 18th century. However, he is also unaware of the Dr Leyden translations.

these works were largely forgotten. The work of Lieutenant Colonel John Malcolm also seems to have been neglected by many writers who followed him. However, his work highlighted the translations of Dr John Leyden, who produced the first major translations of Sikh texts. The skilful Leyden, a master of many languages, produced numerous translations which have also remained neglected up until recently and shed light on historical debates that take place in modern times. Neither was his work considered by Ernest Trumpp, who headed the Sikh scripture translation project. His translation work on the Guru Granth Sahib was seen as the first work on scriptures, but he was unable to translate the Dasam Granth as it was beyond his abilities and he found excuses not to continue the project.[13] If Leyden had managed to translate the Dasam Granth this would have been a unique feat in Anglo–Sikh relations, as it would not only have been the first translation but probably the most accurate. This can be seen from the one translation from the scripture, that of the *Bachitra Natak*, for which he should be commended.

The increase in the knowledge of the mannerisms and religious practices of the Sikhs all fed into the creation of Sikh regiments from within the Panjab, and predominantly from the Cis-Sutlej states, providing personnel for the British Indian Army. New recruits would become indoctrinated with British Army practices and subjected to 'martial races' conditioning, the selection of races based on their physical and military attributes, resulting in their participation in many campaigns in the Indian subcontinent. The Indian Mutiny was one of the pivotal moments which gave justification to employing Sikhs in the British Indian Army. Another was the Battle of Saragarhi, which was a notable achievement with the laying down of Sikh lives for the British Empire. These examples dismiss the notion that the Sikhs were originally employed in the World Wars only, and this rich military history continues today with Sikhs serving across the Indian Army.[14]

Interestingly, this Anglo–Sikh relationship has also extended to Sikhs joining the British Army; however, the numbers are still very limited.[15] There have been calls on many occasions for a specific Sikh regiment, something which would have its advantages and disadvantages.[16] Whilst the Great War centenary commemorations between 2014 and 2018 highlighted the contributions of the Sikhs and Indian soldiers during that time, the Sikh support of British campaigns across the world still suffers from

---

13   This included finding the text too difficult and trying to pass off the scripture as not being important enough, something that was repudiated by other commentators at the time. See Nazer Singh, *Guru Granth Sahib Over to the West.*

14   In 1984, in the aftermath of the attack on the Golden Temple by the Indian Government, there were mass Sikh resignations in the army. There were also many Sikhs fighting against the Indian state during the turbulent period. It was seen for many years that Sikhs were reluctant to join the Indian Army.

15   It has been discovered that there are around 170 serving Sikhs in the British Army.

16   It was not noted in a question-and-answer session at the commemoration of Saragarhi Day that many Sikhs in the present-day Sikh army see their role as facilitating in different areas, as opposed to a distinct Sikh regiment.

the lack of exposure it justly requires. Whilst in military circles the Sikhs and their contribution to the British Indian Army is well known, to the wider general public it is something which rarely gets mentioned.

In conclusion, there was continuous and constant discovery between both the British and the Sikhs, with direct warfare only becoming apparent after the death of Maharajah Ranjit Singh. The annexation of the Panjab whilst resented resulted in the employment of Sikhs within the British Indian Army which solidified a new friendship. The relationship between the two groups in the 20th century would lead to a different perspective of Anglo–Sikh relations, something which is beyond the scope of this work. Many writers have been unable to draw out the relationship between the two groups, as many of the papers which shed light on links between them remain unexamined. Some of the examples we have looked at show how there was a relationship during the 18th century, and how the Sikhs during that period had taken formidable steps to protect their religion and their domination, directly in the face of the British. However, Ranjit Singh's treaty of 1809 with the British heralded a juncture where the British became more familiar with the Sikhs. This treaty is probably the most important of its kind, as the Panjab had effectively been split into two with some areas still paying tribute to the Sikh Empire. While the Anglo–Sikh Wars have been ingrained into military history, they have not received a great degree of understanding among the general public; this is a topic which deserves further examination. The employment of Sikhs from across the Panjab and further away in the British Indian Army was the catalyst for a better understanding between both groups, leading to the Sikhs being given wider coverage in Anglo–Sikh relations. However, the first contact between both groups in the 18th century not only show signs of discovery but actually a great understanding of what both empires would become. The conquest of Delhi by the Khalsa in 1783, in my mind, was one of those events which highlighted that both groups would aspire for a larger control of the Indian Subcontinent. These lessons from the 18th century are important to Sikhs who want to better understand statesmanship, dialogue and warfare, ideas of which could be applied in modern times. I would contend that the developing relationships prior to the 18th century are just as important and set the scene for various important discoveries amongst both groups.

Appendix I

Letters of friendship

---

1. Copy of an undated letter from Jassa Singh Ahluwalia, a chief of the Sikhs, to the Nawab Mayeen ud Dowla James Browne, highlighting their friendship and alliance.

    Your Good Qualities, and fidelity to Engagement, and firmness in Sincerity and Unanimity have reached my knowledge by the writing of Laleh Lukbut Rai, and become the cause of Joy to my heart, and the Establishing of the Duties of friendship is known to be the means of tranquillity to the People, and improvement of the Empire, and arrangement of important affairs, and is clearer than the Sun. Formerly when the Chain of friendship was established between us and the Nobles of the Empire no failure or deviation arose from this quarter in the Compact between us, but from the Variety of the Times, which continue not always alike, the Disposition of the Omras of this time becoming altered. They remained not firm to their mode of Conduct; it is well, it is past, it is forgotten; Now if you have a value of our friendship and good will, Such Counsel must be taken as may dayly increase it. Having Understood that all the Affairs of the English Sircar are entrusted to your Management, I haye rejoyced to excess at the Circumstance; God almighty make you happy! After the Duties of Concord and friendship shall have acquired Solidity (for there cannot be a nobler work than this in the world) great advantages will come to light: what should I write more, besides my Wishes? All Circumstances will be adorned with your Intelligence from the writings of the Vakeels; make me happy by Constant Letters of your prosperity, for Letters are half an Interview.

2. Copy of a draft to Jassa Singh Ahluwalia, a chief of the Sikhs, in answer to his letter. Written 6th Ramzan of the year 1197 (5 August 1783)

    On the Receipt of the favoring Letter full of Joy for every Letter was filled with variety of friendship and every Line with a thousand affections, great Joy, and Chearfulness unlimited was acquired, the Contents were distinctly understood,

I have not intruded on you for Some time with Letters by reason of the great distance, otherwise my friendly heart would be always desirous of the excellent methods of fraternity, and after my arriving in these parts that it was yet remitted and delayed merely in the information that many of your Sirdars had chosen the bad habit of Opposition to his Majesty, and the Omrahs and Nobles of the Presence and were laboring in oppression and Injury to the people, and the English Gentlemen consider no other work but Submission to his royal Majesty, and union with the Omrahs, and the arrangement of the Empire and quiet of the People; Therefore considering the Disobedience, in so much that Certain Chiefs are employed in evil works, I have neglected correspondence which in truth is half an Interview. Now that that Cream of Omrahs is employed in forwarding the Chain of Affections I am grateful for the favors and on understanding the good qualities, and excellent dispositions, and Surpassing Kindness of one unequalled in the whole world which were understood in detail from the writings of Laleh Lukbut Rai Joy was occasioned to my affectionate heart. Whereas I was merely appointed to these parts, that whatever the propriety of the affairs of the Empire and the Chain of Friendship between the Nobles of Hindostan and the Sirdars, and the Gentlemen, might depend on, I should labour fully at, Since by the Grace of God your kind Heart is also inclined to this purpose, by God's favor the endeavors will succeed perfectly with mutual Advice, in the arrangements of the important affairs of the Empire from Calcutta to Atak.

Now being near arriving at the Capital, becoming gladdened by an Interview with the said Laleh [Lukbut Rai], and with Laleh Mungul Sein, and being informed of the whole of Particulars, I will send to attend on you a person of Confidence, discreet, and ingenious, to construct the edifice of friendship. I hope that you will bestow Chearfulness on my anxious heart with Writing constantly Letters which are the means of increase to friendship.

(Reproduced from *Browne Correspondence*, pp.78–79.)

Appendix II

Sikh Treaties:

Treaty with the Rajah of Lahore – 1809

Whereas certain differences which had arisen between the British Government and the Rajah of Lahore have been happily and amicably adjusted, and both parties being anxious to maintain the relations of perfect amity and concord, the following Articles of treaty, which shall be binding on the heirs and successors of the two parties, have been concluded by Rajah Runjeet Sing on his own part, and by the agency of Charles Theophilus Metcalfe, Esquire, on the part of the British Government.

Article 1. Perpetual friendship shall subsist between the British Government and the State of Lahore. The latter shall be considered, with respect to the former, to be on the footing of the most favoured powers; and the British Government will have no concern with the territories and subjects of the Rajah to the northward of the Sutlej.

Article 2. The Rajah will never maintain in the territory occupied by him and his dependants, on the left bank of the River Sutlej, more troops than are necessary for the internal duties of that territory, nor commit or suffer any encroachments on the possessions or rights of the Chiefs in its vicinity.

Article 3. In the event of a violation of any of the preceding Articles, or of a departure from the rules of friendship on the part of either State, this Treaty shall be considered to be null and void.

Article 4. This Treaty, consisting of four Articles, having been settled and concluded at Amritsar, on the 25th day of April, 1809, Mr. Charles Theophilus Metcalfe has delivered to the Rajah of Lahore a copy of the same, in English and Persian, under his seal and signature, and the said Rajah has delivered another copy of the same, under his seal and signature; and Mr. Charles Theophilus Metcalfe engages to procure, within the space of two months, a copy of the same

duly ratified by the Right Honourable the Governor-General in Council, on the receipt of which by the Rajah, the present Treaty shall be deemed complete and binding on both parties, and the copy of it now delivered to the Rajah shall be returned.

Seal and signature of C.T. METCALFE
Signature and seal of RAJAH RUNJEET SING
Company's Seal MINTO (Sd)
Ratified by the Governor-General in Council on 30th May, 1809

Treaty between the British Government and the State of Lahore

Whereas the Treaty of amity and concord, which was concluded between the British Government and the late Maharajah Runjeet Sing, the Ruler of Lahore, in 1809, was broken by the unprovoked aggression, on the British Provinces, of the Sikh Army, in December last; and Whereas, on that occasion, by the Proclamation, dated 13th December, the territories then in the occupation of the Maharajah of Lahore, on the left or British bank of the River Sutlej, were confiscated and annexed to the British Provinces ; and since that time hostile operations have been prosecuted by the two Governments, the one against the other, which have resulted in the occupation of Lahore by the British Troops; and Whereas it has been determined that, upon certain conditions, peace shall be re-established between the two Governments, the following Treaty of peace between the Honorable English East India Company and Maharajah Dhuleep Sing Bahadoor, and his children, heirs and successors, has been concluded on the part of the Honorable Company by Frederick Currie, Esquire, and Brevet-Major Henry Montgomery Lawrence, by virtue of full powers to that effect vested in them by the Right Hon'ble Sir Henry Hardinge, g.c.b., one of Her Britannic Majesty's Most Hon'ble Privy Council, Governor-General, appointed by the Hon'ble Company to direct and control all their affairs in the East Indies, and on the part of His Highness Maharajah Dhuleep Sing by Bhaee Ram Sing, Rajah Lal Sing, Sirdar Tej Sing, Sirdar Chuttur Sing Attareewalla, Sirdar Runjore Sing Majeethia, Dewan Deena Nath and Fakeer Noor-oodeen, vested with full powers and authority on the part of His Highness.

Article I. There shall be perpetual peace and friendship between the British Government on the one part, and Maharajah Dhuleep Sing, his heirs and successors on the other.

Article II. The Maharajah of Lahore renounces for himself, his heirs and successors, all claim to, or connection with, the territories lying to the south of the River Sutlej, and engages never to have any concern with those territories or the inhabitants thereof.

Article III. The Maharajah cedes to the Honorable Company, in perpetual sovereignty, all his forts, territories and rights in the Doab or country, hill and plain situated between the Rivers Beas and Sutlej.

Article IV. The British Government having demanded from the Lahore State, as indemnification for the expenses of the War, in addition to the cession of territory described in Article III., payment of one and half crore of Rupees, and the Lahore Government, being unable to pay the whole of this sum at this time, or to give security satisfactory to the British Government for its eventual payment, the Maharajah cedes to the Honourable Company, in perpetual sovereignty, as equivalent for one crore of Rupees, all his forts, territories, rights and interests in the hill countries, which are situated between the Rivers Beas and Indus, including the Provinces of Cashmere and Hazarah.

Article V. The Maharajah will pay to the British Government the sum of 50 lakhs of Rupees on or before the ratification of this Treaty.

Article VI. The Maharajah engages to disband the mutinous troops of the Lahore Army, taking from them their arms – and His Highness agrees to reorganize the Regular or Aeen Regiments of Infantry, upon the system, and according to the Regulations as to pay and allowances, observed in the time of the late Maharajah Runjeet Sing. The Maharajah further engages to pay up all arrears to the soldiers that are discharged, under the provisions of this Article.

Article VII. The Regular Army of the Lahore State shall henceforth be limited to 25 Battalions of Infantry, consisting of 800 bayonets each with twelve thousand Cavalry – this number at no time to be exceeded without the concurrence of the British Government. Should it be necessary at any time – for any special cause – that this force should be increased, the cause shall be fully explained to the British Government, and when the special necessity shall have passed, the regular troops shall be again reduced to the standard specified in the former Clause of this Article.

Article VIII. The Maharajah will surrender to the British Government all the guns – thirty-six in number – which have been pointed against the British troops – and which, having been placed on the right Bank of the River Sutlej, were not captured at the battle of Subraon.

Article IX. The control of the Rivers Beas and Sutlej, with the continuations of the latter river, commonly called the Gurrah and the Punjnud, to the confluence of the Indus at Mithunkote – and the control of the Indus from Mithunkote to the borders of Beloochistan, shall, in respect to tolls and ferries, rest with the British Government! The provisions of this Article shall not interfere with the

passage of boats belonging to the Lahore Government on the said rivers, for the purposes of traffic or the conveyance of passengers up and down their course. Regarding the ferries between the two countries respectively, at the several ghats of the said rivers, it is agreed that the British Government after defraying all the expenses of management and establishments, shall account to the Lahore Government for one-half of the net profits of the ferry collections. The provisions of this Article have no reference to the ferries on that part of the River Sutlej which forms the boundary of Bhawulpore and Lahore respectively.

Article X. If the British Government should, at any time, desire to pass troops through the territories of His Highness the Maharajah, for the protection of the British Territories, or those of their Allies, the British Troops shall, on such special occasion, due notice being given, be allowed to pass through the Lahore Territories. In such case the Officers of the Lahore State will afford facilities in providing supplies and boats for the passage of rivers, and the British Government will pay the full price of all such provisions and boats, and will make fair compensation for all private property that may be endamaged. The British Government will, moreover, observe all due consideration to the religious feelings of the inhabitants of those tracts through which the army may pass.

Article XI. The Maharajah engages never to take or to retain in his service any British subject – nor the subject of any European or American State – without the consent of the British Government.

Article XII. In consideration of the services rendered by Rajah Golab Sing, of Jummoo, to the Lahore State, towards procuring the restoration of the relations of amity between the Lahore and British Governments, the Maharajah hereby agrees to recognize the Independent Sovereignty of Rajah Golab Sing in such territories and districts in the hills as may be made over to the said Rajah Golab Sing, by separate Agreement between himself and the British Government, with the dependencies thereof, which may have been in the Rajah's possession since the time of the late Maharajah Khurruck Sing, and the British Government, in consideration of the good conduct of Rajah Golab Sing, also agrees to recognize his independence in such territories, and to admit him to the privileges of a separate Treaty with the British Government.

Article XIII. In the event of any dispute or difference arising between the Lahore State and Rajah Golab Sing, the same shall be referred to the arbitration of the British Government, and by its decision the Maharajah engages to abide.

Article XIV. The limits of the Lahore Territories shall not be, at any time, changed without the concurrence of the British Government.

Article XV. The British Government will not exercise any interference in the internal administration of the Lahore State but in all cases or questions which may be referred to the British Government, the Governor-General will give the aid of his advice and good offices for the furtherance of the interests of the Lahore Government.

Article XVI. The subjects of either State shall, on visiting the territories of the other, be on the footing of the subjects of the most favoured nation. This Treaty, consisting of sixteen Articles, has been this day settled by Frederick Currie, Esquire, and Brevet-Major Henry Montgomery Lawrence, acting under the directions of the Right Hon'ble Sir Henry Hardinge, g.c.b., Governor-General, on the part of the British Government, and by Bhaee Ram Sing, Rajah Lai Sing, Sirdar Tej Sing, Sirdar Chutter Sing Attareewalla, Sirdar Runjore Sing Majeethia, Dewan Deena Nath, and Fuqueer Noorooddeen, on the part of the Maharajah Dhuleep Sing, and the said Treaty has been this day ratified by the Seal of the Right Hon'ble Sir Henry Hardinge, G.C.B., Governor-General, and by that of His Highness Maharajah Dhuleep Sing.

Done at Lahore, this Ninth day of March, in the year of Our Lord One Thousand Eight Hundred and Forty-Six, corresponding with the Tenth day of Bubbee-ool-awul, 1262 Hijree, and ratified on the same date.

.. (Sd.) H. Hardinge (L.S.)
.. (Sd.) Maharajah Dhuleep Sing (L.S.)
.. Bhaee Ram Sing (L.S.)
.. Rajah Lal Sing (L.S.)
.. Sirdar Tej Sing (L.S.)
.. Sirdar Chuttur Sing Attareewalla (L.S.)
.. Sirdar Runjore Sing Majeethia (L.S.)
.. Dewan Deena Nath (L.S.)
.. Faqueer Noorooddeen (L.S.)

Articles of AGREEMENT Concluded between the British Government and the Lahore, Durbar, on the 11th March 1846.

Whereas the Lahore Government has solicited the Governor-General to leave a British Force at Lahore, for the protection of the Maharajah's person and of the Capital, till the reorganization of the Lahore army, according to the provisions of Article 6 of the Treaty of Lahore, dated the 9th instant; and whereas the Governor-General has, on certain conditions, consented to the measure; and whereas it is expedient that certain matters concerning the territories ceded by Articles 3 and 4 of the aforesaid Treaty should be specifically determined, the following eight Articles of Agreement have this day been concluded between the aforementioned contracting parties.

Article I. The British Government shall leave at Lahore, till the close of the current year, a.d. 1846, such force as shall seem to the Governor-General adequate for the purpose of protecting the person of the Maharajah and the inhabitants of the City of Lahore, daring the reorganization of the Sikh Army, in accordance with the provisions of Article VI. of the Treaty of Lahore. That force to be withdrawn at any convenient time before the expiration of the year, if the object to be fulfilled shall, in the opinion of the Durbar, have been attained – but the force shall not be detained at Lahore beyond the expiration of the current year.

Article II. The Lahore Government agrees that the force left at Lahore for the purpose specified in the foregoing Article, shall be placed in full possession of the Fort and the City of Lahore, and that the Lahore troops shall be removed from within the City. The Lahore Government engages to furnish convenient quarters for the Officers and men of the said force, and to pay to the British Government all the extra expenses in regard to the said force, which may be incurred by the British Government, in consequence of the troops being employed away from their own Cantonments, and in a Foreign Territory.

Article III. The Lahore Government engages to apply itself immediately and earnestly to the reorganization of its army according to the prescribed conditions, and to communicate fully with the British Authorities left at Lahore, as to the progress of such reorganization, and as to the location of the troops.

Article IV. If the Lahore Government fails in the performance of the conditions of the foregoing Article, the British Government shall be at liberty to withdraw the force from Lahore at any time before the expiration of the period specified in Article I.

Article V. The British Government agrees to respect the *bona fide* rights of those jaghiredars, within the territories ceded by Articles III. and IV. of the Treaty of Lahore, dated 9th instant, who were attached to the families of the late Maharajahs Runjeet Sing, Kurruk Sing, and Shere Sing and the British Government will maintain those jaghiredars in their *bona fide* possessions during their lives.

Article VI. The Lahore Government shall receive the assistance of the British Local Authorities in recovering the arrears of revenue, justly due to the Lahore Government from the kardars and managers in the territories ceded by the provisions of Articles III. and IV. of the Treaty of Lahore, to the close of the khureef harvest of the current year, viz., 1902 of the Sumbut Bikramajeet.

Article VII. The Lahore Government shall be at liberty to remove from the forts, in the territories specified in the foregoing Article, all treasure and State property, with the exception of guns. Should, however, the British Government desire to retain any part of the said property, they shall be at liberty to do so, paying for the same at a fair valuation, and the British officers shall give their assistance to the Lahore Government in disposing on the spot of such part of the aforesaid property as the Lahore Government may not wish to remove, and the British Officers may not desire to retain.

Article VIII. Commissioners shall be immediately appointed by the two Governments to settle and lay down the boundary between the two States, as defined by Article IV. of the Treaty of Lahore, dated March 9th, 1846.

(Sd.) H. HARDINGE (L.S.)
(Sd.) Maharajah Dhuleep Sing (L.S.)
.. Bhaee Ram Sing (L.S.)
.. Rajah Lal Sing (L.S.)
.. Sirdar Tej Sing (L.S.)
.. Sirdar Chuttur Sing Attareewalla (L.S.)
.. Sirdar Runjore Sing Majeethia (L.S.)
.. Dewan Deena Nath (L.S.)
.. Faqueer Noorooddeen (L.S.)

Treaty of Bhyroval
Articles of Agreement concluded between the British Government and the Lahore Dubar, on the 16th December 1846.

Whereas the Lahore Durbar and the principal Chiefs and Sirdars of the State have in express terms communicated to the British Government their anxious desire that the Governor General should give his aid and assistance to maintain the administration of the Lahore State during the minority of Maharaja Duleep Sing, and have declared this measure to be indispensable for the maintenance of the Government; and whereas the Governor-General has, under certain conditions, consented to give the aid and assistance solicited, the following Articles of Agreement, in modification of the Articles of Agreement executed at Lahore on the 11th March last, have been concluded on the part of the British Government by Frederick Currie, Esquire, Secretary to Government of India, and Lieutenant-Colonel Henry Montgomery Lawrence, C.B., Agent to the Governor-General, North-West Frontier, by virtue of full powers to that effect vested in them by the Right Honorable Viscount Hardinge, g.c.b., Governor General, and on the part of His Highness Maharajah Dhulleep Sing, by Sirdar Tej Sing, Sirdar Shere Sing, Dewan Dena Nath, Pukeer Nooroodeen, Eai Kishen Chund, Sirdar Runjore Sing Majethea, Sirdar Utter Sing Kaleewalla, Bhaee

Nidhan Sing, Sirdar Khan Sing Majethea, Sirdar Shumshere Sing, Sirdar Lall Sing Morarea, Sirdar Kher Sing Sindhanwalla, Sirdar Urjun Sing Rungrungalea, acting with the unanimous consent and concurrence of the Chiefs and Sirdars of the State assembled at Lahore.

Article I. All and every part of the Treaty of peace between the British Government and the State of Lahore, bearing date the 9th day of March 1846, except in so far as it may be temporarily modified in respect to Clause 15 of the said Treaty by this engagement, shall remain binding upon the two Governments.

Article II. A British Officer, with an efficient establishment of assistants, shall be appointed by the Governor-General to remain at Lahore, which Officer shall have full authority to direct and control all matters in every department of the State.

Article III. Every attention shall be paid in conducting the administration to the feelings of the people, to preserving the national institutions and customs, and to maintaining the just rights of all classes.

Article IV. Changes in the mode and details of administration shall not be made, except when found necessary for effecting the objects set forth in the fore-going Clause, and for securing the just dues of the Lahore Government. These details shall be conducted by native officers as at present, who shall be appointed and superintended by a Council of Regency composed of leading Chiefs and Sirdars acting under the control and guidance of the British Resident.

Article V. The following persons shall in the first instance constitute the Council of Regency, viz., Sirdar Tej Sing, Sirdar Shere Sing Attareewalla, Dewan Dena Nath, Fukeer Nooroodeen, Sirdar Runjore Sing Majethea, Bhaee Nidhan Sing, Sirdar Utter Sing Kaleewalla, Sirdar Shumshere Sing Sindhanwalla, and no change shall be made in the persons thus nominated, without the consent of the British Resident, acting under the orders of the Governor General.

Article VI. The administration of the country shall be conducted by this Council of Regency in such manner as may be determined on by themselves in consultation with the British Resident, who shall have full authority to direct and control the duties of every department.

Article VII. A British Force of such strength and numbers, and in such positions as the Governor-General may think fit, shall remain at Lahore for the protection of the Maharajah and the preservation of the peace of the country.

Article VIII. The Governor-General shall be at liberty to occupy with British Soldiers any fort or military post in the Lahore Territories, the occupation of which may be deemed necessary by the British Government, for the security of the capital or for maintaining the peace of the country.

Article IX. The Lahore State shall pay to the British Government twenty-two lakhs of New Nanuck Shahee Rupees of full tale and weight per annum for the maintenance of this force, and to meet the expenses incurred by the British Government. Such sum to be paid by two instalments, or 13,20,000 in May or June, and 8,80,000 in November or December of each year.

Article X. Inasmuch as it is fitting that Her Highness the Maharanee, the mother of Maharajah Duleep Sing, should have a proper provision made for the maintenance of herself and dependants, the sum of one lakh and fifty thousand Rupees shall be set apart annually for that purpose, and shall be at Her Highness' disposal.

Article XI. The provisions of this Engagement shall have effect during the minority of His Highness Maharajah Dulleep Sing, and shall cease and terminate on His Highness attaining the full age of sixteen years or, on the 4th September of the year 1854, but it shall be competent to the Governor-General to cause the arrangement to cease at any period prior to the coming of age of His Highness, at which the Governor-General and the Lahore Durbar may be satisfied that the interposition of the British Government is no longer necessary for maintaining the Government of His Highness the Maharajah.

This agreement, consisting of eleven articles, was settled and executed at Lahore by the Officers and Chiefs and Sirdars above named, on the 16th day of December, 1846.

(Sd.) F. CURRIE H.M. LAWRENCE (Sd.)
.. Sirdar Tej Sing (L.S.)
.. Sirdar Shere Sing (L.S.)
.. Dewan Deena Nath (L.S.)
.. Fukeer Nooroodeen (L.S.)
.. Rai Kishen Chund (L.S.)
.. Sirdar Runjore Sing Majethea (L.S.)
.. Sirdar Utter Sing Kalewalla (L.S.)
.. Bhaee Nidhan Sing (L.S.)
.. Sirdar Khan Sing Majethea (L.S.)
.. Sirdar Shumshere Sing (L.S.)
.. Sirdar Lal Sing Morarea (L.S.)
.. Sirdar Kher Sing Sindhanwalla (L.S.)

.. Sirdar Urjan Sing Rungurnungalea (L.S.)
.. (Sd.) Hardinge (L.S.) & (Sd.) Dulleep Sing (L.S.)

Ratified by the Right Honorable the Governor-General, at Bhyrowal Ghat on the left bank of the Beas, twenty-sixth day of December, One Thousand Eight Hundred and Forty-Six.

(Sd.) F. CURRIE, Secretary to the Government of India

Treaty of Lahore 1849

Terms granted to the Maharajah Duleep Singh Bahadoor, on the part of the Honourable East India Company, by Henry Miers Elliot, Esq., Foreign Secretary to the Government of India, and Lieut.-Colonel Sir Henry Montgomery Lawrence, K.C.B., Resident, in virtue of the power vested in them, by the Right Honourable James, Earl of Dalhousie, Knight of the Most Ancient Order of the Thistle, one of Her Majesty's Most Honourable Privy Council, Governor-General, appointed by the Honourable East India Company, to direct and control all their affairs in the East Indies; and accepted, on the part of His Highness the Maharajah, by Rajah Tej Singh, Rajah Deena Nath, Bhaee Nidhan Singh, Fakeer Nooroodeen, Gundur Singh, agent of Sirdar Shere Singh Sindunwallah, and Sirdar Lai Singh, agent and son of Sirdar Uttur Singh Kaleewallah, members of the Council of Regency, invested with full powers and authority on the part of His Highness.

I. His Highness the Maharajah Duleep Singh shall resign for himself, his heirs, and his successors all right, title, and claim to the sovereignty of the Punjab, or to any sovereign power whatever.

II. All the property of the State, of whatever description and Chapter whereso-ever found, shall be confiscated to the Honourable East India Company, in part payment of the debt due by the State of Lahore to the British Government and of the expenses of the war.

III. The gem called the Koh-i-Noor, which was taken from Shah Sooja-ool-moolk by Maharajah Runjeet Singh, shall be surrendered by the Maharajah of Lahore to the Queen of England.

IV. His Highness Duleep Singh shall receive from the Honourable East India Company, for the support of himself, his relatives, and the servants of the State, a pension of not less than four, and not exceeding five, lakhs of Company's rupees per annum.

V. His Highness shall be treated with respect and honour. He shall retain the title of Maharajah Duleep Singh Bahadoor, and he shall continue to receive during his life such portion of the above-named pension as may be allotted to himself personally, provided he shall remain obedient to the British Government, and shall reside at such place as the Governor-General of India may select.

Granted and accepted at Lahore on the 29th of March, 1849, and ratified by the Right Honourable the Governor-General on the 5th of April, 1849.

(Signed)
Dalhousie – Maharajah Duleep Singh
H. M. Elliot – Rajah Tej Singh
H. M. Lawrence – Rajah Deena Nath
Bhaee Nidhan Singh (Head of the Sikh religion)
Fakeer Nooroodeen
Gundur Singh (Agent to Sirdar Shere Singh, Sindunwallah)
Sirdar Lal Singh (Agent and son of Sirdar Uttur Singh, Kaleewallah)

Appendix III

Diwan Mul Raj's Proclamation To The Khalsa

[date unknown]
Sarbat Khalsaji
After [compliments] Wahi Guru Ji ki Fateh.

You may read [this]: Now that the question of dharma has risen, three things are being written [placed before you]. If you know that the dharma of the Hindus and of the Khalsajio shall remain safe and the lives of the family of ours shall also be safe, and Mai Sahiba [Maharani Jind Kaur] shall be released, and Maharaja [Duleep Singh] Sahib – may he live long – shall reign in his own right, then the keys of the fort [of Multan] are at your disposal. You may give them to whomsoever you wish. But if the situation does not appear to be like this, then it is incumbent upon them [Khalsajio] that, remaining firm in their dharma, they should come to this side [join us], receive their rewards and salaries, so that with the grace of Sri Maharaj [God], all the above four things may come about, and that after the army accompanying Mr. Edwardes is defeated we will move towards Lahore with the grace of God, as in the house of God it is not much that He may grant sovereignty to an ant. But if you cannot do any of the two, then come out openly in the field to fight so that both sides, having been freed from the misery of this world, go to heaven, because there is no other [better] occasion than this.

(Sd) Didar Singh, Commandant	(Sd) Jagat Singh Nihang
(Sd) Jaimal Singh	(seal) Mul Raj
(Sd) Baba Anandgir Sannyasi	(seal) L. Singh
(Sd) Sardar Attar Singh	(seal) Gosain … Gir
(Sd) Sucha Singh (seal)	(Seal) …

[From Ganda Singh, *Maharaja Duleep Singh Correspondence*, p. 26. According to Dr Ganda Singh, the proclamation was in Persian and there was also a Panjabi translation of the text which was in his collection.]

Appendix IV

The Sikhs

'ALL THAT CAN BE SAID ABOUT THEM, FROM A MISSIONARY POINT OF VIEW.' Essay by the Rev. William Keene, B.A., Church Missionary Society, Umritsur, from *Report of the Punjab Missionary Conference: held at Lahore in December and January, 1862–63*

The subject assigned me by the Committee of this Conference, is – "The Sikhs;" and "all that can be said about them, from a missionary point of view."

I shall say a few words, by way of introduction, on the character and genius of Sikhism. It must be borne in mind, that four centuries ago, the religion known by this name did not exist. It was in the neighbourhood of this ancient city, in the precincts of which we are now holding our first general Conference of missionaries, in the year of our Lord 1469, in the village of Talwandi, that Baba (otherwise Father) Nanak, the founder of the Sikh religion, was born. His parents were of the once warlike caste of Khattris; and his father, Kalu, was perhaps a petty trader in his native village. After Nanak, the founder of the religion, Govind, the tenth and last of the Sikh Gurus, calls for a few remarks. Govind was a lineal descendant of Amar Das, the third Guru. His father, Tegh Bahadur, was executed as a rebel, in the year 1675, at Delhi, by the stern and bigoted Aurangzeb; and this circumstance, in the effect it had on his son Govind's mind, led to a great change in the religion which Nanak had instituted.

Nanak's desire was to know God, to become inwardly pure, to escape from every earth-born trammel. It was an out-going of the soul after her heavenly and primeval heritage, freedom. We, as Christians and Anglo-Saxons, all know the import of this word, in its various, as well as its highest, acceptation. True; but "He who hath made of one blood all nations of men," has planted the desire deep in the heart of collective humanity. It was Nanak's desire; it was the very object of the reformation which he introduced, – freedom, for himself and his followers, from mental and spiritual bondage. He did much, but it was imperfect: it is reserved for the disciples of the only and true redeemer to know, that – "If the Son make you free, ye shall be free indeed."

150

Nanak struggled to free the mind; but had no desire to carry his principles farther. The great aim of Govind, on the contrary, was to free his followers from the hated Moslem rule; and he was ready to sacrifice anything, and everything, which interposed to hinder the accomplishment of this great design. His reform, and the spirit he infused into his followers, ultimately resulted in the establishment of the Sikhs, as an independent and powerful nation.

Both of these great men have left us a record of their tenets: the one, in the work called the *Ad Granth*, or First Book; the other, in the *Daswen Patshah da Granth*, or The Book of the Tenth King, as Govind is sometimes styled. Nanak's aim was to free the mind. We accordingly find him, in his writings, assailing many of the gross errors of the Hindoo religion. And just in proportion as the teaching of Nanak diverges from the gross errors of the popular Hindoo belief, and reverts to the simplicity of natural religion, so far must we look on it as favourable to the success of the labours of the Christian missionary, among that interesting people, the Sikhs.

I intend, therefore, at this stage of my essay, to bring before this Conference of Christian brethren, some of the chief points on which Nanak is decidedly at issue with the popular faith of the Hindoos. The points in question are – the Godhead, idol-worship, caste, and the immolation of the Hindoo wife, on the funeral pile, at the decease of her husband.

1st. – The Godhead
The following passage forms the opening words of the *Ad Granth*, and is also the formula of the Sikh baptism, called the *pahul*: – "The true name is God, the creator, without fear, without enmity, the immortal being, the unborn, the self-existent, that is understood by the good favour of the Guru. – Repeat this, that God is such: in the beginning true, before all ages true, true now, and, says Nanak, ever will be true."(Jap Ji, 1 pauri.)[1]

The writers of the Granth acknowledge only one creator, styled in the above passage "Kartapurkh;" while, in the Hindoo books, many creators are spoken of. The following sayings are, if anything, more explicit on this point: Arjan, the fifth Guru, writes: – "My mind dwells on One, – Him, who gave the soul and the body."

One more passage, taken from the writings of Guru Govind, will suffice: – "God is one image (or being): how can He be conceived in another form?"

2nd. – Idol-worship
This also Nanak forbids; – "Read not that which creates doubt in the mind. Worship not another than God; go not to the tombs of the dead." (Sorth di Ast-padi, 1 mahal, 1 tuk.)[2]

1   *Japji Sahib*, Verses by Guru Nanak, Guru Granth Sahib.
2   Guru Nanak, Guru Granth Sahib.

And Arjan says, "He who calls a stone 'God,' he and the stone will sink together into the ocean of this world." (Suhi, 5 mahal, 9 sabd, 4 tuk.)[3]

Lastly, hear with what contempt and boldness Govind speaks of idolatry: – "fool, fall at the feet of God. In stone God is not."(Bichitr Natak, 1 dhiay, 99 sawayya.)[4]

We, as Christians, believe in one God, the God of Abraham, Isaac, and Jacob – and the Father of our Lord Jesus Christ. Such a glorious Being Nanak could not believe in; because it is by revelation only that we know God as such. But he believed in one God. Again, he, with Govind, discountenanced idolatry. Such teaching being found in the Sikh books, is, I conceive, all in favour of the Christian missionary, in his work amongst the Sikhs.

The Hindoo, on the contrary, prostrates himself before sense-less stone, and believes the Divine Being to be in such idols. A few remarks are necessary here, on the present practice of the Sikhs. Some of them, although they do not discard the teaching of the Granth, have yet returned to the Hindoo belief of many creators: and since the taking of the country by the English, several have gone back to idolatry.

Such a state of things shews the necessity of more active efforts, on the part of the Christian Church, in disseminating, and preaching, the Word of God to these people.

3rd. – Our next subject is caste

In caste, as such, Nanak places no dependence, although he does in the works of caste: – "Caste, as such, does not avail: your righteousness will be put to the test: [as] no one dies by taking poison in the hand, but by eating it." (Majh ki war, 10 pauri, 1 tuk.)

Caste, among Hindoos, is not a social, but a religious institution. It forbids the members of one caste to eat with, or inter-marry with, those of another. It is one of the monster evils of Hindooism. The ancient Sikhs, I understand, ate together, in common. To do so with those of a different creed, and also with Mazhabi Sikhs, was, however, never their practice.

In the time of Ranjit Singh, indiscriminate marriages were not contracted; but Brahman Sikh married with Brahman Sikhni; and so of the other castes. Now, the Sikhs do not even eat in common, much less contract indiscriminate marriages. The next point of difference which I shall notice, between the teaching of Nanak and that of the Hindoo books, is on the self-sacrifice of the Hindoo wife, called sati, or suttee. Sat means true; and consequently sati, a true and virtuous wife.

This monstrous practice Nanak assails in the following lines: – "Those women are not called satis, who burn on the funeral pile: Nanak says those are satis, who die from the blow of separation." (Suhi ki war, 6 pauri, 1 slok.)

On the death of Ranjit Singh, four of his wives, and seven concubines, immolated themselves at Lahore. Under that monarch's rule, however, a sati, neither among

3   Verses by Guru Arjan Dev, Guru Granth Sahib.
4   Verses by Guru Gobind Singh, *Bachitra Natak*, Dasam Granth.

Hindoos nor Sikhs, was common. The order of the Hindoo Shasters is not for all wives, whose husbands die, to burn themselves; but only for those who are childless,

A few more passages, in which is exhibited the general teaching of the founder of the Sikh religion, must suffice for this part of my essay: – "Murder, love of the world, covetousness, anger, are four rivers of fire. Into these rivers all mankind fall and consume away. By the grace of God alone any escape." (Majh ki war, 20 pauri, 2 slok.)

"Men are born in sin, live in sin."

"When God forgives, says Nanak, then are they forgiven: otherwise they are obnoxious to punishment." (Majh ki war, 23 pauri, 1 slok.)

To show the futility of ceremonial ablutions, Nanak says: – "Wash as you will; if you wash a hundred times, not a single sin can you remove." (Suhi, 1 mahal, 3 sabd, 2 tuk.)

And again: – "The heart of man is as a drunken or lustful elephant; whatsoever it does, is nothing but sin." (Asa-rag, 1 mahal, 8 sabd, 1 tuk.)

The Granth abounds in passages of this kind, – of which the greatest use could be made, in preaching the Gospel to the Sikhs. The above extracts will suffice to show the character of the religious writings of the Sikhs.

Doubtless, Nanak's extensive intercourse with men did much to enlarge his mind; and it may be reasonably supposed, that he was not a stranger either to the teaching of Mahomed, or to that of the Hindoo reformers, Ramanand, and his pupil Kabir the weaver.

The question now arises – Has the teaching of Nanak, in any way, prepared the Sikhs for the reception of Christianity? The Christianity teaching of Moses and the prophets was designed by God, to prepare the Jewish people, if not the world, for the reception of the Gospel. What has Sikhism done, to this end, amid modern heathenism?

This appears to be the question proposed for discussion by this Conference. Some may be ready to answer, that it has done nothing; – judging from the depraved morals of the Sikhs with whom they have come in contact; thereby fallaciously drawing an universal conclusion from a particular premise. Others, again, looking at the comparatively pure teaching of the *Ad Granth*, may, from the very purity of such teaching, draw a conclusion adverse to Sikhism; in the same way, (as it is acknowledged,) that it is more difficult for a moral, upright man, to come to Christ, than for one who is openly profligate.

There is no doubt that Nanak's tenets, where understood and believed, must dispossess the mind of many gross errors, superstitions, and prejudices, which have taken firm hold of the Hindoo. His spirit of toleration, too, cannot be without its good effect. As the influence of Nanak's teaching was for good, so was that of Govind for evil. He abused the principles of Nanak, to lay the foundations of Sikh independence; and in so doing, he roused the very worst passions of the soul; and his influence, on the whole, did but demoralize and corrupt the peaceful followers of Nanak.

In conclusion, let me inquire if any systematic efforts have the Sikhs been made for their conversion?

In answering this, I must make a few remarks on the labours of our brethren of the American Mission, who first planted the standard of the cross at Lodiana; and there commenced the first systematic efforts for the conversion of the Sikhs. They made themselves acquainted with the colloquial dialect of the Sikh people. To the Lodiana Mission we are indebted for a Grammar, and a most valuable Dictionary of the Panjabi language. At different times, 39 works in the Sikh colloquial have issued from the Lodiana Press. Three of these are portions of the Word of God; the rest, with a few exceptions, are tracts on the Christian religion.

Here I must not omit to mention, that the indefatigable Carey translated and published the whole of the New Testament, and the Old Testament up to the 40th chapter of Ezekiel, besides a few small tracts, in the Panjabi language.[5]

Turning next to the labours of our own Society, we have rather made use of the materials made ready to our hand by our American brethren, than added to the stock of that material. My brethren, who founded the Umritsur Mission, made themselves more or less acquainted with the Sikh language; and there has been done a good deal of work for the conversion of the Sikhs, by the missionaries and native assistants of the Umritsur mission, both at that place, and in the neighbouring district of the Manjha, – which has the honour of being the cradle of Sikhism. In enumerating what has been done for the conversion of the Sikhs, I must draw attention to the movement in the 32nd Native Infantry of Mazhabi Sikhs; and which was retarded, for a time, by an order issued by the Supreme Government. This movement was fostered and stimulated by the Umritsur and Peshawur missionaries. Altogether there have been baptized some 40 individuals (men, women, and children) out of that corps, at Khairabad and Attock. Besides these, there have been baptized three Sikhs at Lahore, ten at Lodiana, and one at Umballa. Our brethren also at Rawulpindee and Sealkote can doubtless give instances of Sikhs who have been baptized at these stations. At Umritsur eight, or more, have been admitted into the visible Church, besides a considerable number of Mazhabis – of the above named Regiment. One has been baptized at Kotgur, two at Cawnpore, and one, that I know of, at Benares. There doubtless are several more that I am not aware of. I have numbered above 60 Sikhs who have been baptized into the Christian Church.

Now what is the character of Sikh converts? I can only speak so far as I am acquainted. They are docile, easily attached, out-spoken, and warm-hearted. They are not generally so quick and intelligent, as the Mahomedan and Hindoo converts, but they are pains-taking, and anxious to learn. They do not fraternize well with Mahomedan converts: this is partly owing to their old hereditary hate. We have our prejudices, and they have theirs; and we must bear with them.

I would now throw out some suggestions, for the more effectual evangelization of this interesting people. I am strongly in favour of missionaries taking up a particular

---

5   Reference to the *Bible* translations made by William Carey at Calcutta and eventually sent to the Panjab.

line of study. There should be distinct evangelists for the Mahomedans, the Hindoos, and the Sikhs. Now the cradle of the Sikhs is the Manjha, – the country between Umritsur, Kussoor, Hurikighat, and Byrowal. The next great tract of country inhabited by this people, is the Malwa – beyond Ferozepore. Itinerating missions should be planted, or extensive itinerations made, in both of these districts. For this object one or two missionaries should take up the Sikhs, as their work. They must learn Panjabi – both to speak and read it – as indispensably necessary.

Such evangelists should also make it their business to acquaint themselves with the books most commonly read by Sikhs; especially should they study the Vedant system of philosophy, as taught in the Mokshpanth. They should also be well acquainted with the biographies of Nanak and Govind.

Lastly, the substance of our preaching must be the person and the work of Jesus. All the distinctive doctrines of Christianity must be much insisted on; otherwise the Sadhs and Vedantista will surely tell us, that they have just as good teaching in their Granth; or, that after all our preaching, we have been teaching them Vedantism.

Another point, I would especially urge on the missionary to the Sikhs, is this – the all-importance of maintaining a holy life; otherwise the Sikh will see nothing in the Christian Guru, which he does not see in his own saints and Gurus. Preaching there must be; but I am perfectly sure, that the most effectual preaching to the heathen is the power of a holy, loving, Christ-like life. The Gospel preached is indeed a mighty power; it is the power of God unto salvation, to everyone that believeth. But let that Gospel be lived, as well as preached, in the sight of the heathen, and I believe its power will prove irresistible.

Glossary

Adi Granth	*See Guru Granth Sahib*
Akal Purakh	The One beyond time. The concept of the timeless Creator, a name for God.
Akal Takht	Literally the timeless throne; seat of temporal authority of the Guru. Also known as the Akal Bunga, meaning the tower or palace of Akal. Located in the complex of the Harimandir Sahib or Golden Temple at Amritsar. It is the highest seat of Sikh temporal authority; this was declared by Guru Hargobind Sahib in 1609. Traditionally only the Buddha Dal Jathedar was the historical leader of the Akal Takht, for example Akali Phula Singh.
Akali	Worshiper of Akal. A warrior Sikh, clad in blue and high turbans, with steel weapons. The term was copied from this traditional order and used by political parties, such as the *Akali* Dal. The term is synonymous with the word Nihang.
Akali Nihang	The traditional Singh warrior guardians of orthodox Sikhism. Under the British, this order suffered heavily. A high-ranking Nihang Singh who has a plume on top of a high conical turban.
Akhand Path	Unbroken reading; uninterrupted recitation of a Sikh scripture by a relay of readers, normally comprising of five Sikhs only.
amrit	Immortal. Also the nectar of immortality used in the initiation ceremony of the Sikhs and Khalsa.
ardas	A prayer or invocation at the end of every Sikh ceremony. This is from the first stanza of the Dasam Granth composition *Chandi di Var* – The ballad of Chandi.
baba	A term used for an elderly father or grandfather. It is a term of affection and respect used for holy figures and saints, e.g. Baba Baghel Singh.
Bachitra Naṭak	The autobiography of Guru Gobind Singh, the composition forms part of the Dasam Granth. This historical composition narrates his lineage and the battles he fought.

bani	The word or utterance; works of the Gurus and the Bhagats recorded in the Sikh scriptures. This can also mean Bhai Gurdas *Vars* and *Kabitts*, as well as other compositions that are sung in *kirtan*.
bhai	An address, to mean brother or friend. Also given for piety and learning, e.g. Bhai Mani Singh.
brahmin	The members of the Indian high caste. They are normally priests. In Sikhism, a Brahmin is irrespective of caste but a person who knows Braham. This is in line with ancient Indian texts such as *Bhagavad Gita*.
Chakravarti	Always on the move. A reference to the Nihangs who would move from place to place. Reminiscent of the Misls from the 18th century.
Buddha Dal	The moving throne (*Takht*) of the Akali Nihangs Deriving its name from Baba Buddha, the martial instructor of the sixth preceptor, Guru Hargobind. Various Akali Nihangs Dals are all subordinate to the Buddha Dal. The leader of the Buddha Dal was traditionally seen as the head of the entire Sikh nation and commander of the Sikh army, as well as being the custodian or Jathedar of the Akal Takht.
darshan	The vision or experience of being in the presence of God. To have an audience. The appearance of an eminent person. To have the audience of the Guru.
Dasam Granth	The scripture written by the 10th Guru. A text of various themes, mostly focussing on fighting a righteous war. It is respected by the non-martial Sikh orders Udasis, Nirmala and Seva Panthis. It is worshipped as equal to Guru Granth Sahib by the Akali Nihangs and the school of learning the Damdami Taksal. It is enthroned at two of the thrones of Sikh polity and was also enthroned at the Akal Takht and numerous Gurdwaras across the Indian subcontinent prior to 1920.
Dasam Padshah ka Granth/ Dasven Patshah ka Granth	Panjabi. Lit. the scripture of the 10th King. The original name of the secondary Sikh scripture, Dasam Granth, the compositions of which instil warrior spirit into the Sikhs.
dastur-al-amal	A collection or body of directions, rules or ordinances; especially a book of directions for the conduct of worship. Governing document.
degh-tegh-fateh	A popular slogan used by the Khalsa in the 18th century.
Dhai Phat	Lit. two-and-a-half strikes. A military manoeuvre where you strike and retreat twice, and then finally attack wholeheartedly.
Dhal	Shield.
Durbar	The court of a ruler.
Farman	A royal or governmental decree.

Fauj-i-Khas	Special royal corps in the Sikh Empire. Trained in the French system of drill and other military matters.
Ferengi	A Western person. A reference to the Western generals in Ranjit Singh's army.
Ghallughara	Holocaust. A reference to the two holocausts in the 18th century known as the *Vadhha/Choota Ghallughara*, or big/smaller holocausts.
Ghorcharhas	Lit. horse-riders, cavalrymen who formed the bulk of the irregular divisions in the *Fauj-i-Khas*.
Guru	The Divine Master, Enlightener or Teacher.
Gurdwara	Lit. Guru's door, a Sikh place of worship; in which the Sikh scriptures are venerated.
Gurmukhi	Lit. from the Guru's mouth; the script in which the poetry of the Gurus is written. It has become the script in which Panjabi is written by Sikhs in India.
Guru Granth Sahib	The first scripture of spirituality compiled by Guru Arjan Dev in 1603–04. The sacred scriptures of the Sikhs are known as Granth. The Granth is the paramount Sikh scripture that enshrines the spirit of peace (*Shanti ras*). Also referred to as *Sri Guru Granth Sahib* and *Guru Granth Sahib*. To differentiate one from later scriptures, this recension was known as the first Granth, i.e. Adi Granth. When the Granth received Guruship in the form of the *Damdami* recension, it was then termed *Sri Guru Granth Sahib*, literally translated as the first Granth, in relationship to the Dasam Granth being the second.
Harimandir	The Temple of God. The most sacred Sikh shrine in Amritsar, referred to as the Golden Temple under the British.
Hukumnama	An edict originally sent by the Gurus. In modern days a reference to the taking of a verse from a randomly selected left-hand side page from the Guru Granth Sahib each morning. This is then published by the Gurdwara.
Janamsakhi	Hagiographic accounts or birth stories of the founder of the Sikhs, Guru Nanak. Reference to the manuscripts of this tradition.
jap	Repeat name, meditate.
Jap ji Sahib	The first composition within the Guru Granth Sahib. Composed by Guru Nanak. It forms part of the daily *nitnem*.
Jathedar	The leader or commander of a Takht; or the leader of a military army.
Kalgi	Plume.
Kalgidhar	Wearer of the plume. A reference to Guru Gobind Singh.
katha	Exegesis of the Sikh scriptures by a Giani. The rendering of verses of the Sikh scriptures followed by the explanation.
kaur	Lit. princess, a name used by female initiates of the Khalsa, as an equal to Singh (lion) for men.

kirpan	A reference to the sword of the Sikhs. This is one of the '5Ks' or prescribed symbols worn by a Sikh initiated into the Khalsa.
kirtan	Singing praises, spiritual music, one who performs *Kirtan*.
khalsa	A religious/chivalrous order established by Guru Gobind Singh in 1699. Lit. the pure, the ones from one source, the sovereign.
khande ki pahul	Mystical 'knighthood' and 'initiation of the double-edged sword'. The ceremony where five compositions are read (from the Guru Granth Sahib and the Dasam Granth) and a cauldron of water and sugar is stirred with a sword. The initiation ceremony which new spiritual aspirants/warriors undergo to enter the Khalsa fraternity.
Kurehats	Conduct from which an initiated Sikh should refrain, including the use of tobacco, consumption of alcohol etc.
koftgari	A type of gold/silver decorative inlaying on metal objects
langar	The Gurdwara kitchen from which sacred food is served to all, regardless of caste or creed; the sacred food from such a kitchen.
manjis	Diocese. A chapter or Sikh administration centre Sikhs could preach in various parts of India. Set up by Guru Amar Das, the third Sikh Guru.
mughal	Dynasty of Muslim rulers of India. During the time of the Sikh Gurus, the rise of the Sikh Misls up to the time of the EIC domination in India.
nitnem	The liturgy of Sikh prayers that are recited daily.
panj piare	The five beloved. A reference to the five Sikhs who were willing to give their head to the Guru.
panth	This keyword refers to the Sikh community; the path, way or system of religious belief.
pauri	Stanza of a *Var* or ode.
Pothi	Sikh breviary. Generally containing religious verses. Condensed use of verses from the Sikh scriptures.
rahit	The code of chivalry or conduct of the Khalsa.
rahitnama	A Gurmukhi record of the *rahit*. There were several *rahitnamas* written by the Guru's followers. These early codes of conduct were used to form the modern-day Sikh Rahit *Maryada*.
Raja	A chief of a certain area or battalion within India. Sometimes short for Maharajah.
SGPC	Shiromani Gurdwara Parbandhak Committee (S.G.P.C.). The Sikh organisation which controls the main Gurdwaras in Panjab. It was formed in the early 20th century during the British Raj.
Sabrah	Caretaker/custodian. Reference to the keeper of keys at the Harimandir Sahib.

sahib	Master/lord; term of respect.
Sakhi	A story or an account. Also see *Janamsakhis*.
sant sipahi	Lit. saint soldier. A reference to the Khalsa, which is an amalgamation of the saintly and soldierly aspect.
Sawa Lakh	The Khalsa concept of one Sikh being equal to 125,000 on the battlefield.
Shastarvidia	The science of weapons. Seen as a martial art of the Sikhs. Seldom practised by the Sikhs in the modern age, but some Akali Nihangs still preserve this old tradition.
Singh Sabha	A reform movement initiated in 1873. The Singh Sabha became an open area for a debate between the conservative Sikhs and the radical Tat Khalsa.
Sirdar	A reference to a Sikh (turbaned), title of nobility to describe princes, nobles and aristocrats. Leaders of the Sikh Misls, equivalent to the senior British generals.
Svaiye	Stanza.
Takht Hazur Sahib	Situated at Nanden, Maharashtra, India, where Guru Gobind Singh ascended to heaven. It was here that the Guru Granth Sahib was declared to be the Guru of the Sikhs.
Takht Keshgarh Sahib	Situated at Anandpur Sahib, Panjab, where Guru Gobind Singh gave birth to the fraternity of the pure or Khalsa.
Takht Patna Sahib	Situated in Patna, Bihar, India, the birthplace of the Guru Gobind Singh.
Takht	Throne; one of the five centres of temporal power within the religion. The five takhts are situated at Amritsar, Anandpur Sahib, Damdama Sahib (Bhatinda district), Patna Sahib (Bihar) and Hazur Sahib, Nanded (Maharashtra). Traditionally there were four physical Takhts: Akal Takht Sahib, Patna Sahib, Keshgarh Sahib, Hazur Sahib and the Buddha Dal (Khalsa), traditionally seen as the fifth.
Taksal	Lit. mint. A reference to a Sikh educational centre, Damdami Taksal, where the scriptures are taught.
Taruna Dal	In 1734, Kapur Singh split the Khalsa into the *Buddha Dal* (superior and comprising older, wiser and battle-hardened warriors) and the *Taruna Dal* (comprising younger warriors).
tisra panth	The third way or path; to distinguish the faith from both Hindu and Muslim. A reference used in Dasam Granth compositions like *Ugradanti* referring to the third path separate from the Hindus and the Turks, i.e. the Khalsa.
Toshkhana	*Persian.* Treasury. Reference to the Treasury of the Sikhs in Lahore built up by Maharajah Ranjit Singh.
Udasis	Journeys taken by Guru Nanak. As described in the *Janamsakhis*.

Vahiguru	Wonderous praise to the Guru/God. An expression of the awe-inspiring God. There are various English spellings, including Waheguru, Vahiguroo, Vahiguru, Vaheguru, Vaheguroo and Vahguru. What most Sikhs use as a name for God.
var	Ballad. One of the most famous compositions is the *Vars* attributed to Bhai Gurdas, scribe to Guru Arjan Dev. These are in the poetic form of an ode. In the Guru Granth Sahib, these are poetical compositions consisting of stanzas (*pauris*) with preceding *saloks*. *Var* is used in the Sikh scriptures.

Bibliography

Ahluwalia, M.L., *Bhai Maharaj Singh* (Patiala: Punjab University, 1972).

Aijazuddin, Fakir S., *The Resourceful Fakirs: Three Muslim Brothers at the Sikh Court of Lahore* (New Delhi: Three River Publishers, 2014).

Anon., 'Biographical Memoir of Dr Leyden, M.D.', *The Edinburgh Annual Register For 811*, Vol Fourth, Part Second (Edinburgh: Longman, Hurst, Rees, Orme and Brown, 1813).

Anon., *Inscriptions on the Seikh Guns Captured by the Army of the Sutledge 1845–46. Volume of 64 hand-coloured engravings by and after C. Gomeze* (Calcutta: 1846).

Anon., *Papers Relating to the Punjab, 1847–1849* (London: Printed by Harrison and Son, 1849).

Anon., 'Works/Bible Translations', William Carey University https://www.wmcarey. edu/carey/bib/works_bible.htm (accessed 10 November 2018).

Arnold, Edwin, *The Marquis of Dalhousie's administration of British India, Volume the First* (London: Saunders, Otley and Co., 1862).

Asiatic Annual Register, vol. XI – for the Year 1809 (London: printed for T. Cadell and W. Davies, etc., 1811).

Aufrecht, T.H., *A Catalogue of Sanskrit Manuscripts in the Library of Trinity College* (Cambridge: Deighton, Bell, & Co. etc, 1869).

Bance, Peter, *Sovereign, Squire and Rebel: Maharajah Duleep Singh and the Heirs of a Lost Kingdom* (London: Coronet House, 2009).

Barstow, Major A.E, *A Handbook for the Indian Army: Sikhs* (Calcutta: Govt of India, Central Publications Dept, 1928)

Bayly, C.A., *Empire and Information: Intelligence Gathering and Social Communication in India, 1780–1870*, Cambridge Studies in Indian History and Society, No. 1. (Cambridge: Cambridge University Press, 1996).

Bhargava, Krishna Dyal (ed.), *Browne Correspondence* (Delhi: Pub. for the National Archives of India by the Manager of Publications, Government of India, 1960).

Bonarjee, P.D., *A Handbook of the Fighting Races of India* (Calcutta: Thacker, Spink and Co, 1899).

Brice, Christopher, *Brave As a Lion: The Life and Times of Field Marshal Hugh Gough, 1st Viscount Gough* (Solihull: Helion & Company, 2017).

Brown, Kerry (ed.), *Sikh Art and Literature* (London: Routledge, 1999).

Browne, Major J., *India Tracts: Containing a Description of the Jungle Terry Districts, Their Revenues, Trade, and Government: with a Plan for the Improvement of Them. Also an History of the Origin and Progress of the Sicks* (Black-Friars: Logographic Press, Printing House Square, 1788).

Building News and Engineering Journal, Volume The Twenty Second, January to June 1872 (London: Office for Publication and Advertisements, 1872).

Butalia, Brig. R.C., *The Evolution of the Artillery in India: From the Battle of Plassey 1757 to the Revolt of 1857* (New Delhi: Allied Publishers, 1998).

Caldwell, Rev. J., 'Journal of a Missionary tour amongst Towns and villages in the neighbourhood of Lodhiana', *The Missionary Chronicle*, Volume 11 (New York: Mission House, 1843).

Campbell, George, *Memoirs of my Indian Career* (London: Macmillan and Co, 1893).

Campbell, Christy, *The Maharajah's Box – An Imperial Story of Conspiracy, Love and a Guru's Prophecy* (London: Harper Collins, 2001).

Carey, William, *et. al.*, *The Holy Bible, Containing the Old and New Testaments, Translated from the Originals into the Punjabee Language*, Vol. V. Containing the New Testament (Serampore: Printed at the Mission Press, 1811).

Carey, William, *A Grammar of the Punjabee Language* (Serampore: Printed at the Mission Press, 1812).

Chopra, Gulshan Lall, *The Punjab as a Sovereign State (1799–1839)* (Lahore: Uttar Chand Kapur & Sons, 1928).

Clarke, Caspar Purdon (Intro. Robert Elgood), *Arms and Armour at Sandringham: The Indian Collection Presented by the Princes, Chiefs And Nobles Of India … In 1875–1876* (Cambridge: Ken Trotman Publishing, 2008; reprint of the original from 1898).

Clarke, Caspar Purdon (Intro. Robert Elgood), *Indian Art in Marlborough House: A Catalogue of Indian Arms and Objects of Art presented by the Princes and Nobles of India to H.R.H. the Prince on the Occasion of His Visit to India in 1875–1876* (Cambridge: Ken Trotman Publishing, 2008; reprint of the original from 1910).

Cook, Hugh, *The Sikh Wars* (London: Leo Cooper Ltd, 1975).

Crust, Robert Needham, *A Sketch of the Modern Languages of the East Indies* (London: Trubner & Co., Ludgate Hill, 1878).

Crust, Robert Needham, *Linguistic and Oriental Essays. Written from the year 1840 to 1901*, Sixth Series (London: Luzac & Co., 1901),

Cunningham, J.D. and Garret, H.L.O. (eds), *A History of the Sikhs* (Delhi: S. Chand and Co., 1955).

Dalhousie, E. Login, *Lord Login's Recollections: Court Life and Camp Life 1820–1904* (London: Smith, Elder & Co, 1916).

Daly, Major H., *Memoirs of General Sir Henry Dermot Daly G.C.B., C.I.E., Sometime Commander of Central India Horse, Political Assistant for Western Malwa, etc., etc.* (London: John Murray, Albemarle Street, 1905).

Dhesi, Narindar Singh, *Sikh Soldier – Gallantry Awards*, Vol. 2 (Uckfield, East Sussex: Naval & Military Press, 2016).

East India Company, *An Authentic Copy of the Correspondence in India: Between the Country Powers and the Honourable the East India Company's Servants: Containing Amongst Many Others the Letters of Governor Hastings, J. Macpherson, Esq., J. Stables, Esq. … &c., Together with the Minutes of the Supreme Council at Calcutta: the Whole Forming a Collection of the Most Interesting India-papers, which Were Laid Before Parliament in the Session of 1786*, Volume 4 (London: Printed for J. Debrett, 1787).

Eden, Emily, *Portraits of the Princes & Peoples of India by the Honorable Miss Eden, Drawn on the Stone by L. Dickinson* (London: J. Dickinson & Son, 1844).

Eden, Emily, *Up the Country: Letters Written to Her sister from the Upper Provinces of India* (London: Richard Bentley, 1867).

Edwards, William, *Reminiscences of a Bengal Civilian* (London: Smith, Elder And Co., 1866).

Falcon, Capt. R.W., *Handbook on Sikhs for the use of Regimental Officers* (Allahabad, Pioneer Press, 1896.)

Faroodi, Main Bashir Ahmed, *British Relations With The Cis-Sutlej States(1809–1823)* (Delhi: Punjab National Press, 1942).

Forster, George, *A Journey from Bengal to England: Through the Northern part of India, Kashmire, Afghanistan, and Persia, and into Russia by the Caspian Sea* (London: Printed for R. Faulder, 1798; 2 volumes).

Francklin, William, *The History of the Reign of Shah-aulum, the present emperor of Hindostaun: Containing the transactions of the court of Delhi, and the neighbouring states, during a period of thirty-six years: interspersed with geographical and topographical observations on several of the principal cities of Hindostaun* (London: Cooper and Graham, 1798).

Fraser, James Baillie, *Military Memoir of Lieut-Col. James Skinner, C.B.: For Many Years a Distinguished Officer*, Vol. II, (London: Smith, Elder and Co., 1851).

Friedlander P., *A Descriptive Catalogue of the Panjabi Manuscripts in the Library of the Wellcome Institute for the History of Medicine* (London: The Wellcome Institute for the History of Medicine, unpublished).

Fox, Richard G., *Lions of the Punjab: Culture in the Making*, 1st Edition (Berkeley: University of California Press, 1985).

Gill, D.S., 'Relics of Guru Gobind Singh ji', *Sikh Review*, Issue 548, 47 (August 1999).

Gott, Richard, *Britain's Empire: Resistance, Repression and Revolt* (London: Verso Books, 2011).

Gough, Sir Charles and Innes, Arthur Donald, *The Sikhs and the Sikh Wars: The Rise, Conquest, and Annexation of the Punjab State* (London: A.D. Innes & Company, 1897).

Grierson, G.A., *The Modern Vernacular literature of Hindustan* (Calcutta: Asiatic Society, 1889), p.128.

Griffin, Sir L.H., *Ranjit Singh and the Sikh Barrier Between Our Growing Empire and Central Asia* (Oxford: Clarendon Press, 1905).

Griffiths, Charles John, *A Narrative of The Siege of Delhi with an Account of The Mutiny at Ferozepore in 1857* (London: John Murray, 1910).

Gupta, Hari Ram, *History of the Sikhs* (New Delhi: Munishiram Manoharlal Publishers Pvt. Ltd, 2014, 5 volumes).

Hasrat, Bikrama Jit, *Anglo Sikh Relations 1799-1849. A reappraisal of the Rise and Fall of the Sikhs*, (Hoshiarpur, V. V. Research Institute Book Agency, 1968).

Heath, Ian, *The Sikh Army 1799–1849* (Oxford: Osprey, 2005).

Humbly, William Wellington Waterloo, *Journal of a Cavalry Officer: Including the Memorable Sikh Campaign of 1845–46* (London: Longman, Brown, Green, and Longmans, 1854).

Imperial Record Department, *Calendar of Persian Correspondence: Volume 2 (1767–9)* (Calcutta: Superintendent Government Printing, 1914).

Indian News and Chronicle of Eastern Affaire (London: 24 April 1848).

Iyangar, Rao Bahadur, 'Manucci in Madras', *The Madras Tercentenary Commemoration Volume* (Chennai: Asian Educational Services, 1994).

Keay, Julia, *Farzana: The Woman Who Saved an Empire* (London: I.B. Tauris, 2013).

Keene, Rev. William, 'The Sikhs: All that can be said about them, from a Missionary Point of view', *Report of the Punjab Missionary conference held at Lahore In December and January 1862–63* (Lodiana: American Presbyterian Mission Press, 1863).

Khera, Paramdip Kaur, *Catalogue of Sikh Coins in the British Museum* (London: The British Museum, 2011).

Kipling, Rudyard, *Kim* (New York: Doubleday Page and Company, 1912).

Kohli, Sita Ram, *Catalogue of Khalsa Darbar Records*: Volume 1 (Lahore: Printed by the Superintendent, Government Printing, 1919).

Kohli, Sita Ram, *Catalogue of Khalsa Darbar Records*: Volume 2 (Lahore: Printed by the Superintendent, Government Printing, 1927).

Kohli, Sita Ram, *Sunset of the Sikh Empire* (New Delhi: Orient Blackswan Private Limited, 2012).

Lafont, Jean-Marie, *Fauj-i-Khas: Maharajah Ranjit Singh and his French officers* (Amritsar: Guru Nanak Dev University, 2002).

Leitner, G.W., *History of Indigenous Education in Punjab Since Annexation and in 1882* (Calcutta: Printed by the Superintendent of Government Printing, India, 1883).

Leyden, John, *Journal of a tour in the Highlands and Western Islands of Scotland in 1800* (Edinburgh and London: W. Blackwood and Sons, 1903).

Leyden, John, *Scenes of Infancy: Descriptive of Teviotdale* (Edinburgh: J. Ballantyne for T.N. Longman and O. Rees, 1803).

Login, Lady, *Sir John Login and Duleep Singh by Lady Login with an introduction by Colonel G.B. Malleson, c.s.i.* (London, W.H. Allen & Co., 1890).

Lowrie, Rev. John. C., *Travels in North India: Containing notices of the Hindus; journals of a voyage on the Ganges and a tour to Lahor; notes on the Himalaya mountains and the hill tribes, including a sketch of missionary undertakings* (Philadelphia: Presbyterian Board of Publication, 1842).

Macauliffe, Max Arthur, *The Sikh Religion: Its Gurus, Sacred Writings and Authors* (Oxford: Clarendon Press, 1909, 6 volumes).

Mackenzie, C., *Life in the Mission, the Camp, and the Zenana, or, Six Years in India*, Vol. 1 (London: Richard Bentley, 1853).

Mcleod, W.H., 'Reflections on Prem Sumarag', *Journal of Punjab Studies*, Volume 14, No. 1 (Spring 2007).

Mcleod, W.H., *The A-Z of Sikhism* (Plymouth: The Scarecrow Press, 2009).

Malcolm, Lt Col John, *The Sketch of the Sikhs: A Singular Nation Who Inhabit the Provinces of the Punjab Situated Between the Rivers Jamnu and Indus* (London: John Murray, 1812).

Mann, Gurinder Singh, 'Descriptions of the Dasam Granth from the Sketch of the Sikhs in view of Sikh History', *Sant Sipahi* (April 2008).

Mann, Gurinder Singh, 'Sri Takhat Harimandir Sahib Patna Sahib: A Perspective of its History and Maryada', *Sant Sipahi* (September 2008).

Mann, Gurinder Singh, 'The Role of the Dasam Granth in Khalsa' (unpublished MA thesis, De Monfort University, Leicester, 2001).

Mann, Gurinder Singh, and Singh, Kamalroop, *Sri Dasam Granth: Questions and Answers* (London: Archimedes Press, 2011).

Manucci, Niccolao, *Storia Do Mogor or Mogul India 1653–1708 By Niccolao Manucci, Venetian, Translated with Introduction and Notes by William Irvine* (London: John Murray, 1907, 4 volumes).

Martin, Robert Montgomery, *The History, Antiquities, Topography, and Statistics of Eastern India: comprising the districts of Behar, Shahabad, Bhagulpoor, Goruckpoor, Dinajepoor, Puraniya, Rungpoor, & Assam, in relation to their geology, mineralogy, botany, agriculture, commerce, manufactures, fine arts, population, religion, education, statistics, etc* (London: W.H. Allen and Co., 1838).

Maunsell, Colonel E.B., 'An Historic Durbar', *Journal of the United Service Institution of India*, Vol. LXII, Jan.–Oct. 1932,(Lahore: Printed by E.A. Smedley at the Civil and Military Gazette Press, 1932).

Meghani, Kajal, *Splendours of the Subcontinent: A Prince's Tour of India 1875–76* (London: Royal Collection Trust, 2017).

Morton, Rev. James, *The Poetical Remains of the Late Dr. John Leyden: With Memoirs of His Life, by The Rev. James Morton* (London: Longman, Hurst, Rees, Orme, and Brown, 1819).

Osbourne, W.G., *The Court and Camp of Runjeet Singh* (London: Henry Colburn Publishers, 1840).

Owen, Edward Farley, *European Travellers in India: During the Fifteenth, Sixteenth and Seventeenth Centuries, the Evidence Afforded by Them with Respect to Indian Social Institutions, & the Nature & Influence of Indian Government* (Delhi: Asian Educational Services, 1991; originally published in 1909).

Pal, M.K., *Historical Gurdwaras of Delhi* (Delhi: Niyogi Books, 2013).

Pall, S.J.S., *The Beloved Forces of the Guru* (Amritsar: B. Chattar Singh, Jiwan Singh, 2007).

Pandey, V.C. and Khattri, U.S., *Modern India: Based on Dr Ishwari Prasad, Dr Tarachand, Majumdar, Raychaudhuri, Datta, and H.H. Dodwell, Etc* (Lucknow: Prakashan Kendra, 1978).

Pearse, Major Hugh, *Soldier and Traveller; memoirs of Alexander Gardner, Colonel of Artillery in the service of Maharaja Ranjit Singh* (London: William Blackwood and Sons, 1898).

Prakash, Dr Ved, *The Sikhs In Bihar* (New Delhi: Janaki Prakashan, 1981).

Panjab Cultural Association, *Dr Leyden's Panjabi Translations* (London: Archimedes Press, 2011).

Prinsep, Henry Thoby, *Origin of the Sikh Power in the Punjab and political life of Maharaja Ranjit Singh; with an account of the Religion, Laws, and Customs of Sikhs* (Calcutta: G.H. Huttmann, Military Orphan Press, 1834).

Randhawa, T.S., *The Sikhs: Images of a Heritage* (New Delhi: Prakash Book Depot, 2007).

Reith, John, *The Life of Dr John Leyden, Poet and Linguist*, (Galashiels: A. Walker & Son Publishers, 1923).

Rennell, James, *Memoir of a map of Hindoostan; or The Mogul Empire: with an introduction, illustrative of the geography and present division of that country: and a map of the countries situated between the head of the Indus, and the Caspian Sea* (London: Printed by M. Brown for the author, 1788).

Richardson, Thom (ed.), *East Meets West: Diplomatic Gifts of Arms and Armour between Europe and Asia* (2013).

Roebuck, Thomas, *The Annals of the College of Fort William* (Calcutta: Printed by Philip Pereira at the Hindoostanee Press, 1819).

Roy, Kaushik, 'Race and Recruitment in the Indian Army: 1880–1918', *Modern Asian Studies*, Volume 47, Issue 4 (July 2013).

Russell, William Howard, *The Prince of Wales' tour: A diary in India; with some account of the visits of His Royal Highness to the courts of Greece, Egypt, Spain, and Portugal* (London: Sampson Low, Marston, Searle & Rivington, 1877).

Sandhra, Sharanjit Kaur, 'The Nihangs within the Great Sikh Court of 19th Century India' (unpublished MA thesis, The University of the Fraser Valley, 2005).

Sandhu, Gurmukh Singh, *Maharaja Duleep Singh, The King in Exile* (Chandigarh: Institute of Sikh Studies, 2006).

Sandhu, Jaspreet Kaur, *Sikh Ethos: Eighteenth Century Perspective* (Delhi: Vision & Venture, 2000).

Scott, George Batley, *Religion and Short History of The Sikhs – 1469 to 1930* (London: The Mitre Press, 1930).

Sessional Papers of the House of Lords, Session 1849, (12 & 13 victoria), Vol. Xv (London: Harrison and Sons, 1849).

Seth, Mesrovb Jacob, *Armenians in India, from the Earliest Times to the Present Day* (New Delhi: Asian Educational Services, 2005).

Shackle, C., *Catalogue of The Panjabi and Sindhi Manuscripts in the India Office Library* (London: India Office Library and Records, 1977).

Siddons, Capt., 'Translation of the Vichitra Natak', *Journal of the Asiatic Society of Bengal*, Vols xix. (part 1) and xx (part 2) (Calcutta, 1851–52).

Sidhu, Amarpal Singh, *The First Anglo–Sikh War* (Stroud, Gloucestershire: Amberley Publishing, 2010).

Sidhu, Amarpal Singh, *The Second Anglo–Sikh War* (Stroud, Gloucestershire: Amberley Publishing, 2016).

Sikh Review, Volume 31, Issues 355–60 (Calcutta: Sikh Cultural Centre, 1983).

Simpson, William, *India Ancient and Modern: a series of illustrations of the country and the people of India and adjacent territories; executed in chromo-lithography from drawings by William Simpson; with descriptive literature by John William Kaye* (London: Day and Son, 1867).

Singh, Attar, *Sakhee Book: or, the Description of Gooroo Gobind Singh's Religion and Doctrines* (Allahabad: The Indian Public Opinion Press, 1876).

Singh, Attar (trans.), *The Travels of Guru Tegh Bahadar and Guru Gobind Singh* (Lahore: Indian Public Press, 1876).

Singh, Bhagat, *A History of the Sikh Misals* (Patiala: Punjabi University, 1993).

Singh, Colonel Iqbal, *The Quest for the Past – Retracing the History of the Seventeenth-Century Sikh Warrior* (US: XLIBRIS, 2017).

Singh, Darshan (ed.), *Western Image of the Sikh Religion – A Sourcebook* (New Delhi: NBO, 1999).

Singh, Duleep, *A Reprint of two sale catalogues of jewels & other confiscated property belonging to his Highness the Maharajah Duleep Singh (1837–1893): which were put up to auction and sold at Lahore, in the years 1850 and 1851 by the government of India. With introductory remarks* (Privately printed, 1885).

Singh, Ganda (ed.), *Early European Accounts of the Sikhs* (Calcutta: Indian Studies, Past and Present, 1962; reprint).

Singh, Ganda, *A Select Bibliography of the Sikhs and Sikhism* (Amritsar: SGPC, 1965).

Singh, Ganda, *Guru Gobind Singh's Death at Nanded: an Examination of Succession Theories* (Faridkot: Guru Nanak Foundation, 1972).

Singh, Ganda (ed.), *Maharajah Duleep Singh Correspondence* (Patiala: Punjabi University, 1977).

Singh, Harbans, *Guru Nanak and the Origins of the Sikh Faith* (Bombay: Asia Publishing House, 1969).

Singh, Harbans (ed.), *The Encyclopaedia of Sikhism* (Patiala: Punjabi University, 1992, 4 volumes).

Singh, Harpal, 'An European Surgeon Who Attended Satguru Gobind Singh in 1708', https://satguru.weebly.com/european-surgeon-who-attended-satguru-gobind-singh-in-1708.html (accessed 10 June 2018).

Singh, Kamalroop and Mann, Gurinder Singh, *The Granth of Guru Gobind Singh: Essays, Lectures and Translations* (New Delhi: OUP, 2015).

Singh, Khushwant, *Ranjit Singh Maharaja of the Punjab* (London: George Allen and Unwin Ltd, 1962)

Singh, Kulwant (trans.), *Sri Gur Sobha Sainapati* (Chandigarh: Institute of Sikh Studies, 2014).

Singh, Nahar and Singh, Kirpal (eds), *Rebels Against the British Rule (Guru Ram Singh and the Kuka Sikhs)* (New Delhi: Atlantic Publishers and Distributors, 1995).

Singh, Nahar and Singh, Kirpal, *Two Swords of Guru Gobind Singh in England (1666–1708 A.D.)* (Delhi: Atlantic Publishers and Distributors, 1989).

Singh, Navtej, 'British efforts to gain control of the Golden Temple, 1844–63', in Singh, P. *et. al.* (eds), *Golden Temple* (Patiala: Punjabi University, 1999).

Singh, Dr Nazer, *Guru Granth Sahib Over to the West, Idea of Sikh Scriptures translations: 1810–1909* (New Delhi: Commonwealth, 2005).

Singh, Sikandar (Bhayee) and Singh, Roopinder, *Sikh Heritage: Ethos & Relics* (New Delhi: Rupa & Co., 2012).

Singh, Trilochan, 'Guru Gobind Singh's Ascension', *Sikh Review*, October 1963.

Smith, George, *Life of William Carey: Shoemaker & Missionary* (London: John Murray, 1909).

Smith, R. Bosworth, *The Life of Lord Lawrence, 1849–1852* (London: Smith Elder & Co., 1883).

Smyth, G.C., *A History of the Reigning Family of Lahore: with Some Account of the Jummoo Rajahs, the Seik Soldiers and their Sirdars* (Calcutta: W. Thacker and Co., 1847).

Sotheby's, *Sotheby's Coulston Auction Catalog, May 21–22, 1990*.

Steinbach, H., *The Punjaub; Being a Brief Account of the Country of the Sikhs, its Extent, History, Commerce, Productions, Government, Manufactures, Laws, Religion, etc.* (London: Smith, Elder, & Co., 1846).

Stern, Philip J., *The Company-State: Corporate Sovereignty and the Early Modern Foundations of the British Empire in India* (USA: Oxford University Press, 2011).

Streets, Heather, *Martial Races: The Military, Race and Masculinity in British Imperial Culture, 1857–1914* (Manchester: Manchester University Press, 2005).

Stronge, Susan (ed.), *The Arts of the Sikh Kingdoms* (London: V&A Publications, 1999).

Tanner, Brigadier J.K., 'Immortal Fame – The 80th (Staffordshire Volunteers) at Ferozeshah', *Soldiers of the Queen – Journal of the Victorian Military Society*, Issue 130, September 2007.

Taylor, F., 'The Oriental Manuscript Collections in the John Rylands Library', *Bulletin of the John Rylands Library*, vol. 54 (1971–72).

Trumpp, Ernest, *Adi Granth, or the Holy Scriptures of the Sikhs, Translated from the original Gurmukhi, with introductory Essays* (London: W.H. Allen, 1877).

Verma, Devinder Kumar, *Foreigners at the Court of Maharaja Ranjit Singh* (Patiala: Arun Publications, 2006).

Watson, J. Forbes and Kaye, John William (eds), *The People of India: A series of photographic illustrations, with descriptive letterpress, of the races and tribes of Hindustan, originally prepared under the authority of the government of India, and reproduced by order of the secretary of state for India in council*, Vol. 4 (London: W.H. Allen and Co., 1869).

Wheeler, George, *India in 1875–76: The Visit of the Prince of Wales* (London: Chapman and Hall, 1876).

Wheeler, J. Talboys, *Early Records of British India* (London: Trubner, 1878).

Wilkins, Charles, 'The Seeks And Their College At Patna, 1st March 1781', *Transactions of the Asiatick Society*, Vol. 1 (Calcutta: 1788).

Williams, Monier, *Religious Thought and Life in India. An Account of the Religions of the Indian Peoples, Based on a Life's Study of Their Literature and on Personal Investigations in their Own Country* (London: John Murray, 1885).

Wilson C.R., *The Early Annals of the English in Bengal*, Volume II, Part II (Calcutta: The Asiatic Society, 1911).

Wilson, H.H., *The Journal of the Royal Asiatic Society of Great Britain and Ireland*, Vol. 13 (1852).

Special papers and Manuscripts

McKenzie Papers, India office, British Library.

MS 241, University of Leicester.

Mss Eur F236/216, British Library.

Mss Panj. E1, British Library.

Mss Panj. E2, British Library.

Panjabi MS. 5, John Rylands Library, Manchester.

Websites

The Encyclopaedia of Sikhism: www.advancedcentrepunjabi.org/eos/

www.anglosikhmueum.com

www.anglosikhwars.com

www.Bl.org.uk

www.britishmuseum.org

www.hathitrust.org

www.rct.uk

www.sikhmuseum.org.uk

www.sikhscholar.co.uk

www.vam.ac.uk

www.vanda.org.uk

www.worldcat.org

Index

Electronic L
Production: The Advanced
Guide On How to Produce
Music for EDM Producers

Copyright Notice

Disclaimer

Claim This Now

Music Business Skills for Musicians:

If you're in the music business, read on. Today you need to view yourself through the new rules of the music industry.

Those who play by them will succeed.

Gone are the old days where you would hope to get signed and then become a star (i.e., everything would be done for you).

Do you wonder why other artists are getting breaks and you are not?

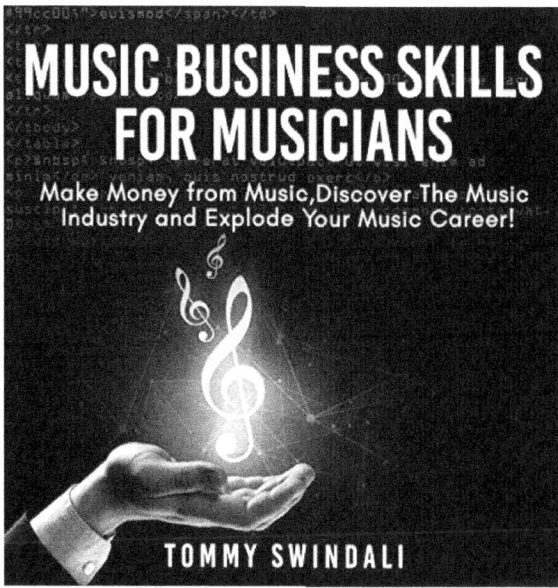

Discover How To Find Your Sound

Find Out More

Swindali music coaching/Skype lessons.

Email djswindali@gmail.com for info and pricing.

INTRODUCTION

Welcome to *Electronic Dance Music Production: The Advanced Guide On How to Produce Music for EDM Producers.* Your about discover what it takes to make an EDM song from idea, to finished song, to getting signed and more. Whether your a beginner or a more experienced producer your going to find value from this book.

When you think of EDM you will probably imagine big festivals, huge anthems and epic productions. All of that might well seem a million miles away from what you believe is possible for yourself. But let me tell you what those big name DJs do is not all that different from what most bedroom producers do. That is all easily achievable with the right knowledge, techniques and a few tools. The biggest difference between you and the big stars is in ideas and quality. Skillset, knowledge and tools are almost the same.

All you need to know and more will be covered in this book. From the knowledge of music to getting inspired and creating an epic EDM song. I'm even going to show the steps to get that song signed and out there for the world to hear.

Imagine the possibilities of having your song signed to a major label.

It's no secret that the top DJ's got there because of the music they make. You could be there too. Mainstage Ultra Music Festival, playing in clubs worldwide and getting your songs heard. Or maybe you just want to learn how to make an EDM

track from start to finish. There are so many possibilites. All of that will be covered and much more.

The flow of this book will begin with an outline of EDM, then it will focus on the journey of a song from concept to production, mixing, mastering and then how to get it out there. You can decide to go through this chapter by chapter or you can jump straight to the parts that interest you the most. Remember that learning something takes repetition so always come back and refresh your knowledge. Now let's get started producing EDM.

THE MAIN GENRES OF EDM

EDM is a broad way of defining dance music. As a whole it encompasses music that is suited for the dance floor. Within that umbrella genre there are many more genres that vary massively from each other. Let's take a look at some of the most popular ones. This will give you a clearer picture of what to expect when producing within that genre. You can also check out how difficult each genre is to produce within the descriptions. Don't be put off by that though, learning curves can be quite steep at the start but once you climb them your flying.

higher scores mean it is more easy to produce.

Big Room: (126 - 130 BPM)
Big room is one of the most popular sub genres of electro house music and EDM. It was popularized by the likes of artists such as Hardwell, Martin Garrix, KSHMR and R3hab.

The music is very formulaic and one of the easiest to produce. All tracks will include a long techno style build up that goes into a big drop with a 4/4 hard, bass thumping kick. Minimal musical elements, synths and percussion usually fill in space but most of the room is left for a huge kick.

Difficulty to produce: 8/10

Drum and Bass: (160 - 180 BPM)
Drum and bass also known as D'n'B, is a subgenre of EDM which was born in the UK jungle and rave movements during

the early 90s. Fast breakbeats, with big bass lines, samples, and synths characterize the genre.

A major influence on D'n'B comes from the Jamaican dub and reggae sound. It also incorporates a number of scenes and styles, from highly electronic, industrial sounds the jazz-influenced end of the spectrum. From its UK roots, the style has gained worldwide recognition and has influenced many other genres.

Difficulty to produce: 4/10

Dubstep: (140 - 155 BPM)

Dubstep is a subgenre of EDM that originated in London. It is generally characterized by syncopated rhythmic patterns and strong sub bass lines. The drums of Dubstep tend to be simple one shot kicks and snares with some hats. This simplicity makes a nice contrast for the wobbly, complex basslines.

Difficulty to produce: 3/10

Electro House: (126 - 130 BPM)
Electro house is a subgenre of house music that is distinguished by heavy basslines that are usually creating with lots of distortion and automation. In addition to a large bass drum in a 4/4 pattern. As with Dubstep the drums are usually simple to contrast complex basslines. It can also include melodic elements, samples and synth work. Generally the tempo falls around 130 BPM.

Difficulty to produce: 3/10

Future Bass: (145 - 160 BPM)

Future bass is a sub genre of electronic dance music that features elements of Trap music and is characterized by modulated synthesizer bass sounds. Sounds are modulated with automation or LFO's to create choppy effects. Arpeggio chords, vocal chops and vocoders are also popular in the genre. More mainstream Future bass music uses supersaw chords, whilst underground sounds experiment more with other sounds.

Difficulty to produce: 2/10

Hardstyle: (150 - 160 BPM)

Hardstyle is takes characteristics from hardcore and techno. Typically consists of a distorted, hard sounding kick drum. Multiple layers are combined to create a big and lead style kick. Hardstyle also utilises harsh and distorted synths, detuned and distorted sounds accompanying the main instruments.

Hardstyle has influenced many other styles of EDM, Most notably Big Room. This shares similarities with hardstyle such structure, rhythm and pitched kicks.

Difficulty to produce: 6/10

Psytrance:(135 - 150 BPM)

Psytrance also known as psychedelic trance or psy is a subgenre of trance music. Psytrance is easily recognizable with its use of a strong bass beat that usually occurs throughout the whole song. This is interlaced between the kicks on a fast and varying rhythm that might be in triplet or standard form.

Typically it falls between the 135 to 150 BPM range and is usually faster than trance. The layouts are usually long, sometimes well over ten minutes. These are progressive with various elements and layers coming in at regular intervals and leading to breakdowns.

The mood can vary from minimal to progressive, chill and dancefloor.

Difficulty to produce: 7/10

Trap: (140 - 160 BPM)

Trap is an amalgamation of dubstep and classic trap hip hop. As a subgenre it emerged around 2012. It is categorized by the use of 808 basslines, big subs and some minimal melodic elements. The BPM of a typical trap beat is around 140 to 160 BPM. Typically has strong bass drops and hard sounds.

Difficulty to produce: 5/10

THE ELEMENTS

When your producing EDM regardless of sub genre there are going to be some consistent elements that appear. Let's take a look at how to create and work with those.

THE KICK

In EDM the kick is the most important element. Remember kick sounds are dependent on the genre. Some things works well for different genres. For example big room favours bigger kicks whilst electro house goes with smaller kicks.

Using samples is the best solution for getting great sounding kicks, fast. These can be found within sample packs or on Splice which hosts a huge library containing billions of amazing samples.

Use my invite: https://splice.com/vip/Tommyswin

Every kick sample can essentially be cut into three different sections.

Tic/click: This is the transient starting sound. Usually it's going to be around five ten milliseconds long and contains quick attack, high frequency content. In essence this is what allows the kick to kind of jump out of the mix. Without the tick it will be very hard to hear any kick. Especially on speakers that are smaller such as headphones, laptop speakers and so on.

Body: Next section, will be anywhere from a hundred to one hundred and fifty milliseconds. This is where you start to move away from the high frequency content of the tick into the kind of low mids. In essence it's the punch and is what gives the kick energy.

Tail: The last section is where you can start to perceive the pitch of a kick. The tail can be as long short as you want. The

longer it is, the more easily it will be to tell the keys. 808 Kicks usually have quite long tails and are often used as a bassline playing a melody.

Understanding how these sections work will make mixing and creating kicks a lot easier and quicker because you will be making informed decisions. Let's say you take your kick to a smaller speaker environment such as your car laptop speakers and you can't hear it. That may mean that your kick tick isn't strong enough. Or it might mean that your punch is too short or it has too much low frequency content. Tweaking the different sections can help to fix things. If all else fails try a new sample.

Tune Your Kicks
To make sure your kicks work the best with your songs always tune them to the root note of the key of your song. Now if you like having kicks that are in perfect tune with your song then there are plugins which will create kicks such as, Sonic Academy kick. Otherwise your going to be using a sample of which you will need to know the key.

To determine the key of the sample you can use a free plugin named Span by Voxengo. This is an analysing plugin which will display the frequency and key of an input sound. The way to identify key is to look for where the waveform peaks a little bit higher on the analyzer screen. Press play and then scroll over to the peak amplitude. Then you will see the key reading at the bottom of the screen.

Once you know the key of a kick you can change it as you wish. Normally it's best to stick within the required key or within a range of two semitones. If you want to pitch kicks up or down you can load them into any sampler and transpose

them up or down. Samplers are also great for loading multiple samples and then drawing them out in midi. Another way to pitch your samples is to use the built in tools of your DAW or plug ins such as soundshifter from Waves.

Best Frequencies to EQ a Kick

There are some magic frequencies for kick drums which work pretty well. For the best results use a parametric EQ. Using this you can set a wide of narrow Q band to add or remove frequencies. Here are some useful frequencies to consider with your kicks.

100 to 200 Hertz: Kicks consist of dominant low frequencies. In some instances the kick drum might low frequency impact. The Waves Renaissance bass can come in here. It sounds great it's easy to use and you'll get fast results. You can also boost in this frequency range for good results. Always high pass the very lowest frequencies (below 30 HZ) since these usually clip limiters and cause distortion.

200-500 Hz: Boxy sound. Generally something we don't want. Many kicks have a lot of energy here so we usually have to take it out a little bit.

Around to 2 KHZ: The attack / click of the sound. Enhancing this helps to to define the kick more clearly. Many people assume kicks are all about bass but the mids are very important for rhythm. If your song has a fast rhythm you will benefit from short kicks with well defined mids.

THE LEAD

The real secret to a great lead is the melody. A melody is by definition monophonic which means that it is one voice without any chords. A melody can be characterized by four elements:

- **Contour**

A contour can be thought of as a line that ascends, descends, dips or arches. Different contours evoke different emotions and how they are used is down to preference.

- **Range**

The range of a melody is the distance between it's highest and lowest note. Most EDM melodies work well on a smaller range (half to full octave) because EDM is dependent on sounding big and powerful. Bigger ranges mean shifting in pitches which weakens sounds as they move from the root note. Just remember that narrower ranges are less musical. Focus on smaller ranges for the drop and wider ranges for melodic breakdowns.

- **Intervals**

Melodies always use more than one note and so there will always be at least one melodic interval. Think of this as the blueprint and it will help you create alterations for different parts of your melody. Does the melody jump down to certain notes or move to them incrementally?

- **Structure**

Melodies are based on a structure too. You can have different sections of your melody. That could be call and response, up and down, etc.

- **Scales**

Scales form melodies and there are numerous types:

- Modal: Variable patterns of major/minor scale.
- Major and minor: The majority of Western music.
- Chromatic: All twelve notes.
- Pentatonic Scale: 5-note scale. Often used in blues and rock.
- There are others, but those are irrelevant to EDM production.

In EDM with a little theory and structure you can create a melody more quickly and easily. Try these five steps.

1. Scale

Work with a scale and this limits the amount of notes you can use. EDM producers usually work with one scale most of the time. F Minor is particularly popular. Learning and sticking to a scale will help you to know which notes will work.

2. Rhythm

After deciding on a scale you need a rhythm for your melody. A bunch of notes is nothing but with a simple rhythm a melody is born. You can tap out a rhythm or try some percussion to map the rhythm out.

3. Contour

Once the rhythm is locked in, it's time to outline the melody. This is where you get creative and imagine where the note falls. Is it up, down or the same? Follow your vision.

4. Sound

If you have a great melody it will sound amazing with pretty much any instrument. Spend time getting that right with basic sounds and then develop the sound design. It's better to do that first otherwise your wasting time trying to turn something average into something spectacular. Start with good sources. Later on you might wish to move and vary notes as you please.

If you get stuck try using silence, changing instruments, shifting octaves or moving notes around. Try to get a decent four to eight bar melody. Take inspiration from other music and even use MIDI files.

The Best Synths For Making EDM Leads

Nowadays there are so many synths available to make leads with. The best option is to find one that you feel comfortable with and can easily get great results with. Results won't come instantly until you master the synth. So for starters, try to use less instead of spreading your skills across a bunch of different synths. To help you decide, let's take a look at three of the best currently on the market. These are used by some of the top producers in the EDM world.

Sylenth

Sylenth is a legend and has been around since 2007. But it has continued to develop and has stood the test of time with it's huge array of soundbanks and amazing sonics. Every EDM producer should have it installed.

It is capable of making almost any sound from bass, pads, percussion and more. But the real highlight is how good it is at making EDM leads.

- Spec: Subtractive synthesizer with four oscillators, two filters, two envelopes, and two LFOS.
- Artists: Afrojack, Hardwell, Avicii, Skrillex, The Chainsmokers and more…
- https://www.lennardigital.com/sylenth1/

Serum

Serum is the EDM synth to have and right now is one of the most popular synthesizers on the market. It is a beast at making EDM leads and hosts hundreds of soundbanks plus a library full of high quality presets. Excels at sounds for Dubstep, Trap and Future Bass. It's unlimited LFO's are great for making hard and interesting leads. Add this to your EDM arsenal.

- Spec: Wavetable Synthesizer with three envelopes, unlimited LFOS, two Filters, ten built in effects, and thousands of wavetables.
- Artists: Dyro, Deadmau5, Morgan Page, DJ Snake, Skrillex and more...
- https://xferrecords.com/products/serum

Spire

A hidden gem that is a strong contender for making the best EDM leads. Easy to use with a plethora of customizable presets. Great for trance and progressive sounds with lush textures or Big Room leads. Anthems sound great with this. Offers almost everything as Sylenth and Serum but in a different package that should be part of your EDM production arsenal.

- Spec: A subtractive, wavetable, FM and AM Synthesizer with two Filters, and standard modulations.

- Artists: Hardwell, Armin Van Buuren, Dimitri Vegas & Like Mike and more…
- https://www.reveal-sound.com/

Samples

Making lead sounds with synths can be a long and arduous task. If you struggle with it you can always make use of samples. Splice is a great resource.

https://splice.com/vip/Tommyswin

You can browse the library for synth sounds as one note samples. Load the samples into a sampler such as Kontakt or the built in sampler of your DAW. You can then play in your lead melody and have that sample play it. Amazing sounding results almost instantly!

Layering

Want to make huge leads? If you are looking to create epic leads then layering multiple synths is the way to go. The trick to layering synths is in knowing what type of synths to layer together. For that to work you need to choose sounds that will compliment each other and sound great as one.

The first sound you use should be a simple synth sound and usually that would be in mono. This works great on big sound systems so having it as your base sound is perfect. The init sound in Sylenth is a great starting point. If your melody sounds good with basic sounds then you're onto a winning track because its then going to sound amazing when you add in all the layers and effects processing.

Normally layers won't sound great on their own so avoid using the solo button. The next layer to add can be a nice wide lead

to fill out the stereo field. Then you will have a good mix of mono and stereo for making a huge full lead. You can keep adding more layers but just be conscious of having a purpose for them. A trick you can use with the layering is to have them dropping in and out. This can work really well with progressive EDM styles.

Want more distortion? Add a distorted layer. Want more realness? Add some live world instruments. Just make sure they all compliment each other. You can EQ layers individually to remove any unwanted or clashing frequencies or even add effects processing as you please. It's a good practice to send all those layers to a bus so they can all be controlled as one. Finally add some master effects such as reverb, compression and so on. Sidechaining on the leads helps to make them fit in more with the kick.

BASS

Bass is without a doubt at the core of EDM music. It might be subtle or extremely exaggerated but regardless without it EDM would sound dead. In layman's terms it is the low pitched instrumental part of a song. In some cases such as with trap it might be an 808 kick drum. In other cases it might be lower register of an instrument or a synthesizer.

Without a good bass line to back your drop, your song won't get to the next level. Great basslines consist of an awesome sound and a great groove. Here are some tips to make your bass lines sound awesome. You can also apply some of the tips you learned to create melodies.

- *Match the bassline with the kick*. A good relation between these will provide a strong foundation for the track. Adding in other instruments later will be a breeze.
- *Get inspired*. Listen to other songs how does the bass sound, what is it's rhythm? Don't be afraid to copy a little because it will help your bass lines sound great and get you inspired. Just make sure you add in some originality.
- *Layer*. Again this will help you basslines become much fuller, fatter and bigger. Most sounds on their own are not enough. You can even add in some modulated layers to make your bass sound super interesting. Use tools such as compression and distortion to gel the layers together.
- *Slide notes*. This will create nice transitions between notes. Almost all synthesizers come with the portamento/legato function that can be adjusted to

make notes slide into each other. This will work wonders on basslines.

- *Harmonizing*. Most bass lines follow the root notes of the chords played by other instruments. Try changing the bass notes to others that are in harmony with your chords and you will get a whole new flavor of bass.
- *Bouncy*. If the rhythm sounds good but it's boring, make it bouncy. Simply putting certain notes up an octave and elongating some of them will give you a more bouncy and interesting bass line. Remember to turn on the legato as with sliding technique.

The Best Synths For Making EDM Bass

Now when it comes to the sound of the bass your going to need a solid, reliable synth. You could go with bass guitars or pianos on the low riff but that's less common in EDM. Here are some of the best virtual instruments for bass.

Novation Bass Station

If you're looking for warm, fat and dirty basslines then Bass Station will deliver. It's two distinct analogue filter types offer massive variation in sonic possibilities. The sounds can be strong or soft as you wish. Crank the distortion for more hardness or tweek the filters to soften. Comes with sixty four diverse patches to get you started.

- Spec: Analogue Monosynth emulation with two oscillators and one sub oscillator.
- Artists: Soul Clap, Brohug, Vini Vici and more…
- https://novationmusic.com/synths/bass-station-ii

Native Instruments Massive

Massive is a hugely popular synth with EDM producers. Instead of taking direct inspiration from vintage hardware, Massive uses a combination of wavetable synthesis technology and a simple drag-and-drop interface for programming. It practically gave birth to dubstep with its wobbly bass lines and has gone onto be a go to synth for future house and bass house producers. Great at creating traditional analogue style tones to complex evolving sounds.

- Spec: Wavetable Synthesizer with multiple envelopes, LFOS, two Filters, built in effects, and thousands of wavetables.
- Artists: Sub Focus, Knife Party, Dannic, Swedish House Mafia and more…
- https://www.native-instruments.com/en/products/komplete/synths/massive/

Rob Papen SubBoomBass

This is one of EDM basses best kept secrets. The design might scream "80s", but inside is a modern and powerful sound engine. In addition the standard sine, square, saw and triangle waveforms are many sampled waveforms for adding texture to your bass. The result is an organic-sounding and powerful bass plug-in. Comes with a huge bank of great presets.

- Spec: Dual Oscillator Synthesizer with envelopes, LFOS and sequencer
- Artists: Junkie XL, DJ Khaled, DJ Mustard and more…
- https://www.robpapen.com/subboombass.html

DRUMS

EDM is built on its drums which entice people to dance. A bad beat will ruin a song.

Why Tuning Your Drums is Essential

Tuning your drum and percussion parts is essential to achieving a great song. Like all other instruments, the drums need to be in the same key as the song.

Use a key and frequency chart to identify specific notes. This will help you identify the key for your individual drum hits. For example, if you have a song in the key of A, it would sound best to boost at frequency ranges matching the A note. The frequency note chart will show you all those ranges for each of the notes across the spectrum. Use other notes in the same key to give your drum hits different character and help them stand out. Many EDM producers tune their snares up a fifth from the root note.

Everyone has their own unique mixing process music. Depending on the music style we have our default ways that define us. A big influence on mixing is how we use Equalizers (EQ) for different instruments. EQ is a tool used to enhance or remove frequencies from sounds. Another way to use an EQ is to tune drum hits so that they match the key of your song. Use a tuner whilst EQ'ing. When applied to a channel a tuner will identify what key your drum hit is. If it's out of key, you can shift your EQ settings until it matches the right key. Alternatively you can use a frequency shifter to tweek the specific part without losing any clarity or tonality.

Drum Programming

Drum programming is the process of composing with drums. Instead of playing drums live you are actually drawing them out in a sequence. This is different drum synthesis since you are not actually creating the sounds. Instead you're using drum samples. As you can imagine this can take a while because you have to pick the right samples, layer and then construct sequences.

Fundamentally drum programming is easy. Anyone can create a basic kick-hat-snare drum pattern. But when you go deeper and want to create more interesting, complex and great sounding drums it becomes more complicated. Learning is an ongoing journey. You can always learn from other songs. Analyze them, consider the different elements and what makes them good. Be an active listener and take notes.

Great drums begin with sourcing the best samples. With better samples, less work will be required. Then you won't need to rely on layering multiple hits together. Sometimes if all that is needed is one hit then that's fine. Layering drums can be a complicated task and often it's best to choose just one good sample.

There really is no secret method or technique for finding great samples, it's all about trusting your ears. Developing your listening skills is critical to becoming better at that. Unfortunately out there are many low quality samples. If you're considering to buy a sample pack download a demo first. This way you can test out the samples first. Truthfully you will only need a few great samples anything more and you'll waste time searching for the perfect sample. Don't waste time searching. Choose the one that works, and then process it so it becomes perfect. One of the best websites for samples is Splice. It's a

paid monthly service that offers you millions of sounds for all EDM genres.

Add Interest and Variation to Your Drums
Repeating the same drum loop for sixteen bars gets boring really quick. You do need the main drum loop but you also should make it more interesting.

Try the following techniques
- Every two bars, introduce a new drum hit
- Every four bars, introduce a new drum hit that's stronger or louder
- Every eight bars create a drum fill or roll

These techniques aren't the only ones you can try. Experiment and it will turn a boring loop into an interesting one. Analyze the drums in your favorite EDM and apply it to your productions.

In addition you can add swing to your drums to give them a natural feeling. This is essentially small variations in velocity and time to enhance the groove and rhythm. You can apply this manually to individual hits, changing velocity, timing and so on or in some DAWs they have a setting that you can apply in intensity. This will make your drums more funky and exciting. Experiment with it.

Big Room
Big room is pure simplicity when it comes to drum programming. It's designed for festivals and clubs, not for home listening. Typically it will have a sub bass, distorted kick tuned to the root note of the song. Often this is combined with a clap that has reverb added to it which is sidechained with

the kick. Also you will often have a high passed ride cymbal on the top. Sometimes you will hear some percussion playing on off beats. Every eight or sixteen bars the patterns will have a fill. When selecting samples choose big and simple hits.

Drum and Bass

Drum and bass is fast and is one of the hardest genres to make drums for. Having the snare right is an important thing to get right. Get this right and the foundation is solid. Then you want a hard hitting tuned kick. The next thing is to layer in many different hi hats and breakbeats to fill up the drums. Create diversity and interest with new drums every so often then progressing into fills and rolls every sixteen bars.

Dubstep

Drums in dubstep are there to support the bassline and are often very simple. Often they will consist of a very strong kick and snare combined with shuffle style hi hats which break up monotony. All are of course tuned to the key of the song. Remember to tune your snare up a 5th for diversity. Add in some subtle percussion to create more interest. Every so often add in some new hits or even modulate the snare by making it shorter, longer or changing pitch and so on.

Electro House

Electro house drums are often using very simple patterns. In most cases it's simply just a kick, snare and hihat. The purpose of simplicity is usually to contrast with the complex arrangements of bass and synths. Generally the drums sound dirty and rock style. Select samples that have a rough characteristic. Rolls and fills are less common in elector house in some cases there will be a pause and some fx take their place.

Future Bass and Trap

Drums in Future Bass and Trap are quite similar. The drums are almost always consisting of a kick drum, snare, and hi-hats. Kicks are usually coming from a tuned 808 sample to the root note of the song. Often this will also play some kind of a melody. Then the snare would probably be pitched a 5th up from the root. Hi-Hats are very important to the character of trap. Percussion sounds in Trap are quite experimental and will often include unique sounds to give more character. Normally Future Bass songs have more real world sounding drums. You can get really creative with the variations, add in breaks or new hits as you please. Just make sure to keep the rest of the song in mind and help the track as a whole.

Hardstyle

This is very similar to the simplicity and arrangement of Big Room. The main difference is obviously the tempo but going further Hardstyle is actually even more minimal. Often the only drum programming is the kick. This is left alone because it is the focal point. Hardstyle kicks are multiple layers or resampled and distorted kicks to create a huge monster of a sound that fills the whole spectrum. This would be tuned to the root note and usually play a melody. Fills take the place of any areas where the kick doesn't play. Usually every sixteen bars or so.

Psytrance

Psytrance is very kick driven. Short and low frequency full sounding kicks work well here. They play a 4/4 beat and are usually supported by some light percussion or hi hats. You have to keep things minimal but full sounding with Psytrance otherwise you move away from the character of the genre.

Tips

- Make samples fit by applying Attack, Decay, Sustain, Release (ADSR)
- Adding effects won't improve a bad sample
- Apply swing for complexity and a human feel
- Keep it simple. Always make sure you have a reason to add new samples
- Create interest through variation. Vary your drums every eight to sixteen bars
- Practice. Remake some of your favourite tracks.
- Compliment the track and make space for the instruments.

VOCALS

Some of the biggest EDM songs feature vocals. Vocals capture your heart, mind and emotions. Having the vocals right is going to make EDM production awesome. With that said here are some fundamentals to achieving great vocals. Remember to add on a healthy dose of, experimentation, inspiration, and creativity.

Processing EDM Vocals is one of the most important skills a producer can develop. At the start you need to make sure your vocals are great without any processing. The number one way to achieve this is to find a good singer. Someone with experience and talent is going to give you a great vocal performance. Maybe you have a song idea you can send them. Or it could be a cover, your own lyrics or maybe their ideas. Ideally find someone who is creatively sharing your mindset. Harmonious working relationships will produce great results.

Now the singer doesn't really need to have a big vocal range but some experience is required. Ideally, you should find someone who fits your song and has an original vocal character. Screening for these attributes will ensure a great vocal performance.

Once you have your vocalist it's time to get into the technicalities. First of all select the right microphone. Condenser microphones are generally more suitable for recording vocals because of their sensitivity to high frequency detail. However dynamic microphones will work fine if your budget is lower. Famous artists have achieved great results with both. Make sure you set the microphone up at a distance

that captures them effectively. Not too close but not too far. Finally add on a pop shield to attenuate plosive sounds.

Avoid any effects processing for now. EDM songs usually have heavily process vocals but all that should be saved for later on. If you do it now you can't undo it so it's better to capture a raw and well recorded vocal. You don't even need compression or limiting going in. Just make sure you use a good quality recording interface, cables and microphone. Save the effects for later.

Capture the best performance. Remember that the one thing above all else is to record the greatest vocals possible. Your job is to make sure the singer delivers their best performance. Make sure they are comfortable, that their monitor feed is at the right level and even small things such as if they need water or a short rest. Some of the best vocal recordings happen on first takes so be focused on the results and don't waste time if you get the result early on. If things aren't working out then take a short break.

Once you have recorded a good vocal performance you can begin to clean things up. Often there will be some low level noise on recordings. You can use a noise reduction plug-in to clean that. Have the settings light so that you aren't muting out parts. If there are long empty sections you can trim out those. But keep it natural and retain any breathing because this will help to maintain the natural vocal characteristics.

The next thing to clean up is everything below 100 HZ as that is likely rumble and not part of the vocal. Apply a simple high pass filter set at 100 HZ here. Once we have done this it's time to remove any unwanted resonating frequencies. These usually occur in very small rooms. The way to find them is by

using an EQ with high Q band set and then sweeping it across the spectrum to listen for any areas that jump out. Once you find those all you need to do is then reduce the gain where you found them and that will be all for the cleaning portion.

It's time to start beefing it up. EDM vocals need to sound strong and clear. Compression will help to achieve that because a singer will never deliver a performance where their voice is loud all the time. This is where compression comes in by making the dynamic range of the vocal smaller. However compression must be used carefully because you don't want to take the life out of a vocal. Too much and it will result in a dead sound.

Adjust the threshold to catch the sound and the ratio to control how much to compress. Next, have the attack set so that the first transients keep their punchiness. Then again tweek the threshold and ratio controls as preferred. The result will be a more consistent vocal that will stand out in the mix. Also, De-ess your vocals to get rid of high frequency sibilant sounds and help make the vocal shine through the mix. Waves have some great presets adjusted for male and female singers.

The last step is to polish the vocals. Apply reverb, delay, and all the effects that make vocals sound amazing and powerful. First up add a little bit of warmer or saturation to warm up the vocals. Next use a simple delay to add a bit of a delay effect to make them sound more wide. After this apply a reverb to the vocal via a return. Using a return will maintain the clarity of the vocal and keep the effects clean. A return can be created in every DAW. Normally you just click send to a group. The best reverb for EDM vocals is a Hall style. However you can always flick between presets and then adjust the one you like.

When mixing your vocals make alternate mixes. Try creating three mixes:

- One where you feel the vocal should be
- One more upfront
- One pulled back

Chances are, one of these will be right. In addition make sure you mix the vocals in the rest of the mix. Avoid mixing in isolation because this will sound different to how it will sound in the mix. Mixing decisions should always be done within the mix of the whole song. Only solo the vocals in order to remove problematic frequencies or to fine tune.

This is just one way of mixing vocals. It's up to you to experiment and find unique ways to be more creative. Come up with your own ways of vocal processing and develop your sound.

FX

Add in some FX sounds to make your tracks sound more interesting. Maybe your song feels a bit empty. Trust me and add some FX. They will make all the difference. Get creative here and follow your intuition. To help you here are some of the most commonly used FX.

- **Atmospherics**

These are light and ethereal sounds with lots of ambience. Work great for intros or maybe in the background of more emotionally driven music. Create your own with simple or layered sounds that have lots of reverb on.

- **Background**

It's great to have some long sustained and evolving sounds going on in the background of an intro or drop. This keeps the listener hooked in. Try some tuned effects here to stick with the key.

- **Downers**

Whenever you come to a breakdown or build up it's a good idea to use a downer. This is simply a long sound pitched to the root note of the song that then glides down in pitch. Typically this will be a sub or low bass sound. Creates a great atmospheric effect.

- **Fills**

These are normally sixteen to one bar drum rolls but they could be things such as short bass notes that roll down the scale or anything your imagination can conceive. Place these

every sixteen bars or more to break things up, introduce new sections and keep it interesting.

- **Impacts**

Use these with your downers or on their own. They are loud fast attack sounds with a long sustain and release. Snare drums and impact sounds with reverb work well here.

- **Lazers**

High pitched lfo sounds that work really well over the top of bass heavy music or breakdowns. They work really well when you introduce an important new section of your song such as a breakdown or drop.

- **Make Your Own**

Get creative. Buy yourself a microphone and use household objects your voice or anything else you think would be cool to record. Add it to your songs and make them original.

- **Risers**

The highlight of an EDM banger. When it comes to building up to a huge drop a riser is going to make sure the damage is done well. Take a long sound and pitch it up slowly or quickly over a whole octave or two. Always use risers in the key of your song.

- **Rolls**

Similar to fills but would only be one drum hit or sound repeated and speeding up. Great for going into drops.

- **Stabs**

Sounds with a fast attack and long release. Often a staccato horn sound is used, this is the case in 80% of trap. These can

be a feature at the front or work well in the background. Always make sure they are in key.

- **Sweeps**

Can be long or short depending on how dramatic you want the effect to be. Use them to transition between sections of a song. Reversed cymbals or white noise work well as sweeps.

- **Tonal FX**

Anything that has strong resonant peak in the key of your song. These are great as atmospherics or can even be a main feature.

- **Vocal Samples**

If your song has vocals then it can be a great idea to create some vocal FX from the main hook. You could do some kind of pitched drops such as DJ Snake does or maybe just resample the vocals as atmospherics. Get creative and follow your imagination.

EDM SONG CONSTRUCTION

All You Need to Know About Music Theory

When you start out producing your going to hear about key a lot. So what is a key? Musically speaking key is the name given to a group of musical notes that will sound good when used together. When you use the notes within a particular key your songs will probably sound good. The first or lowest note in the key gives it the name. This is commonly referred to as the root or tonic note.

There are major keys and there are minor keys. In the simplest of terms. Major keys sound happy, and minor keys sound sad. The differences in these keys are in the intervals between each of the notes in the scale. Intervals consist of whole steps and half steps. The smallest interval between each note is half-step which is the equivalent of a semitone. You can identify all the notes of any key by counting the intervals from the root note. All major and minor keys are based on configurations of intervals.

- **Major Key**

Root Note (or Tonic) --> 2 (half-steps) --> 2 --> 1 --> 2 --> 2 --> 2 --> 1

- **Minor Key**

Root Note --> 2 (half-steps) --> 1 --> 2 --> 2 --> 1 --> 2 --> 2

The easiest way to know both is to consider the keys of C Minor and A Major. Both use the same notes (all the white keys) but use the intervals of major or minor respectively. So if you want to write in a particular major or minor key you can

draw out all the notes used in either C Minor or A Major and then shift the root note to the key you wish to use. Alternatively you can just count the intervals using the above guides.

There are many other keys and scales too and there is much more to theory than this but for now this is the most important. Play and experiment with writing in different keys. This should help you to quickly and easily build your EDM tracks in key. It doesn't matter which genre you choose because it will work just as well for Drum and Bass as it will for House, Trap, Dubstep and so on.

Chords
The core of a song are the melody and chords. You don't need to be an expert in Music Theory to compose chords for your songs. As we now know every song is in a specific key and all of the other chords will revolve around it. For example a song could be in the key of C Major which uses all the white keys on a piano roll. Each one of the notes can be given a number which you will often see represented by Roman numerals.

Imagine chords like the building blocks of a story. Some will sound happy, some sad, some exciting, some relaxing and so on. Your job is to arrange these in a way that evokes the emotion you want. In a song the way chords move from one to the next is called a chord progression. The chords can evoke different feelings and there are many ways to combine chords. To start building a chord progression pick a key you like. Have a clear start and finish in mind when writing a chord progression. There also needs to be a degree of emotional development and movement which comes from using different

chord progressions. Alternatively you could use the same chord progression but with a different melody.

EDM songs usually feature simple chord progressions that are easy to memorize. Often those will be only two to three chords. The foundation of EDM is usually simple but the complexity comes in arranging or sound design. A great way to start a song is to find a midi file of a chord progression you like or if you feel confident enough recreate it. Then focus on the sound design and different variations to make it sound your own. Here are some chords commonly found in EDM.

Triad Chord
A chord is generally when three or different keys are played at the same time. These are based on scales. The most common chord is a triad consisting of three keys, the first, the third and the fifth note of the scale. A triad is made up of a root, a third, and a fifth. Just count up the scale (including the root note) For example:

- C Major Triad Chord: **C, E, G**
- A Major Triad Chord: **A, C#, E**

Triads are the most common chords and you will hear many variations of them. You can switch the order of the notes of a chord from low to high to high to low. For example in C major you can put the C on top so that E becomes the lowest note and the G is in the middle. This is called "inversion".

Minor Chord
The next most common and easy to create chord is a minor. This is similar to the major except the third not is dropped by one half step. This gives it a sad emotional feeling. For example:

- C Minor Chord: **C, D#, G**
- A Minor Chord: **A, C, E**

Diminished Chords

Diminished chords can be used to add tension and a dissonant sound to your music. They are built by adding a minor third and a tritone above the root note. A tritone can be found by counting six semitones from the root note. Whilst a minor third can be found by counting three semitones from the root note. For example:

- C Diminished Chord: **C, D#, F#**
- A Diminished Chord: **A, C, D#**

Suspended Fourth

Suspended Fourth chords create a proud and strong emotion. These can be created by using the root, fourth and fifth note of the scale. For example

- C Suspended Fourth: **C, F, G**
- A Suspended Fourth: **A, D, E**

Major Sixth

Major Sixth chords use four notes to create a triumphant and strong emotion. Works well as a climax. These can be created by using the root, third, fifth and sixth note of the scale. For example:

- C Major Sixth: **C, E, G, A**
- A Major Sixth: **A, C#, E, F#**

Major Seventh Chord:

Nostalgic sounding chord that is created by using the root, third, fifth and seventh note of the scale. For example:

- C Major Seventh: **C, E, G, B**
- A Major Seventh: **A, C#, E, G#**

Dominant Seventh:
Expectant sounding chord that consists of a major third, perfect fifth, and minor seventh above a root. For example:

- C Dominant Seventh: **C, E, G, B#**
- A Dominant Seventh: **A, C#, E, G#**

Ninth Chords and More:
You can even go as far as using five notes in your chords or more. Just add notes on the top of your chords and experiment with sounds. Practice, trust your ears and go with what sounds best.

Try downloading some MIDI files of your favourite songs which will include all the notes of the song. You can use these to look at how the songs are put together and how all the notes work. This will give you a great understanding of music theory or perhaps even a song starter.

ARRANGEMENT

Most songs begin as loops. The hard part is taking a loop and turning it into a song. Many great loops with the potential to be great songs get stuck at the loop phase because of too much focus on perfection. It can be easy to fall into the pattern of looping repeatedly and trying to perfect every detail. But there is no reason to waste your good ideas. Why not turn them into finished songs?

When you develop a framework for how a finished song is constructed it becomes more easy to create finished songs from your loop ideas. In order to achieve this we need to understand the construction of an EDM song. EDM uses song structures that are quite different from the song structure of pop music. This is due to EDM not using vocals as much.

The arrangement of your EDM song is going to have a huge influence on how successful it will be. The end goal of most EDM music is to be played by DJ's and in that regard it needs to fulfill some requirements. As a listener of EDM you will notice some common themes. Most have an intro, build up, drop, break down and then repeat again. This isn't a coincidence, rather it is on purpose to allow DJs to easily mix in and out of the songs. To help you structure your songs it's a good idea to choose a reference track which you will study the structure of.

EDM is constructed to keep the energy going through highs and lows. The result is like a rollercoaster, building up energy, dropping it down and then repeating it again. However you don't have to follow the formulas. Breaking rules can produce

profound results and happy accidents, so be creative as you wish.

Most EDM songs consist of four main structural parts:

- Intro
- Breakdown
- Build up
- Drop

Understanding how the construction of these four parts will help you to build a song. EDM songs will usually build up to a single powerful drop that is the focus of the song. Elements are usually added every four to eight bars and this is how you achieve the buildup effect. With this knowledge you can decide where to place your loop into the overall song structure. For example if your loop is from the drop then you can start to make an intro or build up to it. Now depending on the subgenres of EDM that you work in these four elements may differ. For example, Dubstep usually has quicker build ups than House.

Analyze other EDM songs to help you understand how a song is constructed. You can even copy out their structure so that you create a basic blueprint and know where your loop should be. Then finishing your song is simply a case of building up the other parts which you can change as you please.

Aim for a consistent vibe so all the different pieces work together which can be achieved by using some of the same parts for the whole song. Such as using the drop bassline for part of your build up or using parts of the melody in the intro and so on.

So how do you turn your loop into a song? The best way is to start with the drop. In most cases you start with your best ideas and those will likely make a great drop. When you know which part the song you're working with it will help you flesh out the whole song.

Once you know the section of the song you are working on and have a hot loop going you can split it into two by creating an alternative version of the first drop. This will help keep listeners hooked in and keep things fresh. With the drop done you can move to constructing the other parts of the song.

Intro
The intro of a song otherwise known as the beginning. It's standard practice for the intro to feature a stripped down making it easier for DJ's to mix in with. Sixteen bar intros or around thirty seconds have become more common in EDM as the listeners expect you to get straight to the point. Long intros can be saved for more underground genres.

Usually you can start out with some drums here. Not the full set but maybe the kick and a few hi hats. The drums used in your drop can be made more minimal and stripped down for the intro. Most tracks will also use some FX here as well such as a downfilter or some background ambience and tonal FX. sometimes you could use the lead sounds teasing the melody but not fully out there.

Tease things here and there but don't start off too strong, save that for the drop. The perfect intro will contain a balance of teasing and power. Teasing also aids in introducing the elements of your track to new listeners. For now it's all about progressing to the breakdown which you can sweep into with sweep FX and fills.

Breakdown

The intro is followed by a breakdown. Here the drums will usually stop to create a sense of anticipation for the listener. Breakdowns are often atmospheric and progressively build into the main hook of the song. You can also experiment with a big hit or impact coming in at the start of the breakdown. This gives an explosive and dramatic feeling that really adds energy to the track.

Buildup

When coming out of the break experiment with a small silence right before bringing in the main hook of the song in. This will create a big impact when the main part comes in. Coming out of the breakdown you really want to start to build things up to the drop. Use snares and instrumental elements to build things up. Add in some pitched risers that go up the scale. These can get gradually louder and faster to a climax.

Another common popular technique is to use a drop part, such as the lead or a bass line, and place it into the build up. Which makes for a much smoother transition and prepares the listener. Add in some reverse sounds and fills at the end of the buildup and a crash impact into the drop.

You will need lots of fades and automation to make everything nice and smooth. In addition you could even add a high-pass filter effect or other effects to your master channel to intensify it as you progress in the build up. This will not only help to transition from the breakdown to the drop, but also make the drop hit much harder. Ramp up the energy.

Drop

The last element, the drop, is the most important. It is the main hook of the song and the section where your productions have to really shine. Make sure this is the energetic high point and most memorable part of your song. If your song is all about melody, make sure you use the best melody here. This should be the full arsenal and will play for sixteen or thirty two bars with a some fills in the middle and a slightly different variation for the second half. In a lot of EDM genres the drop will then go into another breakdown, build up and then drop again. You can easily copy and paste those to the second part of your track. It's up you if you choose to introduce a new melody or chord progression later on.

Outro

For the end of your song you can do many different things. The most common thing to do is to gradually fade out. This could be the whole volume going down or taking things out one by one over sixteen bars. For example, take out the lead, the bass, the drums and so on. The volume fade is easier to do but the take out method usually sounds better. Just remember that music production is an art form. There is no ruleset for every song. Have an open mind and experiment with different things.

REMAKE: THE BEST WAY TO IMPROVE

The two essential components to becoming a better producer are time and effort. A great use of time and effort is to remake other music. Of course you can keep making originals but that won't expose you to new ideas and techniques as much as remaking will do. In addition you will rarely be at your full capabilities. For example if you learn piano and try to learn a specific song then you will notice when you make a mistake. When you work on original songs there is rarely a plan for how things will be put together. This will usually lead to going with what you know best and falling into habitual patterns. In that regard your not practicing with intent.

Remaking is no secret, it's been around for years. Beethoven studied Bach, authors study each other and of course nothing is made in a vacuum. You will learn so much from remaking other songs that can't be learned from books or YouTube videos. After practice and remake after remake making your own music will come much more naturally. In addition you will build up a wealth of ideas and knowledge. Then when producing new music, you will have an abundance of techniques and ideas to utilize. This will all lead to much more inspired EDM producing.

Now this has nothing to do with plagiarising or stealing. Because this is not about copying other music and passing it off as your own. Rather it is the process of remaking other songs purely for the purpose of practice and learning. When you set the goal to remake something it gives you a clear direction and forces you to figure out what works and what you

need to accomplish. You will need to figure out how to create sounds, construct melodies, structure and every single component required to make an EDM song.

Remaking songs is almost like having a mentorship. Although it might be indirect, it's unlikely that you can call up an EDM superstar and ask them how they made a particular song. However you can remake their music and get inside of their mindset. Not only that but you will be exposed to their techniques and styles. In turn you might discover that they use a particular key or utilize build ups in a certain way and so on.

There really isn't a method for remaking songs. But there are some things you should consider. First of all, choose decent songs. Remakes can be time consuming so remaking something that's average than it will be time wasted. Ideally, you should only remake quality music in the genre you like. In addition try out other genres to learn more. However consider your skill level and don't attempt to remake more complicated songs. Build up your skill set first. If you are a beginner producer it's better to remake more simple EDM.

You don't need to get it exactly the same. There is no value in attempting to get it exactly the same. Always be focused on the value gained from the time spent. Purposeful remaking is beneficial even if you're just remaking basslines, intros and so on. To gain the most value remake the whole song and you will learn all the parts. Make it easy and find where instruments are in solo during the song. When remaking drums, listen at the start where they are most likely played alone. If your remaking a lead, check to see if it's alone somewhere.

Whist your working on remakes keep working on your originals. Ideally set aside some time to do remakes and some time for originals. With some well spent time of this you will have many projects which are essentially full tracks. By changing things around a little you can even turn them into your own songs. You will then notice yourself improving and developing critical listening skills.

HOW TO REMIX

Remixing is an integral part of EDM culture and as a producer it's a great way to open your mind to new ideas. The sooner you learn this skill, the better. As with remakes those skills and techniques that you learn from remixing can then be used for your originals.

Remixing helps you think creatively because it pushes you to try things you probably wouldn't try if you were working on originals. Add to that remixing brings awareness to your brand. There are many famous DJs who started out making mashups, bootlegs and remixes. It will certainly bring more attention to you.

Working with remixes is much easier than producing original songs. From the outset you will be provided with the melodies, sounds and ideas. This is great if your stuck in a creative rut. Starting with nothing can be daunting and remixing circumvents that fear.

To remix, you will need some source material. Decide on what result you're actually looking for before you start any remix. You can get involved in remix competitions where you will be provided with high quality music elements. This will give you inside knowledge of how the music is constructed and made. When your choosing which remix competitions to work on don't be put off if they don't offer much source material. Incidentally you don't need all the parts to remix a song, something as simple as vocal could be all that you need.

When you enter any remix competition it's important to note that your chances of winning are competitive and even if your

work is good you might not get chosen as the winner. If you don't win then you can't releases it without their permission. Nevertheless working to deadlines and with official stems is a good thing to be involved with.

Finding remix competitions

Follow your favorite record labels or channels. Sometimes they run remix competitions independently. Also follow your favourite artists. Others might be hosted on a website such as Beatport Play. This is one of the most famous platforms and usually features tracks by big artists. Just sign up and you can get started.

Remix Comps (www.remixcomps.con) is another site for finding remix competitions. Additionally you can perform a search on Soundcloud for "remix contests" or "remix competitions". Then activate Google Alerts for "remix contest(s)" or "remix competition(s).

Pitching

If your really into a particular artists song then you can pitch to them or their label to remix it. In that regard you would normally benefit from having established yourself as a producer already. But don't shy away from it, believe in yourself. You could create a great remix and then pitch it. If you really believe in your remix then go ahead.

The best way you can approach them is through YouTube or Soundcloud. If they are huge artists that might be a little bit more difficult to get a reply. First, find their contact details and then send them your remix. If your lucky they might even send you the stems so you can improve on your ideas. Later on when your more famous, labels and artists may very well contact you for remixes. Make sure your branding and profile is strong to improve your chances of this happening.

Besides contacting people and remix competitions you can search Soundcloud for the keyword "stems." This will reveal any songs that have been made available to remix. However if you use them always contact the owner to ask if you can remix them. Alternatively you can sample songs, just remember that you will likely be infringing on the copyright and you would not be able to release it without permission.

Ideas

When your listening to potential songs to remix, you should get an idea of what they feature. Scan through the whole song for ideas. If you produce a particular EDM genre then it's beneficial to work with your strengths and find opportunities in that style. Remixing benefits from various genres but if your style is unique, then some remix styles won't be ideal. For example if your style is hard hitting beats then remixing a melodic trance song would not be a great fit.

Remixing is much easier then starting out with an original song. With a remix you will already have some source material. Maybe some stems, vocals and midi. You will also have some guidelines such as the genre, BPM and key. However those are not set in stone and its upto you to be as creative with your version of the remix as you wish.

If you have a vocal you can try out some new chords, melodies and things with it. Remixes can be as simple as changing some drums or as advanced as you wish. You could even change genres. As mentioned before if your known for a signature sound then this is a great idea. For example what works great with EDM remixes is turning pop songs into dancefloor hits. That could be something as simple as turning the chorus into a drop and making an extended intro. For

example, Tiesto's Grammy award winning remix of John Legend's hit song "All of me". For this Tiesto simply added a kick drum beat to turn the song into something dancefloor friendly. Listen to other remixes for inspiration and to hear how they approached things.

Try stripping the song down to its fundamentals. You don't have to use all the parts. Simply build on the basic ideas. Typically when remixing you go with the key elements of the song such as the vocal or lead melody. This is what defines the track and you want to retain some of that so that people can identify with it. Try taking a minor melody and turning it into something major or take a few notes out of it. Experiment and test your ideas.

Changing Things
If you want to change the tempo of stems or acapellas you can utilize the warping function available in most DAW's. This allows you to go from one tempo up or down in BPM as you wish. Try to retain the quality as you do it. Plus or minus ten BPM is usually fine, anything more and you start to lose audio fidelity. In addition, make sure it's also kept in time. You can play a metronome or click to make sure everything is in it's correct place. If there are timing issues you can cut things and move them around. Most DAW warping functions will offer this tool as part of the warping.

Also with vocals you can do some really cool chop and pitch style effects. DJ Snake does this a lot and in fact it's really easy to do. FL Studio offers the Edison pitch tool to cut up samples and pitch them. Other DAW's you can use the audio editing tools to cut up and rearrange vocals. Or you can cut certain phrases of the vocal and load them into a sampler to play a new melody.

Content

You can also find the MIDI files for most songs through a simple Google search. In addition this method will also help you find acapellas. This will help you with unofficial remixes when your looking for the melodies or vocals of a song. You can then create your own versions of those. If you want acapellas for a typical song you can do one of two things.

- Search for the acapella online
- Create your own

Besides a Google search you can check out Acapellas4U which is one of the best websites for acapellas. Beatport also has a DJ Tools section with stems and acapellas.

Try the phase inversion technique to retrieve vocals from songs. You will need the instrumental of a song and then you can use the phase inversion technique. Essentially you play the instrumental with the original but with the phase inverted to cancel out all instruments and leave you with just the vocal. This isn't that effective though. Try as you wish and see how it sounds.

Legal

Remember that if you remix a song and distribute it online without permission, it's a bootleg. If you upload them to YouTube or Soundcloud without permission expect them to be taken down and your account could get banned. But don't let that put you off, you can still use it in your DJ sets. Just don't try to sell it.

If you really want to work around that legally you can produce a cover. Then you have taken the composition aways from the original without directly sampling it. In that regard you would need to re-record the vocal. However this can be a grey area of law. Seek legal advice before you distribute anything.

MIXING EDM

EDM demands huge synth lines, massive drums and beastly bass. With your song written it's time to start making it sound big. Mixing is the first step.

Prepare

Before you start mixing you need to get in the right mind set. Be well rested and inspired. It's a good idea to take a break from you song for at least a week before you start to mix it. Try mixing in the morning to ensure your energy is highest and your ears are fresh. Remove all distractions such as internet connections on your production computer and have your phone away from you. Also make sure you have sufficient time planned ahead for mixing. Between six to ten hours should be plenty of time and that should include some regular short breaks.

Start with good sounds

The mixing process really starts the moment you begin producing. From the outset you need to be selecting sounds that are of the best quality. This will make the mixdown much better and easier. Choose samples and sounds that hit the right frequencies and work well together. Remember, what matters most is how good it all sounds together and not in solo. A hot lead might sound good in solo but could make your drums dull. Spend the time and perfect your sounds before you start mixing down. You can also switch out some sounds during the mixing stages. This is often a better solution to trying to fix them with mixing.

Stems

Use stems when mixing. This involves bouncing all of your channels down to audio files and then importing them to a new project. Mentally this commits you to how things sound, frees up processing power and makes you more efficient. Organize your projects and it will save you a lot of time. You can group certain sounds together such as all the drums or all the FX and so on. This will also save your CPU power by doing things on one channel instead of multiple repetitions.

Reference

Choose some reference tracks that are mixed well and are a great end result to aim for. These work the best if they are in the same key as your song since instruments sound different in other keys.

Clean

Maybe at this stage you might want to add some things or even take out anything unnecessary. Be critical of what you add, everything needs its purpose and place. The more you add to your track the more frequencies will build up. Be aware that you will need to leave lots of space below 200 HZ for your kick, bass and sub. Use EQ to clean up any sharp resonant frequencies. Nothing should stick out too much. You can sweep a parametric EQ with a narrow Q band to hear those and then attenuate them.

Mono

EDM is destined for the club and most club sound systems are in mono. Therefore your song needs to be mono compatible. Be critical of too much stereo imaging on your sounds. Keep testing your mix in mono by using a mono tool on the master channel. You can still use wideners and so on, just make sure you check if any sounds disappear when doing that.

Vocals and bass tend to work best at the center and are often in mono. You can still create width to them and an easy way to do that is with panning. Pan one sound left and another right. Then detune one up a few cents (increment of a half tone) and the other down a few cents. This will give the impression that its a double take or a stereo recording.

Keep anything under 200 Hz mono. This will avoid phase cancellation and again club sound systems have the bass in mono. In addition bass is omni-directional, which means you can't determine where it's coming from anyway. If you want your bass to sound wide, add a mid bass layer with stereo effects. Again, check in mono to identify any phase cancellation.

Listen in context
When your mixing avoid using the solo button on channels. You need to hear things in context of the mix because they will sound different together. Sometimes you might need to switch the sound to another preset or sample. That can often be a better solution then applying lots of mixing processing.

Hierarchy
When you approach your mix decide on which is the most important element of the mix and then mix around that. From the start you should have an idea of which elements will be needed, what their frequency content is and which are the most important. Experiment with their order to achieve the results you want. Usually it would be something like as follows.

1. Vocals
2. Synth lead
3. Kick

4. Bass
5. Snare

Do a rough guidance mix
This is one of the most important steps to get your track to sound better. The best point to start mixing at is the drop or the most important section of the song. This guarantees that things will hit the hardest here and you can then mix around that.

Set the master fader at 0dB and pull all the channels in your song down to muted. Select the most important channel in the song, usually that will be the kick or vocal in EDM. Have that peak around -6dB. By staying at lower levels it will give you space to bring all the other channels into the mix. Mix them in one by one and follow that sequence by importance. The master channel should not be peaking above -6dB which will help for for mastering later on.

Make sure when you bring sounds in that they don't compromise the most important elements as you add them to the mix. Do they sound good together? If no, change things up. Try out different kick or drum samples, presets and so on. Everything should be tested in the context of the mix.

Group and bus
Make use of grouping and bussing. You can group similar sounds together and process them as one. For example all the drum hits can go to one channel. Or all the vocals to one channel. Then you can apply processing to them as a whole and make it cohesive.

Sidechain Compression

Sidechain compression is an elite trick of the EDM trade. We can use it to clean up a mix and make things stand out. In essence sidechain compression will turn down one sound so that another sound can be heard clearly. The most common use is to sidechain the bass and kick so that the bass ducks every time the kick hits.

Xfer LFO tool is a great plugin for sidechaining. Just apply it to the bass channel with a ¼ rhythm. You can then adjust the envelope for how it ducks. Alternatively if your song is not on a 4/4 beat you can use sidechaining on a send and return to duck parts. Just apply a compressor with the sidechain function to the channel you want to duck. Then choose the input source as the channel you want to be the sound that ducks it. You can then adjust the envelope for the ducking.

EQ

EQ allow us to reduce or boost the gain of specific frequency bands. There are four different EQ shapes commonly used:

- High Pass: Used to remove low-end frequencies.
- Low Pass: Used to remove high-end frequencies.
- Bell: Used to boost or cut at a given range.
- Shelf: Reduce or boost high end or low end.

When using EQ it's better to cut than boost. This reduces the build up of frequencies that can make your mix clip. For example to make a sound brighter, try reducing the bass and mid frequencies. Then increase the channel volume. You should high pass filter the majority of your sounds to give more room in the mix. Many record sounds have unwanted low frequencies. Even sounds such as hi hats. Apply a simple hi pass filter to clean them up.

When you want to boost with EQ have a purpose for doing it. Such a helping something cut through a mix. All EQ decisions should for a purposes not because you got told to by some guide. Listen, test, and then decide.

There are certain frequency ranges that produce characteristic sounds:

- Sub frequencies: Below 100Hz
- Heavy/ Muddy: 180-225 Hz
- Nasal/ Boxy: 400-600 Hz
- Ears Most Sensitive: 1.6-3 kHz
- Airy/Bright: 10 kHz and up

Compression

Compression and EQ are the fundamental tools used to help sculpt a mix. EQ can be used to remove unnecessary frequencies first. After fixing those problems the compressor can even out volume differences and give an overall louder sound. This make it easier to hear in the mix. Essentially it will take the quiet parts of a sound and boost them to be closer to the louder parts. This is a popular effect in EDM but use it sparingly to avoid squashing your sounds too much.

Compressors have the following common functions.

- Attack: When the compressor is activated. If sounds have too much transients you can reduce them with a fast attack. Alternatively you can boost them by letting them through and then compressing the rest of the sound. Some compressors have an automatic attack which will follow a compression algorithm.
- Release: When the compressor lets go of the sound. Sometimes you might want to compress the whole

sound. Sometimes you might want to compress a smaller part. Release can be used to set that. Some compressors have an automatic release which will follow a compression algorithm.
- Threshold: This is for setting the amplitude of when compressor starts to compress. Setting it at the top will catch the very loudest sounds. Pushing it more will squash the sound.
- Ratio: This is the intensity of compression. Higher ratios push the compression more.
- Gain: after compression you will want to bring the reduction in amplitude back up. Gain does that. Some compressors have an automatic gain which will follow a compression algorithm.

Reverb

Todays sound in EDM is pretty dry. However there is still a lot of reverb in use and it is great for adding life and width to your sounds. It works best when applied to a bus send. Set up a new group channel with a reverb on then send your sounds to that. Make sure it is set to wet %100.

Reverbs in EDM are usually heavily ducked with the source sound which will give you a dry source with a nice reverb tail. You can achieve this by sidechaining the reverb with your source. Here are some basic guidelines to using reverb:

- Drums: Try a room-reverb with high damping to make them sound more real.
- Bass: A simple reverb similar to the drums will add life whilst not taking up too much space.
- Vocals: Hall reverb works well. Use sparingly and be careful to check mono compatibility and also that any high frequencies are not washed out.

- Synths: Big reverbs work well. Try sidechaining them to keep the lead clean with some nice reverb tail.
- Pads: Usually benefit from big and lush reverb.

Volume automation

Utilize volume automation to make changes across the whole song. Some sections of your song might require different levels for instruments. For example maybe the drop lead needs to be louder than in the build up. Or the vocals work well quieter in the breakdown. You can use volume automation to turn up or turn down those parts as you wish. Incidentally you can automate pretty much any parameter in most DAWs. Maybe you want to send more reverb or high pass certain sections. Be creative.

Use a Spectrum Analyser

Spectrum analysers will show you a visual representation of your songs frequency content, amplitude and stereo information. This is essential for checking your mix against your reference. However don't rely too much on it, trust your ears first.

Test

Before you move to the mastering phase listen to your mix on all your headphones, speaker setups, cars, and sound systems. Take a break for a few days and come back with fresh ears. Don't mix for more than a couple of hours each time. Otherwise you start to lose objectivity. Take a break, get some air and get back to it later on.

Ask your friends, family and peers for feedback. Fresh ears will give you a new perspective. But don't ask them if they life it because most will say yes to avoid hurting your feelings. Instead ask them for critical feedback. This is vital for your

development. You can also make use of websites such as www.synthshare.com for feedback.

Test the mix down at different levels. For the majority of the time mix at quieter levels to minimize ear fatigue. Now and then turn the levels up and see how it sounds. Human hearing is sensitive to different frequencies depending on their amplitude. Therefore checking your mixes at different levels overall will help you achieve a better mix.

<u>MASTERING</u>

Well mastered EDM is critical to getting DJs to play your songs. The process is often misunderstood and perceived as someone simply cranking a mix through a limiter and adding some shine with fancy gear. Sometimes you may well send your song to be mastered. However it's a good idea to get familiar with the process.

The goal of mastering is to turn a mixed song into a finished a product ready for distribution. Whether that be for streaming, broadcasting, DJ's or downloads. Mastering concerns the final stereo mixdown of a song after it has been mixed.

Good mastering requires an acoustically accurate environment as well as transparent monitoring. Invest in a subwoofer for your studio so you can hear lower frequencies. Alternatively you can use a SUBPAC which is a wearable bass system allowing you to feel the lowest frequencies. In addition make use analyzers so that you can see the lowest frequencies.

The first step is to listen through the song with fresh ears. Listen for any technical mishaps or things that stick out. Usually the common flaws are, excessive bass or excessive sharp high-end frequencies. Often producers also push their mixes too high and clipping or phase issues occur. Mastering can't fix a bad mix. In extreme cases it's best to go back to the drawing board and mix again.

After forming an idea of what you need to do to the track you can start to address things. Try not to go overboard otherwise

you will sacrifice the character of the mix. Remember that these are guidelines and each song will have differences that require alternative approaches and techniques.

How to master EDM with iZotope Ozone

iZotope Ozone currently on its 8th edition is an entire suite of plugins for mastering. It's a great way for beginners to start mastering their own music.

Bass management

Start with bass management. Apply an EQ with a high-pass setting to filter out anything below 30 HZ. Go with the steepest slope.

Exciter

Next add an exciter to brighten things up. The exciter comes as a multiband exciter so you can split the frequency spectrum into four different bands and then boost or cut the harmonics in each band. The difference between an exciter and an EQ is that with an exciter you boost the harmonics. This can be done in many different modes including, warm, retro, tape, tube, triode and dual triode. These emulate analog devices to saturate those areas in a harmonically pleasing way. Experiment with each of the types and apply as required. Use the dry and wet mix to make it more subtle.

Compression

Next add some vintage compressor to control dynamics along with some buss compression. Set the gain reduction, you don't want too much. The two and a half to one ratio is fine. Set the attack time a bit slower to let the transients come through and keep things punchy. Again we are being very subtle. Apply the threshold slowly and hear the results. You can do this in multi band mode also to tame peaks in a

different band. Then add on auto gain to automatically adjust the gain to compensate for the loss of volume encountered in the compression process.

Saturation
Use the vintage tape add effect to add saturation or warmth. You can add this in the different frequency bands as you wish. Be subtle and retain the songs character without going overboard.

Stereo Imager
Use the imager to do a nice spread on the mix. You can spread each individual four different bands. EDM works well with a narrow low end and then spreading out to the high end. It can be tempting to push these wide but it just messes with your with your phase coherence. Make sure the mix is always mono compatible. There's also a built-in correlation meter which you want to more or less stay at zero or above to maintain proper phase coherency.

Maximizer
Use a Maximizer to get some extra gain at the end. This is a brick wall limiter. Just pull your threshold down to get some gain boosting. The limiting is quite transparent across the four available modes. However don't go overboard with it. Try to maintain a transient heavy song. The kick and drums need to come through.

Once the mastering is how you want it to be you can mix out the files for the medium they're to be released on. That could be WAV or Mp3 as required with meta-data embedded) or AIFF and so on. You can deliver a different master for downloads then you would from what you might play at a club. Test those out.

DIGITAL AUDIO WORK STATION (DAW)

The DAW is the central working unit for making EDM. Before we look at the options it's important to note that there is no best DAW. It all depends on how you work and what you like to use. The kind of music you make and the techniques you prefer will influence that.

Try before you buy.
Most DAW manufacturers offer a demo version for people to try. Testing with a demo will reveal whether you are going to like it or not. Consider factors such as the price, resources and workflow. The main factor to consider besides price should be workflow. This is the way you produce and arrange music. The DAW that allows you to do this seamlessly is the best option for you.

There are five major DAW's out there which are really great for EDM production. Each of these are easy to get started with and offer a wealth of guidance. Most come with a manual and online support at the least. Without further ado let's take a look at them.

Ableton Live
Ableton Live is currently the most popular DAW for EDM producers. It is easy to learn for anyone, with or without experience. It was designed for both live performance and music production. Comes with over 11 GB of samples, three instruments and over thirty effects. Simple, intuitive, design and workflow are central to it's design.

Used By: Jack U, Major Lazer, Hardwell, Maddix and More.

FL Studio
FL Studio is the underdog of EDM production. It offers an intuitive approach to making EDM. Popular among dub-step and trap music producers because it is easy to program beats with the sequencer. Comes with some great synths and tools for producers to utilize. Check out the vocal editing options in Edison.

Used By: Makj, Afrojack, Martin Garrix, Jay Hardway, DJ Snake and More.

Logic Pro X
Logic Pro X has been a choice of many EDM producers for a long time. It is stable, reliable and easy to work with. Included with it is a solid library of sounds and some great factory instruments. Logic is available for Mac computers only. Sorry Windows users.

Used By: Calvin Harris, Axwell Ingrosso, Jonas Blue, Swindali, David Guetta and More.

Steinberg Cubase
Steinberg Cubase was technically the first DAW ever made. Viewed largely as a pioneer of music software. Very stable even with large projects. Includes some great tools which make an awesome environment for creating EDM. Also some awesome in built instruments.

Used By: Knife Party, Junkie XL, Chase & Status, Infected Mushroom and more

Reason

Reason can be a bit intimidating at first glance because of its intricate interface. However it is easy to learn. The rack is full of awesome instruments and effects that are all of very high quality. You can mix and mash these together as you please and the processing required is minimal. The only drawback is that third party plug-ins aren't supported as of now.

Used By: Rick Rubin, The Prodigy, Claude Von Stroke and more

MUST HAVE PLUGINS

In EDM production it is easy to get lost in downloading more and more plug ins. However what is far better is to know a few tools really well. The plugins you need really depends on the music you are creating. A one size fits all solution doesn't exist. Incidentally the stock plug ins packaged with your DAW are pretty damn good these days.

As time goes on you will find certain plugins you prefer. That will also depend on the level of skill you are at. Sometimes you will outgrow and need something more advanced. But regardless of your skill level, price is still going to be a huge factor in what plugins you own. The important thing to note here is that an expensive plugin does not necessarily mean it is better or that it's going to make your music sound better.

Nothing beats talent and good sounds.

VIRTUAL STUDIO INSTRUMENTS

Virtual instruments are software versions of an instrument. That could be a real world instrument such as a piano. Or something completely unique for software. There are so many available for you to start making sounds with. Let's take a look at some of the most popular for EDM.

Arturia V Collection
This is a collection of ten virtual instruments that cover analogue style synthesis. If you want to create some fat leads and big bass then this is a great choice.

Kontakt
Every EDM producer needs a good sampler to load up sounds and play them across the scale. Kontakt is one of the best on the market. It also comes with some great sound banks which means you have access to orchestras and more at your fingertips.

Native Instruments FM8
This is a more advanced synth that is used by producers including Skrillex and Knife Party. Has some great presets and ability to create morphed sounds.

Native Instruments Komplete Ultimate
Komplete is a collection of instruments, effects and sounds. Included is a huge library of synths, samples and packs. You can create pretty much any sound with this. Drums, bass, real instruments and synthetic ones. Essential for your productions.

Nexus

Nexus is a ROMpler which means it plays back sample libraries from expansion packs. You can modify those sounds with the inbuilt, EQ, envelopes, filters and so on. The patches are super high quality and are a must have for EDM production.

NI Massive

This is the synth for dubstep. Amazing lfo and modulation section for creating those wobbly basslines. In addition can make so much more with its diverse wavetables and intuitive programming options.

Reaktor 6

If your looking to get advanced and create your own sounds from scratch then Reaktor 6 is the synth for you. Offers tons of flexibility from designing and wiring your own synths to creating unique custom sounds. For advanced users.

Spectrasonics Omnisphere

Omnisphere is a beast of a virtual studio instrument and is epic at making complex sounds and atmospherics. Used mostly by movie composers but can be great for EDM. With over fifty gigabytes of sample libraries it gives you access to incredible instruments. From classical sounds to the most bizarre sounds. Load up some presets and get inspired.

Spire

Spire is a great sounding additive hybrid synth that works really well for creating modern EDM leads. You can even create some complex sounds using the modulation matrix and lush filters.

Sylenth1

This is one of the go to synths for EDM. Has a warm sound and some great factory presets to get you going. Unlimited possibilities for creating everything from the complex to the big, simple sounds. Heard in countless EDM hits.

U-he Diva

Inspired by the classic analogue synthesizer, the Minimoog. Offers an analog-like sound quality and is easy to use. Great for creating big and full sounds.

X-FER Records Serum

Serum dethorned Massive as the king of wavetable synthesis. It is an amazing synthesizer that can create analog style patches and amazing sounds. You can even import your own wavetables to acquire more sound palettes. Great LFO, freedom to program, high quality effects and more.

PLUG INS

Plugins are there to plug into your channels and enhance, modulate or clean up your sounds. They can be used on both midi, instrument, group and audio channels. There are so many different kinds of plug ins and below are some of the most popular listed by category for EDM production.

Analyzers

Voxengo Span, Waves and Izotope
Every project needs a spectrum analyzer. This will help you to understand frequencies and their relationship to pitch. Waves and Izotope also offer some great analyzers.

Delay

Soundtoys EchoBoy
Models classic units and has various delay types.

Waves H-Delay
This is a great delay with an old school analog feel with a modern touch. Use it to give vocals the feeling of more space or add depth to your sounds.

Distortion

Fabfilter Saturn
The perfect blend of complex and simple saturation or distortion. The standard presets are easy to get you going and you can modulate them even more to create your own sounds.

Izotope Trash
A great option for distortion. Smash things to the next level. Used by Skrillex.

Camelphat
Has an amazing distortion section offering four different types.

Dynamics

AOM Invisible Limiter
EDM needs to be big and loud. But you still want it to sound good and not squashed or distorted. The AOM Invisible Limiter comes in with transparent limiting and it can be pushed so hard that your track won't distort.

Izoptope Ozone
Mixing and mastering suite of high quality plug ins. Easy to use and great results.

Oxford Inflator
Make your sounds louder and fuller.

SPL Transient Designer
Add this powerful tool to your plug in arsenal. This weapon can be used to add punch to your drums and plucked sounds.

Sonnox Dynamics
A multi-purpose processor with functions for gating, side-chain, compression, limiting, EQ and a warmth circuit. Dynamics control is an essential part of EDM production. This is a workhorse that gets the job done well.

Sonnox Inflator

Use this to make your sounds bigger. This increases the perceived volume of a sound without affecting dynamic range. The end result is a bigger version of the original signal.

UAD 1176 Classic Limiter Collection
This is a famous modelled compressor based on hardware. Works well on drums. In order to use this you will need a UAD system.

Waves CLA-2A
Waves are an industry leader for creating unrivaled plug-ins. The Waves CLA-A2 is a compression plugin emulated on tube compressors. These are simple to use and work amazing on Leads, Vocals, and Bass.

Xfer Records OTT Compressor
This one is actually a free tool. Use it to add color and gloss to your sounds.

Effects

Camelphat
Distortion, lfos, filters and effect. All can be routed as you wish. Smash things up and make them interesting.

SugarBytes Effectrix
Super cool effects plug in for manipulating your sounds across a grid. Twist your sounds beyond recognition to create something unique.

Filters

FabFilter Pro Q2

One of the best EQ plugins for mixing and mastering EDM. Allows you to enhance or treat frequency bands with clean transparency. The Linear Phase mode prevents any phase issues from occurring when cutting frequencies.

FabFilter Simplon
Filters are essential for EDM production. Fabfilter is one of the best filter plugins available. It offers great sound and harmonically pleasing resonance. Easy to use and affordable.

Misc

Waves One KNOB
A simple to use plug in that offers great quality, saturation, brightness, side chain and filtering.

Musical

Odesi
Music composition software to help you write melodies, chords and add mood to your music. In addition can detect the key and scale of audio.

Reverb

UVI Sparkverb
If you are looking for a clean sounding reverb that can create light ambiences to huge soundscapes all whilst being light on processing then this is your answer.

Stereo Imaging

Mid Side Tool
Control the mid and side of a signal with ease.

Flux Stereo Tool
Great for stereo imaging and panning. Give your sounds space. Waves An amazing stereo imager and panning tool. Waves and Izotope also offer great stereo imaging tools.

Waves S1
Easily spread or narrow your sounds.

Vocals

Melodyne
When your working with vocals there will always be some treatment required. Melodyne comes in to help here. Allows you to clean up the timing and tuning of vocals. Absolutely essential for recording vocals.

GET SIGNED

So you have your EDM song ready. Your happy with it and ready to share it with the world. Begin your journey to EDM superstardom!

The first step to take towards getting signed is to have great music. Finished products that you believe in. After that there are a few more things an EDM artist will need to do in order to get signed

Branding

These days you need more than good music to stand out. Just uploading your music isn't enough. Even if it is really amazing. Your chances of being noticed and then signed will increase greatly if you have professional press materials and strong branding. Take a good profile shot, have a decent logo and a concurrent theme to your profile. If your lost for ideas look at some of your idols and study what you like. Then try to incorporate some of these elements into your designs.

Leave the best possible first impression you can. When labels listen to your music, chances are they are going to analyze your online appearance. If it looks poor then your reputation is mirrored to them so that will influence them to sign your track or not. Keep it professional and music related only. Make an official website, have strong branding and always try to be unique.

Social media is also important to achieving a successful EDM career. You need at least Facebook, Instagram, Soundcloud and Twitter so that you can contact with DJ's, producers and

labels. The majority of big EDM labels listen to music on Soundcloud. In most cases use this to upload your demos and then send to them. Make sure they are set to **private only** before you sign anything.

Contacting Labels

Having connections with labels is the best way to get signed. If your constantly networking with DJs and producers then they can help get you in touch with the labels. Always be growing your network, send your music out for feedback, attend shows and be social. When it comes to formally contacting a label you can send them an email of your demo.

Come up with a list of suitable labels. You can find out how they accept demos through Google. Just type: label naem + demo. Some might have their own page for submitting demos. Others will accept email and it should follow a simple format.

Subject line: artist name - track name.
Then open the email with:
hello, I would like to share with you my latest song for consideration.
Artist name - Track name
Private Soundcloud link
Thank you

Name
Twitter account
Instagram account
Facebook account
Website

Keep it simple and straight to the point. Be patient and wait for them to reply. Don't send any follow up emails. If they are

interested then they will get back to you. Keep the emails private. If you send emails to multiple labels put them in the BCC section so that no one knows about others being contacted. Labels want to feel special and that it is only you contacting them. Replies can take up to a month or more so don't sit around waiting, move on with your producing. If you have more songs to send wait at least another month. You want to avoid bombarding them. Keep an eye on your Soundcloud stats to see who is playing your tracks.

Tips
Only send your absolute best work and never send unfinished, unmastered songs or demos.

Avoid using copyrighted material
Clearing it requires a lot of effort and money. Labels aren't keen on that. I know there is stuff out there that is copyrighted but it is either coming from big labels who cleared it or from smaller ones who fly under the radar.

Don't send remixes or bootlegs
These are difficult to be signed officially. Anything like those save for your own channels and packs.

Send quality over quantity
Only send in your very best tracks and do it every other month or so. Force yourself to filter for the best.

<u>CONCLUSION</u>

There you have it, everything you need to produce EDM! The next thing you need to do is fire up your DAW and use what you have learned. Turn it into a hit EDM song.

Produce it
Apply the techniques from this book then use the mixing and mastering guide to make it sound huge.

Take it out and test it.
Play it to your friends, family and if you spin a club try it out there. How do people react to it? Should you change anything? When your happy you can send it out to some labels. Rinse and repeat.

Become better
Over time you will become a better EDM producer. If you stick with it and keep trying new things then that's a guarantee. Challenge yourself to try new things and learn more.

Mentors
Make sure you have good mentors around you to give you feedback and help you realize your vision. Be a part of the community both online and in the real world.

Feedback
Have an open mind to feedback and never take it personally. View it as constructive criticism to improve.

I wish you all the best and look forward to hearing your music on the mainstage and festivals soon.

Catch up with me at

www.tommyswindali.com

Thanks for Reading!

What did you think of, **Electronic Dance Music Production: The Advanced Guide On How to Produce Music for EDM Producers**

I know you could have picked any number of books to read, but you picked this book and for that I am extremely grateful.

I hope that it added at value and quality to your everyday life. If so, it would be really nice if you could share this book with your friends and family by posting to Facebook and Twitter.

If you enjoyed this book and found some benefit in reading this, I'd like to hear from you and hope that you could take some time to post a review. Your feedback and support will help this author to greatly improve his writing craft for future projects and make this book even better.

I want you, the reader, to know that your review is very important and so, if you'd like to leave a review, all you have to do is click here and away you go. I wish you all the best in your future success!

Keep upto date with me:

www.tommyswindali.com
www.swindali.com

Thank you and good luck!

Tommy Swindali

BONUS: GHOST PRODUCING

Ghost producing is an agreement between a music producer composing a track for another artist who then releases that track under their own name. The ghost producer will normally be paid a flat fee upfront for their work.

For a lot of established EDM DJs they use ghost producers to help realize their visions. That could mean them sitting down with the ghost producer and directing them or just selecting on of their songs which they like. Nowadays there is a lot that goes into being an EDM artist and you will find behind every EDM superstar there are teams of people.

Many producers go with ghost producing because they prefer to stay out of the limelight. Maybe you love producing but want to keep your life private. Well that's a great idea for you to ghost produce for others. That way you can fulfill your passion and still get to see people enjoy your music. The fame isn't for everyone and there is a lot of pressure with it.

Once the big names start supporting your music it's going to open a lot of doors. In fact it's well known that Martin Garrix started out ghost producing and then got introduced to label bosses through that. Who you know is so important these days.

So many big EDM hits were ghost produced. It's the role of the ghost producer to make the vision of the client into a reality. The amount of money you can make depends on a number of factors. That can start as little as $300 and go right over $20,000. It all depends on the calibre of artists you work with and of course your credentials.

If your looking to get started www.edmghostproducer.com is a website where any producer can upload their tracks for sale. They do have an approval process and not every song is listed, but if you have good music try.

BONUS: 18 THINGS EVERY EDM PRODUCER NEEDS TO SUCCEED

One
You will need a computer or a laptop. A laptop is much easier because you can produce on anywhere, anytime. Mac is usually better long term but if you know about specs go with Windows.

Two
You will need a digital audio workstation (DAW). This is at the centre of your computer music production studio. Use it to hold your projects and work on them.

Three
You will need a set of monitor speakers to playback your music. Make sure you set them up correctly in your room. For best results acoustically treat your room.

Four
You will need a pair of monitor headphones. Nowadays the majority of music is played back on smaller speakers such as headphones. If it doesn't sound good on headphones people are probably not going to like it much.

Five
You will need a MIDI keyboard to play in melodies and chords. Invest in some music training and take your EDM to the next level.

Six

Back support, take care of your back and use a pillow or a comfortable chair for those long hours of producing. Live long and strong!

Seven
Obsession. Eat sleep and breathe EDM production. It takes at least ten thousand hours to be professional in something.

Eight
Music theory, learn scales and keys. This is the fundamental of good music. You don't need to be a Mozart but a little helps massively.

Nine
Find a mentor. They will help you to progress and become better much more quickly then on your own. If you can work with someone face to face its best but online is great too.

Ten
You will need, samples. You need samples to construct your song. Sign up for a Splice account. Use the best ones available.

Eleven
You will need, Plug ins and Virtual Instruments to create and control your sounds. Take a look at the chapter in this book about the best plugins.

Twelve
You will need mixing skills to turn your project into a big mix. Practice makes perfect, keep going and push through the challenges.

Thirteen

You will need, mastering to create a high quality finished song. Take ownership of your songs and do it yourself.

Fourteen
You will need a logo so that people can remember who you are and start branding yourself online. Try www.fiverr.com for some affordable designers.

Fifteen
You will need need to join EDM networks to keep upto to date and network. Get on the best forums and engage with members.

Sixteen
You will need to build your social network presence. This will help you get signed. Facebook, Instagram, Soundcloud are all essential. Be active.

Seventeen
Build fans and friends to support your music. Have a good attitude and add value to people. Reach out to new people.

Eighteen
You will need need good music. This is the most important factor for you to grow and succeed as an EDM artist. You can do it!

Claim This Now

Music Business Skills for Musicians:

If you're in the music business, read on. Today you need to view yourself through the new rules of the music industry.

Those who play by them will succeed.

Gone are the old days where you would hope to get signed and then become a star (i.e., everything would be done for you).

Do you wonder why other artists are getting breaks and you are not?

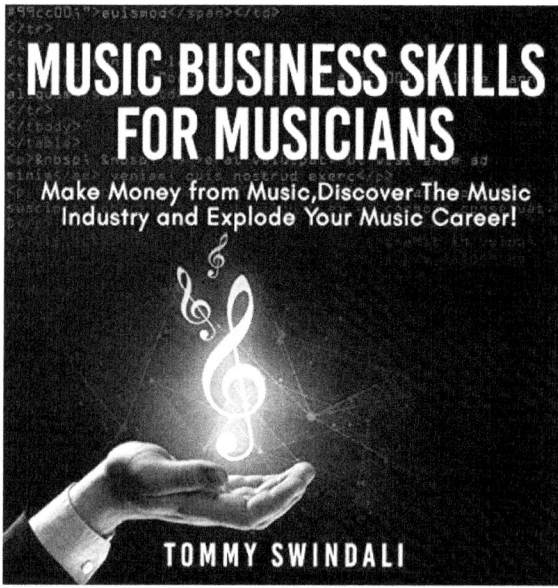

Discover How To Find Your Sound

Find Out More

Swindali music coaching/Skype lessons.

Email djswindali@gmail.com for info and pricing.

Other Books by Tommy Swindali

In The Mix: Discover The Secrets to Becoming a Successful DJ

If you have ever dreamed of being a DJ with people dancing to your music and all whilst having the time of your life then this book will show you how. Find Out More

Music Production: The Advanced Guide On How to Produce for Music Producers

Learn to Produce Music Like a Pro and Take Your Music To a Whole New Level Find Out More

Music Business Skills For Musicians
If Your In The Music Business, Read On Today you need to view yourself through the new rules of the music industry. Those who play by them will succeed Find Out More

Songwriting: Apply Proven Methods, Ideas and Exercises to Kickstart or Upgrade Your Songwriting

Have you ever listened to a song and thought "wow, if only I could write a song like that"? Well, you can now learn all the secrets on how to write beautiful music with this guide to songwriting! Find Out More